The Invisible Girl

A father's moving
story of the daughter
he lost

PETER BARHAM

with ALAN HURNDALL

To my beautiful Debbie

Your smile may be gone, but the laughter

stays with us for ever

HarperElement
An Imprint of HarperCollins*Publishers*
77–85 Fulham Palace Road,
Hammersmith, London W6 8JB

The website address is: www.thorsonselement.com

and *HarperElement* are trademarks of
HarperCollins*Publishers* Ltd

First published by HarperElement 2005
This edition 2006

2

A catalogue record of this book is
available from the British Library

ISBN-13 978-0-00-720543-1
ISBN-10 0-00-720543-0

Printed and bound in Great Britain by
Clays Ltd, St Ives plc

Contents

Acknowledgements

In the writing of this book we embarked on a journey of discovery into the mysterious and very private world of my daughter, Debbie (D. A.) Barham. We have carefully and respectfully tried to reassemble the various elements of her life, and this depended on the assistance of many of her family, friends and colleagues.

I am indebted to my co-author Alan Hurndall, for his inspiration and guidance. Without his hard work and professionalism this book would not have happened.

Thanks also to my wife Sue, whose endless patience and support allowed me the time to concentrate, and without whose love and care Debs would have died three years earlier.

We acknowledge the invaluable help given by many of Debs' former friends and colleagues whose anecdotes and personal memories have brought alive the secretive and mysterious Debs that we all miss. We give special thanks to Nick Thomas, Rachel Swann, Carla Mendonca, Bruce Hyman, Clive Anderson and John Langdon. Thanks also to Robert Kirby at PFD for his support and guidance, and to Belinda Budge and Wanda Whiteley at HarperCollins for giving us the opportunity to share Debs' story.

We also acknowledge with thanks the permission of the BBC, Above the Title Productions, Clive Anderson, John Langdon, and many others, to use excerpts of Debs' material.

Peter Barham

Preface

This is the story of my daughter Debbie and how, from secret writings at the age of 14 for the BBC, she single-handedly created a career as one of the most respected and prolific comedy writers of recent years. She was only 26 when she died in 2003, having struggled for nearly eight years with anorexia.

She was one of the strongest, most complicated, intelligent, funny, cynical people I will ever know, yet sweet and vulnerable – still a child. Her life was created in carefully managed compartments – nobody knew the whole story – and this book allows us access to the real Debbie for the first time.

She lived for her work, literally, and died for it. She flatly refused inpatient treatment for her disorder, because it would have destroyed her one purpose in life – to write.

Yet the inner strength that drove her through so many troubled years to the sort of professional acclaim that most writers can only dream of is absolutely astonishing. Debbie redefined what is physically and mentally possible at dangerously low body weight, but misjudged the invisible inner damage that can be caused by anorexia. At a specialist clinic, to which she was referred in 1997, the consultant psychiatrist wrote:

Emaciated ++ (skeletal)
Pale ++

But also added:

Alert and vivacious

Hers was a life of contradictions and secrecy, but also of extraordinary achievement.

Part One

The Journey

One

It is Easter Monday, April 2003. The war in Iraq is one month old and I'm watching Tony Blair assuring the British public that the discovery of Saddam's weapons of mass destruction is imminent. The phone rings in the study. It is Debs' mother. I sense bad news. Ann and I have been divorced for more than twenty years and we rarely speak. And there is none of the usual formalities of 'Hello' and 'How are you?' Her voice is trembling and the message instant.

'Deborah's dead.'

The news is as unbearable for me to hear as it had been for her to utter. I shut down into numbed silence as the details overwhelm my senses.

Debs had been found slumped on her bed by her Aunt Melanie, Ann's sister. After failing to make contact all weekend, a frantic Melanie had rushed to Debs' London flat. There was no reply. She called 999. The police and fire brigade broke down the door. Debs was lifeless. Her beloved cat, Ellie, and her laptop – still switched on – were beside her. Her two pet hamsters were scurrying around their cage in obvious hunger. She'd probably been dead for several hours. It appears she'd tried to get up and had died instantly and peacefully from heart failure. She weighed a little over four and a half stone.

Debs was 26. She was more than my daughter. I, along with many in her profession, believe she was a genius. She had made a massive impact on the media world in an amazingly short time. Within a few years of packing her bags for London as a starry-eyed 15-year-old, she had become one of the most prolific and wittiest writers in Britain.

Although you probably would not have heard of Debbie Barham, almost certainly you would have laughed at her work. She wrote for most of Fleet Street and for the aristocracy of British comedy – Graham Norton, Rory Bremner, Clive Anderson, Bob Monkhouse, Roy Hudd, Ned Sherrin.

Confirmation of our Prime Minister's growing status as a world statesman came with the revelation that an American toy company is selling a doll based on Mr Blair. Nobody has yet ordered one of the 12-inch figures, but George Bush of course already has his own Tony Blair puppet.

– Ned Sherrin, *Loose Ends*

Say serious issue to me and I say this week's *Hello*;
Say topical and I say fruit;
Say the Royal Family and I say, 'Did you know it's moving to BBC1'?
I hope it's still funny.

– Graham Norton, *So Graham Norton*

Thank you, and this week's Queen's Speech was like watching paint dry – well it was for Brian Mawhinney. Fancy covering the Conservative Party chairman in paint? They might at least have rubbed him down and made him good first.
– Rory Bremner, *Rory Bremner, Who Else?*

Scientists have crossed a Shetland pony with a zebra. The French have amazingly agreed to sell the offspring in supermarkets as one of the first British steaks to come ready barcoded.
– Simon Hoggart, *The News Quiz*

Psychologists argue that eating disorders are all down to your upbringing – specifically the upbringing of your lunch.
– Clive Anderson

Scripts, one-liners, speeches, articles, sitcoms, game shows, stand-ups, 'top-shelf' magazines, sports columns, even technical reviews for computer nerds. One new commissioning editor on receiving her CV could only say: 'Bloody hell!'

But like so many creative giants, she was burdened by frailties, straddling the line between genius and insanity. Debs died making people laugh. Literally. The same rage that fuelled her extraordinary talent also triggered a psychological illness that killed her. Debs suffered from anorexia nervosa, which attacked mind and body alike. She replaced eating with writing. Her food was her gags. And her wilful refusal to eat had damaged her heart beyond repair.

That phone call changes everything. A few moments ago I was in a relaxed Bank Holiday mood; now I'm in despair. As the news of Debs' death sinks in, I fight to control my emotions. My wife Sue passes by the study, sensing instinctively that something is wrong. I mouth to her: 'Debs is dead.' She races in, holds my hand tight and then sits on my lap. She hugs me as the tears start to flow.

Night-time. But Sue and I do not sleep much. So much is going around our heads.

Each time I close my eyes I see images of Debs in sickness and in health and hear the sound of her voice. Whirling around my mind are all the inevitable 'what ifs'.

The previous weekend, Sue and I had travelled from our home near Aylesbury in Buckinghamshire to London to do the 'tourist' thing – museums, the London Eye, and the theatre. We had not seen Debs for some time and had tried to contact her. But she'd retreated into a protective, private shell, alone in her flat, except for her pets. She would only see and communicate with people on her terms. Phone calls, e-mails, and text messages often went into a black hole, unanswered.

We should have been more forceful. We should have kept on phoning. We should have surprised her at her flat. Should have, would have, could have . . .

The next morning we drive through the spring sunshine to Debs' home on the Isle of Dogs, to begin the grim task that no parent should ever have to endure. As I head south on the M40 from Aylesbury, my mood swings between grief and anger. I wonder why God compensates for his gifts by imposing such appalling burdens. There were two Debbie Barhams – the writer and the woman. The tragedy was that as the writer went from strength to strength, the woman became weaker and weaker.

Like so many parents of anorexics, I was a powerless passenger as the juggernaut hurtled towards the cliff edge and certain disaster. Was her premature death such an inevitable consequence of her journey of self-destruction? How could such a happy-go-lucky child, a bright, sparky teenager, and a kind and caring young woman, decline into an emaciated emotional and physical wreck, refusing to eat to the point that she was so weak she could not support the head on her shoulders? What insidious, malevolent force was at work in her mind that allowed her to descend to mere skin and bones, yet encouraged her to write jokes about it?

The two-and-a-half-hour journey to Docklands takes us along the Embankment, near the cafés and bars of Notting Hill and Central London where, for ten years, Debs was a regular and popular nocturnal habitué. She stood out wherever she went. The waiters called her 'The Duchess'. They would scurry to clean a table as my tall, elegantly dressed daughter floated in entirely in designer black. Many things about Debs' life was black, not least her moods, attire, and acerbic humour. Clad top to toe in expensive apparel – full-length coat to keep her frail frame warm, silk gloves to hide her matchstick hands, and matching hat to protect her ulcerated scalp – only her blonde wig and rouge lipstick offered any colour to an otherwise mournful appearance.

She would sit long into the early hours, mostly alone, observing, thinking, reading the day's papers, plotting ideas, firing off rounds of scripts, reviews, and personal e-mails on her palm-sized computer. The millions who enjoyed her work could never have imagined the origins of the material they watched, heard, and read. And no one in those cafés could have known the torment nagging away in the recesses of her mind on her mission to bring a smile to people's faces.

As we approach East London, fear and dread replace the anger and recrimination. I am frightened of what I am about to discover. Frightened how I might react. Frightened of the unknown. Neither Sue nor I had been to Debs' flat since we'd helped her move in three years ago. This was after we had nursed her back from the brink of death when she'd weighed under five stone. She had lived with us for nine months, requiring 24-hour care. Debs survived that crisis and had bought the one-bedroom flat on a wave of optimism and determination that she could put her illness behind her and make a new start.

The Wheel House, a converted wharf off the West Ferry Road, sits at one corner of the Burrells Wharf development. The riverside block is a mix of green-framed glass and cream-painted concrete. It is typical of the flats that sprang up in Docklands in the latter half of the twentieth century – old dock buildings that once formed the bustling gateway to the capital, but now occupied by people from a different world. Yuppy ownership was a stereotype that Debs milked over and over in her comedy routines. Whether she realized or appreciated the irony, she became one herself. Her flat, which she bought for £140,000 in the summer of 2000, is on the fourth floor. It meant so much to her, the realization of a dream, a measure of her personal success. She also saw it as a place where she would be happy to entertain, although, to my knowledge, she never did.

We call at the estates office for the keys and discover the first signs of the warmth and genuine concern that Debs had engendered among people. The staff go out of their way to be courteous and kind. Her death has touched them too – she wasn't just another tenant: they all knew my Debs. A private and lonely person, she was very caring. She once arrived unexpectedly just before midnight on New Year's Eve with a magnum of champagne to celebrate with the security people who had to work while everyone else enjoyed themselves.

Entering the downstairs lobby of her block is eerie. The lift takes us to the fourth floor – and as soon as the doors open we are hit by a strange but very distinctive smell. Not really unpleasant, but not something anyone would want to live with – the overpowering smell of Debs' cooking. What she did to food was unbelievable. Practically everything was microwaved, often to oblivion. Simon in the estates office was later to tell us that he personally had carried up to her flat three microwave ovens in as many years after she had worn the old ones out. Everything was brutally overdone. Broccoli, for example, was best served destroyed. She would microwave it for hours until it was baked brittle and, to most discerning people, totally inedible. Almost certainly this destructive compulsion was a symptom of her irrationality towards food, maybe even an excuse not to have to eat it.

The front door is already open. Here we are greeted by sensations I will never forget.

Strangers in white overalls, rubber gloves and facemasks are making their way out. It could almost be the set of a science-fiction film. In fact, they are cleaners. I will discover later that Debs had become Bulimic during the final months or maybe years of her life. The flush handle on her toilet was too stiff for her frail arms to cope with, and basically the bathroom had become an unpleasant mess. People say that smell is the most evocative of all senses. Whenever I encounter the odour of disinfectant in future I shall remember this moment.

Debs' body has already been taken away for medical examination and her pets were being cared for by neighbours. I stop and look around the flat and try to take in the surroundings where she had spent her final hours. Her home is cluttered and untidy, but not in the state I had feared from my memories of clearing her previous flat in Chiswick at the height of her illness.

In the hall, draped over a coat stand, are her three black overcoats, many handbags, and two distinctive Russian black velvet hats. The rest of the hall is filled with shelving, cases of books and files, and an unopened Tesco Direct food order, containing mostly packets of chocolate and biscuits. Her latest food fad had been Broken Biscuit Cake – a concoction of crushed chocolate biscuits, syrup and melted butter that she learnt as a child from her grandmother. Traditionally, this uses leftover broken biscuits, but typically Debs would only use the best bars of chocolate and expensive shortbread.

So much of the food in the flat is fattening – milk chocolate, white chocolate, cooking chocolate, chocolate fingers, truffles, chocolate mice, and bags of sweets. She wanted to extract every calorie from the merest morsel. There is no sign of any fruit, salad, protein, or vegetables.

The kitchen work surfaces are covered with biscuit crumbs. Otherwise, the kitchen is chaotic but clean, the washing-up dry on the sink. In the racks are wine and Champagne bottles donated to her at end-of-series TV parties, but which she rarely felt celebratory enough to drink. Bucks Fizz and white wine with ice were her favourite tipples – and on form she could drink many men under the table.

I peer into the bathroom. The cleaners have done their job. The floor is soaking, the toilet still doesn't look very appealing, and I can't help wondering what it had been like before. Some of her blonde wigs and ponytails are hanging above the bath. She had started to wear these at the onset of her illness, to hide the poor state of her hair and her ulcerated scalp. We will discover eighteen almost identical wigs tucked in various places around the flat.

The lounge is tightly packed with IKEA-style furnishing: decorative twigs, a settee, coffee table, TV and magazines. Everything is covered in long white cat hair. The floor is littered with box files. And then, in the hall, two very sad and strange mementoes. Hugging the ceiling are two helium-filled balloons, their pink ribbons straddling down to the floor. Between the balloons is a gift-wrapped flower in a jar. I read the embossed inscription on both balloons: 'Get Well Soon'. Attached to them both is the same, handwritten message: 'Chin up babe, it gets easier from now on.'

Later that day, I will discover an Internet order for the balloons. She'd sent them to herself.

I am dreading seeing the bedroom. Leaving Sue in the sitting room, I go inside and stop in the doorway. My emotions are a mixture of heartbreak and trepidation. The room is bright and airy but, like much of my daughter's character, either black or white. Why this preoccupation with black? Was it an expression of her mood or her style?

The curtain pole, bed frame, and rowing machine are all black. The walls, curtains, and bedding are white. The contrast is completed by another black-and-white image. Beside the bed at the end of the room, resting on a wooden easel, is a blackboard-size print of New York's Twin Towers created before the terrorist attack. It was taken in the dark of night, the shimmering lights from the giant buildings casting their white reflection on the Hudson River. This chilling image is strangely contrasted by many large soft toys around the room. I had given her some of these at a time when I felt she needed someone, or something, to cuddle.

Something inside me stops me going any further in. I want to try to take in where she spent those last few moments of her life, to imagine and perhaps share some of her trauma and emotional pain. I step over to the bed and sit on the corner, just where she had lain. I want to be with her and I feel, for a moment, that I am.

I pause to consider my feelings.

I feel completely useless, a total failure as a father, because when she finally needed me most, I wasn't there. And there is anger, too, because I could have been there, if only I'd known how her health was declining. I want to say sorry for letting her die alone. I'd walked out on Debs and her mother when she was a toddler. I wanted to apologize for being an absent parent and for all that I had failed to do for her: for not being there on her first day of school; for missing out on the nativity plays; not being around to help her with her homework; for not chasing off the bullies; not taking her to the panto; for not being a shoulder to cry on during those difficult early years.

Indeed, was I, in some way, a reason for her illness?

In a way, in that moment, I say goodbye to Debs – a contrite, heartbroken father seeking forgiveness and yearning for some post-trauma comfort.

Two

I return to the lounge, pointlessly trying to hide the tears I had shed in Debs' room. I want to just stay there and let it all out, but stupidly feel that I have to be brave. I must try to put personal grief aside and deal with the business ahead.

There is much to be done, and an immediate priority is to inform her many friends and business contacts of her death. This is not going to be easy. There is no such thing as an address book. Debs was a child of the electronic age. All her phone numbers are on this palm-sized personal organizer in front of me. But it is switched off – and I don't know her login details, user-name, or password.

Where do I start? I do not know who her friends are, who she is working for, who is important in her life, who I need to contact about her passing. What I *do* know is that her various other computers are the key to reaching them.

Debs developed a fascination for computer technology at an extraordinarily young age. At secondary school she passed her computer studies exam two years early. She was so good the examiners thought she was cheating. As a 13-year-old, she wrote computer programmes for her Amstrad – even composing a database for her pet hamsters in which she logged their ages, bloodlines, and breeding patterns. She beat hundreds of people in a national competition for developing a computer game aimed at persuading people not to drink and drive. She won the 13–25-year-old category despite the fact she was just 13 herself, travelling down to London to receive the prize from the actor Tom Conti. She became an expert on writing about developments in the computer world and displayed a rare gift for penning lively reviews about new, complicated, and highly technical gadgets and gizmos.

But her wizardry with words and computers also gave her the means to avoid meeting family, friends and business contacts other than on her own terms. By communicating electronically, she did not actually have to meet anyone, and thus expose her true physical and mental state. To a large extent, during her last desperate months Debs existed only in cyberspace, a virtual person in her own specially created virtual world, slowly wasting away – invisible to the people who commissioned her work; invisible to the public who laughed at her gags; invisible to her friends and her immediate family who so desperately tried to help her.

I return to her room to survey the electronic debris. On her bed, somehow, her laptop is still on, her work so rudely interrupted. This is connected to the main computer over in the little alcove in the corner. The screen reveals her last professional act – to e-mail a rough draft of material for the *Daily Mirror* from her bed laptop to the main computer. But the work is unfinished and was never forwarded to the newspaper.

I am about to discover a number of e-mail accounts, all

used simultaneously for different purposes. It will be ages before I realize the significance of one user-name – SKCOL-LOB – achieved by reading it backwards. Another was deb@fuckwitted.com, another dab@joke-shop.com. And she'd mischievously registered the domains of Leo Blair and of the disgraced politician www.neil-hamilton.co.uk – goodness knows what she had planned for those! At the age of 17 she had created her own website – D. A. Barham's Brand Spanking New Homepage – which boasted nearly twenty thousand hits in its first couple of years.

I brush off the worst of the biscuit layer from the key-board, press the space bar, and wait for the computer to burst into life. Suddenly, on the screen flashes the last e-mail Debs ever received. It is from James Steen, the editor of 'The Scurra' column in the *Daily Mirror*, and a close friend. It is a measure of her reliability and absolute deter-mination never to miss deadlines that James should write the following when her copy was only a few hours late.

```
From:       The Scurra
Sent:       21 April 2003 18.16
Subject:    Please Call

Debbie, I'm very concerned not to have heard from
you. Please call me just to put my mind at rest.
```

And then, forty-one minutes later:

From: The Scurra
Sent: 21 April 2003 18.57
Subject: Re Gag Stuff

Debbie, I've clearly got nothing better to do with
my bank holiday, but the more I think about this the
more I feel I should contact the dreaded emergency
services.

He called the police the following day, but they'd already found her body.

I ponder my next move. Without knowing any of her various user-names and passwords, it is vital I do not dismantle the computer systems while going through her correspondence. If I do, everything might be lost forever. I search the computer for Debs' e-mail address book and start typing almost by instinct. Debs is about to announce her own death via her own e-mail account and this is definitely not one of her gags.

From: D. A. Barham (dab@joke-shop.com)
Sent: 22 April 2003 15.08
Subject: Debbie Barham
Importance: High

This message comes from Debbie's father, Peter, and
is being sent to you because you recently, or in the
past, have been an e-mail correspondent of Debbie's.

With the greatest sadness, I have to break the news
that Debbie died peacefully in her sleep on Sunday
April 20th, after struggling for many years with her
health.

I am anxious to make contact urgently with friends
and colleagues to help us make the most appropriate
arrangements to say goodbye. I would be most grateful
if you could e-mail me at the address at the end of
this note or ring me on the following number.

I am sorry that this means of hearing the news is so
impersonal and abrupt but Debbie kept her
professional and personal life much to herself and I
therefore have no other way of starting a search for
those people who were important to her.

With some trepidation I hit the 'send' button. I have no idea
what response, if any, I might get, or how quickly. I have
given my own e-mail address to respond to, and my mobile
phone number; and since I cannot access my own e-mail
from Debs' computers, there is nothing more to do except
carefully close all of the computers down and take them
back home to Aylesbury for some comprehensive backups.

There is a considerable amount of equipment and an
astonishing quantity of cable and other gadgets. There is
still no way of knowing any of her passwords. I can only
hope that essential e-mail logins have saved passwords.

I make two calls, one to her agents, Casarotto, Ramsay
& Associates, in case there are urgent deadlines that will

now not be met, and to her publishers, Summersdale, for whom she is writing a series of compact books. They tell me that, as well as being a beautiful girl, Debs had the greatest talent of comic genius in anyone they have met. These calls are heartbreaking and very emotional, because they are the first indication of the fondness for Debs, her status in the industry, and the real sense of loss at her death.

The news spreads through the media world like a shock wave. As one person receives it they forward it on to other colleagues who knew or may have worked with Debs. An early phone call is from James Steen, the former editor of *Punch*, who had been the first of her professional colleagues to raise the alarm. James is to become a great comfort to me over the next few weeks – caring, understanding, and typical of how her friends are to rally round to help me in the difficult days ahead.

One by one, the recipients of the death announcement respond, with messages of support and condolences. I am overwhelmed by their kind words. There are scores of e-mails. Typical is this from radio producer Bruce Hyman:

    I hope you take comfort from the fact that in her
    short life Deb achieved what most writers would wish
    for in a much longer lifetime. She was prodigiously
    talented, sweet, unwaveringly professional and a
    kind and selfless person. I and so many others will
    miss her, and unsentimental as she was, I think she
    would know that.

And this from the TV presenter Clive Anderson:

> She produced a phenomenal amount of material - on
> any given occasion several times the quantity of any
> other writer I have ever had anything to do with. A
> truly extraordinary person. Obviously I was aware of
> her condition. There was a time when I could
> persuade her to meet for lunch but I had not managed
> that for some time. I am stunned now she has died
> and regret not making greater efforts on her behalf.

From Clive's former producer, Laura Marks, now in Los Angeles:

> Debbie was one of the finest one liner writers I ever
> worked with.

Sam Carlisle, an assistant editor at the *Sun*, replies:

> She was the first person we contacted whenever we
> needed something funny to brighten up the lives of
> ten million readers. And she always, always,
> delivered. Debbie had an amazing wit and ferocious
> intelligence and was one of the most professional
> contributors I have ever worked with.

Lucy Armitage, who worked with Debbie on *The News Quiz*, writes:

> She wrote unbelievably rude and funny gags and
> we invariably ended up down the pub together after
> recordings. She was fantastic company.

Praise and sympathy comes from quarters I did not know even existed. This from online bookmakers, Blue Square:

> We only ever had contact with your daughter, who
> wrote humorous stories for our site, via e-mail and
> so had absolutely no idea she was ill. We enjoyed
> our regular written exchanges which would inevitably
> result in some sort of amusing diatribe about the
> misfortunes of Leeds United.

And an acquaintance from Debs' nocturnal café community:

> I loved spending time with her just chatting. I know
> she was shy, but she had a sweet soul, if a little
> acidic at times! We would meet for coffee and
> dissect London life. It was always the highlight of
> the day to get one of her mails, each one a gem and
> had me laughing out loud.

But it is not just friends and the traditional media who mark her death. Debs was a self-confessed 'geek', a contributor to a number of online publications and a member of numerous newsgroups. Tributes from the online community flow across the ether.

> This is so sad. Debbie was one of the first people
> I met online, when she used to hang out on the
> Vt100-based nightmare that was Delphi Internet
> Services, my first internet job, back in 1994. She
> was startling bright, fun and hilarious. I never

realised that she would have been 17/18 at the time.
A terrible tragedy.
Posted by Stefan.

Another reads:

Debbie's column in the Palmtop Magazine was the
biggest reason I kept subscribing. She was the
'insane' counterpart to the overly serious world of
computers, and I love her ravings and rantings.
Never realized she was that young. I hoped she
realized the joy she brought to a lot of people, and
that is some kind of consolation in the timing of
her illness. May she rest in peace.
Posted by Tim

There is internet empathy, too, from fellow sufferers of eating disorders:

It is truly sad to see yet another sufferer die
from this illness. Not all of us are 'pro-eating
disordered'. There are many legitimate sufferers
out there that do not gloat about the illness and/or
post such forums. I for one, despite numerous
hospital admissions, am quite secretive about my
struggles and live a somewhat reclusive existence.
I send my deepest sympathy to you all that knew Deb.
Posted by Jo.

Three

One week on, but the business of death does not end. I am genuinely shocked at the level of media interest. Sure, I knew how talented she was; but I had no idea of the extent of her popularity and general acclaim within the industry.

Today, 29 April, the first obituary appears. It is in the *Guardian* – ironically, the first national newspaper she ever wrote for, at the age of 18. They had asked for a photo, but there weren't any decent ones that I knew of. I managed to find an acceptable picture from a few years before, and rushed that by e-mail to the paper.

Now other papers are calling for permission to use the picture. By chance, I find a good print in a pile of papers from a series of shots done for the *Sun*. I was in contact with a couple of *Sun* journalists who had known Debs well, and they did everything they could to track down originals, but with no success. So that picture – a particularly elegant and beautiful Debs – will do the rounds of many of the national papers over the next few days.

I am genuinely surprised and impressed by the respect and consideration shown by all of the papers as they handle the story. Everyone consults, checks details with me, or seeks approval before publication. My mobile phone doesn't stop ringing, as journalists politely press me for information or offer magazine exclusives, which I reject. Interspersed with these requests come frequent and touching calls from Debs' friends and colleagues, which bring me to frequent tears.

The *Daily Express* and the *Daily Telegraph* run extended features on her career and untimely death, the latter under the headline: 'The unsung queen of comedy'. The *Guardian* follows up its initial obit with a fuller feature, with a front-page trail above the masthead: 'How anorexia killed a comic genius'. The front page of the paper's G2 section is blank, except for that solitary photograph of Debs, looking radiant with her blonde hair, black headband, piercing blue eyes and rouge lipstick. Inside, an article by Libby Brooks occupies two pages.

Clive Anderson pens an obituary for the *Sunday Times*, written, he says, in the middle of the night with a cup of black coffee out of respect for her and her years of sleepless nights writing comedy. After submitting a lengthy article, even Clive was surprised that the editors demanded yet *more* material. It is the paper's main feature on page three of the News Review section and is trailed on the front. Under the headline 'Funny girl with a fatal obsession', Clive wonders what Debbie might have made of the reaction to her death.

A snort of derision possibly, a string of gags certainly. Rather than wanting us to wax sentimental about her, Debbie would no doubt suggest that her friends and family go out for an enormous meal and then not eat it.

Clive added:

> Unsqueamish post-mortem tributes were a favourite joke
> form of hers: 'The writer of *The Joy of Sex* has died. He's
> now writing a posthumous chapter on how to stay
> permanently stiff.'
>
> Another goes: 'Legendary animator Chuck Jones has
> died. As a mark of respect his body will be splatted with a
> 16-ton weight before being dropped off a clifftop where it
> will remain suspended in the air for several seconds before
> plummeting 300ft down and leaving a body-shaped hole in
> the ground.

I begin to reflect on the whole tragic saga. Hearing the terrible news, going to the flat, the incredible reaction from her friends and colleagues, and the massive media coverage. It strikes me that because of the way Debs led her life – intensely private and packaged in small compartments – no one knows the full picture. She hid behind an electronic wall of deceit.

Driven as much by the need to assuage my own guilt as a yearning for the truth, I am determined to discover the answers to Debs' life and death. I need my own emotional closure. Perhaps I will even be able to offer some knowledge and support to others facing similar battles with a daughter, or even a son.

It isn't going to be easy. Deception is the currency of an anorexic. Whilst she was happy to take advantage of her condition professionally through her writing, thus exposing her illness to the wider public, she created a smoke-screen of lies and half-truths to stop anyone remotely close to her finding a reason. She cunningly and cleverly kept people apart so they could never compare notes and thereby discover the full picture.

There may be barriers, too, from some of Debbie's friends, colleagues, and medical practitioners, anxious not to betray any confidences. But I know in my heart that she was genuinely loved by everyone. And if a father can't trade on his daughter's adoration, then who can? And, united in grief, it is clear that so many of her friends also feel a need to understand our joint loss.

I have valuable leads to go on: Debbie's own writing, not just professionally but in scores of entertaining and illuminating e-mails that I managed to preserve.

Except for the initial stages of her illness, she was never in denial about her condition, physically or mentally. Her denial was more in tackling it. Many victims look in the mirror and see a distorted image. But she had even taken Polaroid snaps of herself when she'd been a 5-stone skeleton.

Debs not only accepted her condition: she did not let it define her. She worked around it, and exploited it in her work for newspapers and television comedy. In a newspaper article she apologized for not meeting friends, writing: 'I have been spreading myself a bit thin lately.' In a Christmas piece for the *London Evening Standard* she wrote: 'It is not the idea of food I object to. I adore food. I just can't bring myself to swallow. But how many girls have said that at Christmas parties? Usually in the stationery cupboard with their knickers around their ankles.'

Will I be able to offer some explanation as to why a funny, gifted girl should starve herself to death? In a way, I feel that Debs has shifted her demons to me. She is finally at peace but I must now do some soul searching for answers of my own. Can I find out for myself and the rest of the family exactly why we lost our loved one? Just as Debs had suffered her own pain, I am ready to share her torment myself through the discovery of facts, however unpalatable.

And if I *have* failed her in life, at least I can seek some salvation by serving her in death.

My story starts just over three years before her death when out of the blue she walked back into my life.

Part Two

Back In My Arms

Four

I am in the kitchen of my home in Buckinghamshire preparing supper. My wife, Sue, has just popped out for some milk. The doorbell rings. She's obviously forgotten her keys. I walk through the lounge and open the front door. I stand in a silent daze for what seems like an age. It isn't Sue at all.

'You don't recognize me, do you?'

Of course, I did. But I am in a state of absolute shock at her appearance. This isn't the healthy, vivacious daughter I know, but an emaciated figure looking like she's stepped out of news footage highlighting Third World poverty.

A young woman of 22, yet looking like a frail pensioner. In truth, she is no more than an animated collection of skin and bones, weighing little over five stone. The muscle of her frame has virtually disappeared and her sculptured, attractive face has wasted away, cruelly exaggerating the rest of her features. Her high cheekbones that once defined her beauty now dominate her facial landscape and protrude like exposed rocks on the shoreline. Her eye sockets seem sunken deeper into her face and her eyes glare at me in a disproportionate, ghostly stare. This is walking death.

It seems an age before I can speak.

'Of course I recognize you. I just wasn't expecting …'

I can't find the words to finish. I'm too busy processing the mental permutations of how and why she looks so ghastly. Starvation diet? Terminal illness? Has she come here to die?

As an absentee father for practically all her life, I don't really know my daughter Deborah at all well. Her mother and I split up when she was just nine months old, confirming the doubts expressed by my father-in-law that I was not the right man for his daughter, albeit for totally different reasons. Even though when she was a child I lived near Debs' home, visits were rare. Certainly I was very focused on striving to prove Ann's father wrong – trying to build a successful career. But I still cared. I just felt, foolishly, that distancing myself would give her a better chance of stability.

Now, from nowhere, on this warm summer's evening, she is on the doorstep. No phone call, no letter, and no e-mail. No warning at all.

I scramble the brain to remember the last time I saw her. Yes, it was at my father's funeral in Amersham two years ago. She had turned up late and missed the cremation service, blaming the trains. Family occasions were not her scene, but she was particularly close to both my parents and she wanted to be there for her grandfather's goodbye.

She'd looked slender and beautiful in her customary black outfit but with a crimson summer top. It was the first time I had seen her with blonde hair – and so wonderfully slim, I thought at the time. I'd told her she looked stunning. I'm sure the compliment registered, but she chose not to react. After the funeral she'd stayed over with me in my rented house in Aylesbury and was ill in the night. In the morning I took her back to the station. She'd waved good-bye, leaving me a bucket of cold sick to dispose of.

Now we meet again, but she is in a far more desperate state. And I am about to discover how stupid I had been not to have spotted that she was in the throes of an eating disorder. The blonde hair had been a wig to hide the wretched state of her hair and scalp, and the sickness had probably been related to her condition.

The ghost on the doorstep speaks: 'My life's a mess, all of it. I didn't know what else to do. Please sort me out.'

With that, she more or less falls into the house. She is so weak, she cannot lift her leading leg onto the nine-inch step. She trips into the hall, and I catch her in my arms. I virtually carry her into the house. Then I put her back on her feet and hug her. And, for the first time that I can ever remember, she hugs me. There is little for me to hold, except for sharp protruding shoulder bones and a rather hard head.

Our cuddle lasts literally two minutes, both of us enjoying silent union, her head nuzzling against mine, clinging to each other as if our lives depend on it, which hers probably does. It is as though after more than twenty years of patriarchal starvation, she suddenly feels safe in her father's arms, intellectually a woman, emotionally a child. Indeed this is more emotional than physical bonding and a milestone for both of us.

Although shocked at what I am seeing, I am selfishly happy that she has turned to me in her moment of crisis. I've longed to be part of her life, and now here she is. A woman, yes, but also my baby back after so many years in the protective embrace of her dad.

Five

Nineteen seventy-six has been declared Britain's greatest ever year by a group of government 'think tank' scientists trying officially to measure the quality of life. It was perhaps fitting, then, that this was also the year Debs was born. It was one of the hottest summers on record. Harold Wilson resigned as Labour Prime Minister, Concorde made its first commercial flight, Abba topped the charts with 'Dancing Queen', and we witnessed the birth of punk rock. Britain had even won the Eurovision Song Contest with Brotherhood of Man. Around the world, it was quite a year too. War waged in the Middle East, there were riots and deaths in South Africa, and, three weeks before Debs was born, Jimmy Carter was elected President of the United States, defeating President Ford.

On 20 November 1976, at the hundred-year-old Jessop Hospital for Women in Sheffield, I watched proudly and nervously as this sweet, shrivelled little thing finally arrived at 2 a.m. after a marathon eighteen-hour labour. Welcome Deborah Ann Barham! She entered a world on the brink of dramatic change: the rise of Thatcherism; the collapse of Communism; the end of the Cold War; and a revolution in the field of communications – mobile phones, personal computers, internet technology and multi-channel television.

On reflection, Debs should never have come into the world at all. Although she had been a planned baby, my marriage to her mother was incompatible with raising a child. We had married very young, more out of defiance than deep-rooted love. Ann and I had got together in the spring of 1971 – five years before Deborah arrived. We were both undergraduates at Cambridge with a shared passion for amateur dramatics. We had no wish to be budding Robert Redfords or Meryl Streeps: we preferred backstage. In those days the ADC building in Park Street was run exclusively by students along commercial lines, mixing Shakespeare and Chekhov with Rodgers and Hammerstein. I became hooked on Ann and the theatre both at the same time. So much so, that I had given up my veterinary course the year before to become the theatre's first full-time employee in its hundred-year-old history.

Sadly, Ann's father did not share our joy. He was a no-nonsense schoolmaster with an intimidating manner. He had high hopes for Ann and was delighted when she gained a place at Cambridge to study for a degree in Geography. In her final year, I remember going to the Lake District to seek his blessing for our planned betrothal. He told me point blank that I, a mere theatre technician, was *not* what he had in mind for his daughter, and that I would never go very far. The snub was to have a profound effect on me for the rest of my life. From that day, I developed a determination to prove him wrong, and it is ironic how much I should now thank him for those disheartening words.

We knew that if we wanted to be together we would have to marry, and so we tied the knot at Sutton Register Office in Surrey that same year. Her parents did not attend.

Ann had been accepted at Sheffield University to do an MA in Librarianship, and I was determined to find a job in professional theatre. Little did I know how difficult that was – without an Equity union card you did not even get interviews. Literally days before the wedding, amazingly, after a London interview, I was offered the job of company manager of the touring company at Sheffield's Crucible Theatre, now better known nationally as the venue of the World Snooker Championships. I was to be one of the lucky few to get a 'provisional' Equity card, from the small ration allocated in the UK each year.

Our luck was in and we headed north in the hope of a successful start to married life and our careers. I was just 20, Ann a year older. We arrived in Yorkshire feeling a mixture of excitement and trepidation, strangers in a strange city. On my first working day I was introduced to a 'chip buttie' – a major culture shock for a sheltered southern public schoolboy. We knew little of the customs and culture of industrial working-class life. South Yorkshire had been the industrial heartland of Britain, a major provider of steel and coal, but its dominance was waning. Sheffield of course is world famous for its cutlery and special steels that built many of the world's railways and bridges. But that industry was suffering and when we arrived there had also been a series of bitter strikes in the coalfield.

Debs was to be brought up in a city of considerable contrast. Sheffield nestles between seven hills. At that time the centre skyline was dominated by ugly tower blocks. To the east, the Don Valley extended through miles of steel works into the heart of the South Yorkshire coalfield. It was smoke-blackened and raw with one of the highest concentrations of derelict land in England, mainly in the older industrial areas affected by steel and colliery closures. However, the 'steel city' has more green space, trees and woodland than any other city in the UK. The south-west of Sheffield is simply beautiful and, not surprisingly, is much favoured by the middle classes. Within ten minutes you can be up on the moors, a million miles from the grime of Britain's fourth biggest city.

This was definitely where we wanted to live. After a couple of rented flats, and a tiny terraced two-up, two-down, we settled in a two-bedroom house in the leafy suburb of Bradway, twenty minutes from the centre, but right on the doorstep of the Peak District with its miles of hilly walks and country pubs.

Sadly, the marriage was short lived. Gradually we became different people with different interests. I spent all hours of the day, and often night, at the theatre, loving every minute, while Ann preferred the company of her academic friends. I remember going to parties and feeling out of their loop, not accepted as one of them. It was the same for her when she came to the theatre. Although she knew that world, it was not what her daily life was about.

It was a very up and down relationship and we did not communicate well. We were different in other ways. Whilst I was a 'touchy feely' person, I found Ann far less physically expressive. By the time Debs was born we'd drifted further apart. Looking back, Ann had got what she wanted – a baby – but I felt pushed aside in her affection.

At just 23 I became Chief Electrician/Lighting Designer of the country's most prestigious regional theatre, but now, only two years later, I was not emotionally mature enough to deal with the widening rifts in my marriage. I remember when Ann's mother came up from Wiltshire to stay after Debs' birth feeling shunned by both of them, and not involved at all with our new baby.

My loneliness and sense of isolation led me quite quickly into a relationship with a colleague called Joanne (a stage name – her real name is Sally), who was deputy stage manager at the Crucible where I worked. She gave me the closeness that I did not have with Ann, but our affair was discovered very quickly. Although Ann was naturally very upset, she did not give me serious grief, something I will always respect her for. Perhaps deep down she knew that things were not right between us.

When Debs was nine months old, Ann and I parted. I set up home with Sally, who was to be my wife for eighteen years. There was no argument over custody or access. I did not want to cause any conflict. At the time I thought it was better that her mother and I should have a clean break, rather than put Debs through any emotional turmoil.

I honestly felt it was in everyone's best interests for me to stay away. There were several notorious 'Tug of Love' stories around at the time, and I remember feeling very strongly that I did not want my daughter to suffer in that way as a result of our failed marriage.

Today, of course, I know differently, and realize how stupid I was to take that view.

Six

I know this long, bony hug means as much to her as it does to me. Debs had always shied away from any contact and you could almost feel her stiffen inside. The only real physical closeness we ever had was my protective arm around her shoulder on family photos when she came to stay. Now I sense her relief, her need to be close and safe, but not a single tear is shed. Not from her, anyway.

Our relationship has always been quite formal. Her mother insisted she be called Ann, rather than Mum, and so I became Peter, rather than Dad. I always figured that, since I'd left her at such a young age, one day she would prefer to call someone else 'Dad' instead of me.

I have been through some turmoil of my own – two marriage break-ups and serious financial problems – and up until now felt pretty useless to her. I wrote her long letters at the times of my own crises, wanting to reassure her that I was still thinking of her, and would be there for her. She was one of the few people I felt I could confide in, even though I did not know her that well. I always felt we were on the same wavelength, and that she would understand. She never formally responded, just one or two fluffy e-mails, addressed *Dear Peter*, or sometimes, patronizingly, *Father Dear*, containing some witty throwaway remarks.

I help her through to the sofa and have barely helped her to sit down when I hear the key in the front door. This time it *is* Sue. I race through and, as she steps in, I greet her in a faltering whisper.

'You'll never guess who's here!'

'I know – it's Debs isn't it …'

Sue has never met Debs before, but has seen her face in photographs and picture bylines in various publications. When she left the house for the milk, she'd spotted a woman emerging from a taxi at the bottom of the road. The slight figure was dressed totally in black, with a winter hat and boots, despite this being the height of summer.

Without much flesh to protect her, Debs had dressed to beat the cold. Somehow, she'd struggled 150 yards up the steep hill with her laptop and two overnight bags. One can never explain these things, but Sue knew instinctively that this strange young woman was her stepdaughter. In fact, she nearly stopped the car to ask her if she was Deborah Barham. Debs has not been to this house. Although she never replied to our wedding invitation, she had saved the address.

Seeing Debs on the sofa, Sue bends down to hug her. She is as shocked at her state as me, but nothing is said by any of us. It is almost as if Debs is our normal, healthy ten-stone daughter who has popped in for a cup of tea. We will, of course, discuss her condition in due course, but we judge instinctively that now definitely isn't the time.

The next couple of hours are surreal. We talk about many

things, but not the obvious. I finish making our macaroni cheese supper and optimistically ask Debs if she has eaten, stupidly thinking she might join us. She explains that she has not had anything solid for a fortnight. She has kept going on thin soups. This she reveals in a matter-of-fact way, with no drama and not in the context of any eating disorder or psychological problems. For the rest of the evening we sit and talk, avoiding any direct references to the reasons for her mental and physical state.

I explain the changes in my life, how Sue and I met through our association with the publishing industry but how we were brought together by our interest in aerobics. She had taught for many years and I was to qualify as a teacher later. After living together for two years, we married on the Caribbean island of St Lucia. She has a daughter of her own, Sophie, and the three of us now live in this three-bedroom semi on the outskirts of Aylesbury. Sophie is away at her father's house for the night.

I tell Debs how it has all been rather hectic of late – a life-changing decision to leave the electronics company where I'd run the publications department for nearly five years and that my new employer is a small family print firm, where I manage the pre-press department. I tell her about family troubles, too: how, last year, Sue's youngest sister and her two children arrived one day from Spain needing refuge from an acrimonious failed marriage. She was seeking protection in case the vengeful husband followed them to England. For nine months the seven of us lived in virtual siege, expecting a knock at the door or a brick through the window any day. In the end, the family were reunited, but it had been a very traumatic time, which tested our new relationship to the limit.

Debs sits upright in her easy chair the whole time, her back exaggeratedly stiff and straight, seemingly eager to absorb every detail of my news. But suddenly an horrific truth dawns. Such is her malnutrition, the neck muscles have wasted away. This upright posture is to stop her head falling off her neck. Her head is merely balancing on her frame, like a badly repaired doll's head.

Sue and I glance at each other in equal despair. We change the subject by sorting out the emergency sleeping arrangements. I go to bed in a state of total shock. In times of crisis I am usually able to cast aside some of the emotional feelings and go into practical mode. But my mind is now hostage to today's events. Already I am beginning to think through how to deal with the issues before me. The stakes are alarmingly high. But how and where do I go from here?

I begin to think about those missing years in Debs' life.

Seven

You can never replace the father in a child's life. However, my mother Yvonne did her best to fill the vacuum created by our break-up and my lack of involvement with my daughter. She greeted her first grandchild with immense pride, even surprising her local vicar by toasting the new baby with champagne while attending a church jumble sale two hundred miles away in Sutton, Surrey.

Mum would visit Sheffield once a month, travelling up by car, the 'long-distance granny driver', as Debs once dubbed her, and on birthdays it would be granny arriving with a homemade cake. Mum passed on regular news about Debs to supplement the occasional times that she would spend with Sally and me.

It could not have been easy for Ann, a single working mother, trying to juggle the demands of career, motherhood, and a social life. For her to enjoy any adult friendships at all, Debs would be put to bed at home and wake up on someone's floor, unsettling for any toddler and ingrained on Debs' memory throughout her life.

Academically, Ann was determined to do the best for her child. She sought out a local nursery run under the principles of the Montessori doctrine of education – far more stimulating than the average playgroup and centred on the freedom of the child.

Italian-born Dr Maria Montessori was one of the most influential pioneers in early childhood education. She believed that children are better learners in the years up to the age of six than they will ever be again and that they can learn almost anything provided special techniques are used. Montessori found that once children are accustomed to making their own choices, they are naturally attracted to what will best serve their educational needs. So Debs was encouraged to choose any activity she wanted to work with and to complete it in her own time. Early learning was centred on individual choices and on providing familiar activities linked to home. In addition to conventional nursery school activities, such as painting, cutting and pasting and water play, Debs was given choices such as sweeping the floor, learning to tie a bow, or polishing her shoes.

Ann's sister Melanie, who was so sadly to discover Debs' body many years later, certainly feels the Montessori experience changed her young niece a lot. When Debs began, her ideas were faster than her hands, leading to impatience and frustration; but she emerged a more mature infant, able to focus and persevere and was a more careful, reflective observer on life.

Around the time Debs began school, Ann cemented her relationship with the academic world by moving in with university lecturer John Kingdom. He taught politics and public administration and was known locally for his lively political analysis on local radio and TV. John had two children of his own from a previous marriage, Becky and Jasper, who were five and three years older than Debs respectively. So Debs grew up in a complicated family structure with an absent father, a stepfather, a stepbrother and sister older than herself, and distant grandparents.

To the outside world, however, she was a happy-go-lucky girl, a picture of sweetness and contentment, although there is no doubt the infant resented the arrival of a stepfather who naturally took up her mother's time and attention – a feeling noticed by my own mother and mentioned later in life by Debs in interviews with psychiatrists.

But if Debs was harbouring any resentment, she did not reveal it either to Ann or John. He remembers being greeted with a spontaneous beam the day he first met his stepdaughter. He found her an extremely bright and gifted 5-year-old. Never mind Janet and John. By the time Debs went to primary school she was more interested in the sophisticated magical fantasy world of C. S. Lewis's Narnia stories. Her hobbies were natural history and pets, rather than dolls.

My mum was a former District Commissioner in the Guide Movement, knew how to entertain young girls, and was a warm and motherly influence. Debs shared her passion for animals and wildlife in general and they enjoyed regular holidays and weekends away. Mum had a black Labrador called Ambrose and Debs would ride it like a horse. Poor old Ambrose never complained. My mother recalls taking Debs on a train ride up Snowdon, but rather than taking in the splendid views outside she spent the whole journey studying the movement of an ant on the window.

Mum lived a few miles from Epsom racecourse and Debs liked nothing better than to watch the horses exercise on the Downs. She also had a caravan in Suffolk. They would buy fish and chips in Newmarket and have a 'fishnic' on the Heath, watching racehorses training. Easter and autumn holidays with grandma were often spent in Devon. Ann and John would come down for part of the time and leave Debs with my mum for a couple of extra weeks, enjoying cream teas, flying kites, and exploring rock pools on the beach.

Debs inherited a love of nature from both sides of the family. Aunt Melanie was a botanist at Kew Gardens and a leading authority on nettles. They would spend hours together pottering in the garden looking for slugs and snails. Even in make-believe, Debs' ideas were original and frequently involved animals. In one of her first letters to Melanie, written on Winnie the Pooh notepaper at the age of five or six, she tells her:

I had a nice holiday and found a butterfly stuck in the window so I let it out and showed it to mummy and granny. It was a peacock butterfly. On Friday we went to the shire horses and one of the foals was called Lord because it was born on Easter Sunday. Thank you for the music case. It is very nice. The piano lessons are going well. Now I have swimming lessons.

I found seven snails and made a snail house. But one snail got stood on, one ran away and one got lost. So I got four left. I made an ant hymn book for the ants in Devon and I found two beetles. I made a jigsaw for you. I will give it to you when we come to see you. It is two jigsaws actually and they are very hard.

Love from Deborah.

And a postcard to her aunt from a camping holiday in the Loire Valley in France when she was nine reads:

This is the picture of the river next to our campsite. We have found lots of insects and animals, stag beetles, rove beetles, shieldbugs, leaf beetles, spiders, ants, butterflies, moths, dragon flies, cat fish and huge water skaters.

The gas has just run out half way through the spuds!

With lots of love from Deborah.

Debs was a shy child, very private, very quiet and withdrawn in new situations, but bubbly and sociable with people she knew. Melanie says her niece was alert, quick-thinking, therefore easily frustrated; questioning but reserved, not garrulous; shy and somewhat tense until she became absorbed in a conversation.

She loved the rituals of childhood – Brownies, bedtime stories, entertaining friends and family with puppet shows in her room, even once staging a pantomime with her hamsters. Who would have thought that one day she'd be writing a real pantomime for national radio and getting a reputation for such crude language that she could make the outrageous comedian Graham Norton blush?

She became friends with the girl who lived next door, Catherine Clark, who was slightly older than Debs. They both became members of the children's section of the Sheffield Natural History Society and enjoyed trips to the Peak District. Catherine's parents took Debs on holiday to a farm cottage in Northumberland, where they became aware of her 'wicked' sense of humour. Catherine's mother Jane recalls: 'She was about ten at the time. She was a lively, articulate child, great fun to have around and someone who made jokes well ahead of her years.'

Her formative years were spent in a highly academic environment, surrounded by books and a radio in every room – even the summer house. Politics and current affairs were always being actively discussed. Ann was a staunch Liberal Democrat and campaigned actively for the party, whilst John of course was an expert on the whole subject of politics. Academically, Debs was thriving, top at every subject. Admiring her ability at English, a teacher at the Sir Harold Jackson Primary School told Ann she was convinced they would be seeing Debs on TV one day. Ann decided that it would be a crime to waste this talent, so at the age of eight Debs was 'fast-tracked' through school a year above her age.

At home, Debs was a perfectionist, almost to the point of obsession, at everything she tackled, and displayed amazing patience at making sure things were perfect. She would take her Instamatic camera down the garden and stand for hours waiting to photograph the squirrels, which she tamed with peanuts purchased with her pocket money. The food would be offered in one hand while, in the other, her camera waited to capture the moment.

At Junior School, she organized snail and hamster racing and greyhound derbies using battery-operated toy dogs. She was positively bubbling with ideas, staging plays with her brother and sisters. My daughter Briony remembers Debs acting the fool, putting Barbie pants on her head and writing plays about rubbish or sick! They once made a banner that read: 'We want rubbish – we want it now!' She also formed her own hamster society – Hastings Hamsters – named after the road she lived in. She bred and kept numerous hamsters, with names such as Spice and Strauss, with records of when they were on heat, their mating habits and their litter. All the details were carefully logged and she kept a collection of slides with photographs of the various animals. She attended hamster shows all over South Yorkshire with Ann and her stepbrother Jasper, winning numerous rosettes and trophies for breeding. Her literacy skills came to the fore when, at the age of ten, she wrote a letter of complaint to the editor of the National Hamster Council magazine about a certain brand of hamster cage.

Dear Editor

I am writing about the matter of Rotastak hamster homes. I think these things are really bad. To start with, £32 for a pretty small hamster home is a bit pricey. They are also not much fun inside for hamsters, providing no toys or space for toys except a wander wheel.

These Rotastak homes do not even have bars to climb on and they are not very well ventilated. They are easy to escape from and an energetic hamster could spend the night pushing wide open one of the doors, despite the so-called safety clips. I have lost a good hamster this way. I think the Rotastak Wonder Wheels are hopeless. I bought one in July and by August it was completely worn out around the axle.

Rotastak are no good for breeding hamsters in because the attic bedroom is small and high up and the babies could easily fall down the tubes and be killed.

Seeing as a decent-sized 'hammy home' costs around £7–£8, I strongly advise members not to buy these hamster homes.

Happy Hamstering

Deborah Barham, aged 10.

I played virtually no part in Debs' upbringing until, ironically, I left Sheffield. I had moved south to Oxfordshire when Debs was seven. By then I had remarried and Sally and I had started a family of our own, Sam and Briony. We would have Debs down for the occasional weekend and in the holidays. In a scene familiar to many estranged parents, Ann would hand her over, like some illicit parcel, at a motorway service station and I would take her to my home in Witney for 'quality time' – daughter, dad, and his new family.

Debs would have very little trouble slotting into the routine. She was shy to start with, but that disappeared quickly and she would go along with anything that we wanted to do. Sally was excellent at occupying the children and keeping them amused, and Debs would love visiting wild life parks, swimming or riding. Hours would be spent just messing about with Briony in particular, drawing cartoons and writing little plays. Sometimes she would sit at the piano and pick out tunes – she had learnt violin and piano for a while, but with little enthusiasm.

Mealtimes in the early years were uneventful. Debs had a normal and healthy appetite, although Sally remembers one incident when she was about two and a half – which, in retrospect, demonstrated how food was already a source of tension at home – when Debs flew into an hysterical rage over the size of a piece of cheese. At bath time she was just one of the gang, sharing baths with Sam and Briony, or the three of them with me! We didn't give her special treatment, but encouraged her to feel like one of the family.

But almost overnight, her mood at the end of visits changed dramatically. She became difficult, argumentative, and downright rude to her mother at the time of handover. My own mother said that at the end of holidays Debs would often be in tears at the prospect of returning home. It was clear that, for some reason, she was building up a deep resentment towards Ann. My mum and I both felt this was more than natural disappointment at the end of a holiday, but foolishly I did not feel that it was my place to tackle Ann about it.

Ann herself put it down to pre-adolescent frustration. But I wonder if perhaps it was because Debs felt she was being groomed as some sort of 'super pupil' in an academic hothouse. Sure, she was precociously bright. But was she emotionally ready for such a step up? Were those tears and resentment the early warning signs of the psychological problems she was to encounter in the years ahead?

Eight

25 June 1999

Debs has been in my home for twenty-four hours, and the extent of her decline is becoming clear. A story is emerging of a life completely out of control. Once a vibrant eleven stone and full of spark, she is now bordering on five stone, frail and devoid of energy. Even the simplest task is difficult. Seeing her in a sleeveless, strappy top is pitiful. Mentally she is alert, but she focuses entirely on her work to the exclusion of all else, including her own well being.

She confesses she's been having treatment for her problems but steadfastly refuses to go into any detail. She says her doctor got Social Services involved and that because of her decline in weight she feared being sectioned under the Mental Health Act. This would mean being force-fed and, worst of all, not being able to work. Sue and I will discover later that Debs hid lead weights in the lining of her bra to fool doctors into thinking she weighed more than she did.

Her personal affairs are a mess too. Although money has never been her main motivating force – she has more than £50,000 in her bank account, plus her own property in West London – she has no interest in managing money or keeping paperwork. She has not filled in a tax return or opened a bank statement for years. People like the Inland Revenue are simply a distraction to her work routine.

It has certainly been a busy time. Work commitments have snowballed, along with her reputation as a major writing talent. In addition to various regular newspaper, magazine and Internet columns, she has contributed to several top shows for TV and radio. These included the BBC's *End of the Year Show* starring Angus Deayton, a Bridget Jones Night, and Channel 4's *So Graham Norton*. She was also the main writer for Radio 4's star-studded Christmas Day panto – *Cinderella and Her Very Ugly Sisters* – in addition to the regular output of gags for radio shows and occasional TV pilots.

But despite her emaciated state, she is determined to work, though she is adamant that nobody must know where she is – not her friends, not her work associates, not even her agent, and specifically not her mother. Almost like making a playground pact, we are all sworn to secrecy. She believes her stay will be short term, so nobody need know she is living with her dad, which she feels would be the height of uncool in her media world. Besides, this will only signal weakness, and she insists on total control.

For now, I am prepared to accept her conditions. For me, it is a time for discovery and care rather than recrimination or paternal dictatorship. It is obvious that she needs urgent help, but I know that her stay will be cut short quickly if I make the wrong move. Rather than confrontation, we all buckle down to the practicalities of cramming three adults and a child into a small semi. With Sophie already in the second bedroom, Debs has to make do with the box room above the garage – big enough for a single bed and little else. She commandeers the dining-room table as her new 'office', taking over my computer and hooking up her Psion palmtop and organizer, all linked via infra-red to her mobile phone, which means she can send e-mail to the outside world while on the move.

I am about to get an insight into Debs' obsessional work routine and the way she goes about her craft. I am instruct-ed to go to the newsagent and get various newspapers. These, along with Internet links to a number of news sites, give her the complete picture of the events of the day. I watch as she scans the pages, carefully making notes about the stories that stimulate her wicked sense of humour. This is the fodder for her next round of 'topicals' – newsy gags – that she will send out to various clients in newspapers, TV, and radio.

Some stories she stores away for future sketches, sitcom ideas, even plays. She reads incredibly fast, but misses noth-ing, finishing each paper in minutes, and then, with all use-ful gossip and celebrity misfortune filed away in her photographic memory, consigns the paper to the bin. She rarely needs to refer back to the stories. Notebook after notebook lists each day's headlines, and these offer a fas-cinating snapshot of the important, or bizarre, events of the day. The stories that catch her eye today, 25 June 1999, are:

Dyke appointed Director General of the BBC; 500,000
passport backlog; Clapton guitar goes for £300,000; EU
to block GM research; Glastonbury Music Festival starts;
Baby left at Palace; London traders 'dress down'; Cinema
in car plan; Jonathan Aitken's poetry published;
Eurotunnel sniffer dogs retired; Welsh African to coach
England cricketers; Human cloning ban; world's longest
sermon preached; mad cow disease from contact lenses;
Bush wife smuggles dresses/jewels; Another Marks and
Spencer profit warning ...

We watch in awe as she types at frantic speed, despite the
restrictions of only a palm-sized keyboard. Instead of using
all her fingers, like on a conventional computer, she holds
the small contraption with her hands and types with her
thumbs, her long, slender digits ideal for covering all the
characters.

We also discover the extent of her compulsive personality. Whilst working she insists on a permanent supply of
scorching-hot coffee, which she takes extremely strong.
When it begins to lose heat, she microwaves it again, so
that it is *always* piping hot. Placed beside this is her glass
of freezing cold white wine, full of ice cubes. Just as her
tastes in life are often black and white, so her liquid intake
has to be blowing hot and cold.

I think back to those few times in her mid teens when
she stayed with us. She went through a vegetarian and then
a vegan phase, which was particularly difficult, but she was

always interested in food. She would cook herself sometimes, and once made us a tuna mousse from a recipe. It looked OK, but something obviously didn't quite go to plan. Although in our house you never threw food away and always left a clean plate, this was so repulsive that we all made an exception and spat it out.

I begin to wonder where, when, and why it all started to go wrong.

Nine

Debs sailed through junior school, but described her secondary school as the 'crappiest days of my life'. Even allowing for her flair for melodrama, the experience marked her right into womanhood. Indeed a year before she died, she discovered the website Friends Reunited, where long-lost class pals get back together again and compare their post-school lives. Her entry was typical Debs – exaggerated, deliciously provocative, funny, mischievous, and based on a foundation of truth.

```
Since leaving the unmitigated hell-on-earth which
was Sheffield Girls High, I have mastered 19 new
languages, won the Nobel prize, graduated from
Harvard, represented Britain in the Olympic
Freestyle Hammer Throwing Competition, served six
months in Pentonville for GBH, discovered a cure for
herpes, set foot on the International Space Station,
borne the children of several male pop icons and
been diagnosed as a compulsive liar. Currently
seeking therapy. If you met me now, chances are
you'd probably still not like me.
```

She half jokingly threatened to set up a rival site called BulliesRevenged.com

```
where legions of fat kids, Green Flash plimsoll
wearers and people whose mums made them Spam
sandwiches can be reunited with their teenage
tormentors. Furnished with the e-mail addresses
of my Fourth Form harassers, I can then exact
retribution by keying them into as many 'Register
Now For Free Information!' websites as I can humanly
manage (or for a small charge, I can become a
Bullies Revenged Silver Member and have the site do
this automatically). Hey presto! My former bully's
inbox is now mailbombed with digital junkmail
(though if he's in need of Herbal Erection
Correction, he's sorted). Upgrade to Gold Member
status, and he or she will also receive a free Love
Bug virus.
```

Debs felt a loner from day one. Unfortunately just before starting at the posh, fee-paying Sheffield High School, she contracted chicken pox. It meant that she missed the first few weeks of term – a time when crucial friendships are forged. I had always sensed that this had been a significant issue and was not surprised to find it highlighted in her psychiatrist's notes years later.

Sheffield Girls High School is an exclusive single-sex academic hothouse, attracting some of the wealthiest, brightest, and often snobbiest girls in the city. But Debs seemed to resent everything about the place: the distinctive school uniform – dark brown blazer, cream blouse, brown jumper and a matching brown-and-cream kilt – that made the High

School girls stand out in the city; the fact that some of her clothes were bought second hand, including her brown gym knickers; the bright orange hockey socks; school dinners – she described the paella as 'radioactive rice'; and the fact that her mother made her do violin lessons, which necessitated lugging an old-fashioned case, which Debs called 'the coffin', to school.

Many in Debs' year knew each other from their previous private schools. The other girls, from the state sector, had already fostered alliances in those first daunting days of secondary education. Debs arrived on the scene late, friendless, a year younger than the rest, and, because she was being fast-tracked, with a reputation of being 'a smart arse'. I felt it was a mistake to fast-track her through school. Nobody likes a clever Dick, do they? I felt it was an unnecessary pressure on someone who would have succeeded at any level anyway. There is no doubt in my mind that much of Debs' future unhappiness stemmed from this decision.

Her only real pal at school was Jane Brocklebank, who describes their friendship as 'two loners who gelled'. Jane and Debs had a lot in common. They were both rather shy and reserved, kept themselves to themselves, and were both on the Assisted Place scheme at the £900-a-term school. They also shared a passion for rodents – Debs with her hamsters and rats, Jane with gerbils and mice.

Jane says Debs had a grown-up, dark sense of humour and could be quite blunt and cutting, whispering some funny remark about the teacher or a fellow pupil under her breath. They sat next to each other in virtually every class for five years, usually in the same seats, third row from the front. Despite this closeness, their friendship never got above the level of companionship. At school, the emphasis was on learning, rather than developing any emotional bond. Debs never opened up about anything. Jane's mother even thought her daughter's classmate at times appeared quite rude.

Jane recalls: 'If you asked her, she would respond, but never volunteer or reveal anything about what was going on in her mind or her life. There were numerous things she kept from me, including that she was taking some exams away from school, and her BBC work.' This reticence was despite the fact that Jane occasionally went to Debs' house at weekends, even going horse-riding together, and that they spent many hours eating their packed lunches outside in the fresh air.

'She was good at everything, always in the top two or three. I enjoyed sitting next to her because she would help me with my homework and her ability rubbed off on me. I remember at open evening one teacher telling my mum that Jane's best friend was very clever. Her stories would always get read out. She would get embarrassed and refuse to read them, so either the teacher or another pupil would do it. Her writing had the class in fits of laughter.'

Their English teacher, Pamela Grayson, particularly delighted at Debs' essays, which she says were witty, sharply observed, imaginative, and mature.

I used to put her book towards the bottom of the pile as something to look forward to when I marked her group's work. I believe the class also looked forward to hearing her work read out. At first she was reluctant to read it aloud herself but quite willing to have a friend read it for her. She always sat towards the front of the class, a keen listener rather than a talker. In retrospect, she found the perfect career as a script writer. She was naturally gifted. The wry sense of humour that was so characteristic of her writing had no edge of malice or bitterness, such as one might have expected from an unhappy person, but rather suggested affectionate amusement in her view of situations and people.

Food became an issue in Debs' life. Jane remembers her giving a talk in class about the politics of the diet industry and how women were becoming slaves to food labelling. She had already stopped having school meals in favour of a packed lunch of sandwiches, yoghurt, and a chocolate bar – later that was reduced to just three or four Ryvitas. But there were no signs of any eating disorder.

Jane says that, as early as the first year, Debs made it clear she could not wait to leave school. It came at the annual school leavers' service, held in the nearby church to the sound of hymns, choirs, and music. It was an emotional time, with many tears, as pupils said goodbye to their chums, sometimes for ever. 'I asked Debs if she thought we would both cry when we left school after the sixth form.

She looked at me as if I was mad and said that she could not wait to get out of the place – and she would not even be staying on until the sixth form.'

Part of Debs' unhappiness may have been down to bullying, although Jane says she never heard Debs complain about this. Debs was prone to flare-ups of eczema, which made her a target. Fortunately her 'minder' during this time was her 15-year-old stepsister Becky, who had to step in several times to protect Debs from jealous pupils. But when Becky left to go to university, Debs was alone.

Physically, Debs was quite tall for her age, slightly ungainly, and a bit of a tomboy. She deeply resented the home-styled 'pudding bowl' haircut that her mother felt necessary to impose on her, and she found homework easier than making friends. Socially isolated she might have been, but academically she was still ahead of the rest, despite being put up a year. Ann wanted to do the best by Debs by pushing her to the limit of her academic abilities, although her stepfather feels that any school would have struggled to satisfy her thirst for knowledge and need for stimulation. School did not stretch her. Her classmate Jane agrees: 'Basically she was too clever for her own good. She was bored at school. She found it all too easy and just not stimulating enough.'

She sought outside influences as a vehicle for her imagination. In 1991 her stepfather authored a heavyweight book about government and politics in Britain. Debs helped him compile the bibliography – pages of references, all accurately listed in strict alphabetical order. These were done by hand without the help of a computer. John was so impressed that in the foreword he publicly acknowledged the 'careful work of Deborah Barham, aged 12'.

Even then she was extremely politically aware and described herself a 'news junkie'. John was a frequent radio pundit on various local issues and as Debs grew up her homeland was constantly in the news through its battles with the Thatcher Government. Sheffield, under the leadership of a fiery left-wing local politician called David Blunkett – later to become New Labour Home Secretary – was at the heart of the so-called Socialist Republic of South Yorkshire, whose signature policy of heavily subsidized bus fares was a big hit locally, but despised by Mrs T.

I had started an electronics manufacturing company in Attercliffe, once the centre of Sheffield steel production, which even featured on Yorkshire Television's *Calendar* news programme as a shining example of Sheffield's new industry. Ironically, while successful technically, this business failed partly as a result of a two-year delay in receiving a development grant due to the council's legal disputes with the government.

One Christmas, Ann and John bought Debs and Jasper a second-hand Amstrad 464 computer, one of the earliest personal computers. They soon got bored of the basic games available in those days. Debs then 'bought out' her stepbrother's share. As sole owner, she could now spend as much time on it as she liked, learning about computer technology and devising her own programmes.

At the age of 12, she responded to an article in the *Sheffield Weekly Gazette*, the local giveaway newspaper, which invited readers to enter a national competition designed to warn people about the dangers of alcohol. Debs developed a computer-based arcade game called 'The Booze Game', in which participants played the part of a delivery driver in the town of Boozebury. Hers was nominated the best individual entry in England, for the 13–25 age group. The judges said it was an 'outstanding entry' with potential for commercial exploitation. She received a plaque and a cheque for £500 from the actor Tom Conti, who at the time was starring in the West End hit play *Jeffrey Bernard is Unwell* – a story about a raging drunk journalist. She spent her winnings on a new TV so she could watch Monty Python in the privacy of her room.

Debs went on to take a self-taught GCSE in computer studies, which she entered and sat outside of school at Norton College in Sheffield. Her project was a computer programme based on hamster genetics called 'Hambase' – an extension of what she had been doing manually for several years. Needless to say, she got an A grade, but John received a phone call from the examiners who thought the work so good that they believed it must have been done by an adult. They wondered if Debs had cheated.

Ten

Debs has quickly settled down to a work routine. Her 'day' begins late in the afternoon and she works right through the evening and night with no break until the following morning. The radio is her only companion. She is a particular fan of Radio 5 Live, which could almost have been created especially for her, feeding her passions for sport and news. Mid sentence she breaks off from her work to e-mail *Up All Night* with wry one-line comments about the topics under discussion.

Routinely, she does not turn in until dawn, often needing pills to sleep. Then, after a couple of hours catnapping, she is up for another round of scripts, comedy routines, columns, and topical one-liners. Much of our communication is done by notes left on the fridge, or on the kitchen work-tops. She finds it practically impossible to write anything straight. Even the most mundane messages have at least one witty line. Her notes and e-mails are an extension of her profession and character – entertaining, often overwritten, but never dull.

Peeps

*Sorry not to see you last night, we must meet up
sometime. I have broken back (of work, not self) at
last – should still be working but eyes and brain
refusing to go along with the idea. Having another nap
(Sue – poss whack door before you leave?) and may try
to avoid town again depending on a) how much I can
get done here b) yuckiness of weather c) Yuckiness of
me. If I do go in, it'll probably be after my 4pm
deadline anyway. So don't be surprised to find me here
when you return – either awake or asleep or
somewhere between the two. Have a good day at
work/school. (Soph only) Cheque for Tesco goodies
(thanks x10⁶) enclosed. If you are passing thru later
there is something called Potters Antitis (I think that's
the name – little pot, pale green, lid with the hippy
herbal remedies) which I could use some of but
absolutely no hurry (also copy of the* Sun, *but I may
pop out to cornershop and get one myself, come to
think of it). Balls, this is turning into* War and Peace –
*I shall turn into Snore and Peace for a while. If you
spot my much-loved grey-barrelled pen anywhere,
kindly apprehend the blighter and leave in prominent
location on table. Thank you, thank you, THANK
YOU and yawning heaps of love*
Debszzzzzzzzzzzzzzzzzz

Another time:

> *Ooops! Didn't turn in 'til 5am. Please do not dis-inter. (Don't worry about disturbing, tho' – anything below noise level of small nuclear bomb exploding during Ian Paisley speech and/or Grateful Dead concert is unlikely to wake me). Debszzzzzz …*

And another:

> *Play with your megaphone as much as you like. It's unlikely to wake me up … Debs*

As well as reading and hearing about the day's events, Debs wants to *see* the world go by. Despite being barely able to walk, she decides she is stable enough to resume her London beat.

5 p.m. A taxi arrives at the door and takes her to Aylesbury station for the one-hour journey to Marylebone. She is far too weak to cope with the escalators on the Underground, so she will get taxis everywhere. She plans to hole out at the BBC canteen or, preferably, in the bars and cafés around Notting Hill, where none of her media colleagues will see her.

10.50 p.m. She calls me from her mobile – her train is due in soon. At Aylesbury, the London trains arrive on the far side of the station. Sadly, Debs can't manage the footbridge and has to wait for the train to pull away and struggle over the rail track to a side gate, which fortunately is conveniently unlocked.

She gets in the car, but does not have the strength to close the passenger door. We decide a way around this is to link hands, so we develop this hilarious 'pulley' system, whereby she holds the door handle with her left hand and I pull her outstretched right hand from my position in the driving seat. This will become our routine for the weeks ahead. It is humiliating for her, but it works, and gives us both a rather unconventional moment of closeness each day – something we never had during her troubled upbringing.

Eleven

As a teenager, Debs was not typical of her peers. She shunned the usual pre-pubescent attractions of boys, cigarettes, make-up, teenage magazines, pop music and discos, preferring the solitude of books, the local library, and wildlife. Her classmate, Jane, says that gradually through secondary school Debs became more and more withdrawn. Whatever catastrophe was happening in her life, real or imagined, it was having a major effect. At home she sometimes went days without speaking to anyone. She lived in a secret, private world. Her only soul mates were her pets and radio.

Her room was at the top of the house, with splendid views of the garden and distant hills. It became a retreat from her unhappiness. More and more she escaped there, listening to the radio until the early hours. Her transistor radio was her best friend, a companion that offered no complications, merely hours of pleasure. Her world was Radios 2 and 4, where she became intoxicated by the mix of news, current affairs, comedy, and politics.

Debs developed an obsession for the topical comedy radio shows *The News Huddlines* and *Week Ending*. She would scour the *Radio Times*, ringing each transmission time to make sure she did not miss a programme. Each show was taped and meticulously logged in her journal. She amassed more than 350 cassettes, containing thousands of jokes, which she organized into a mini audio library and updated weekly. She later told an interviewer: 'I was a very depressed teenager who happened to listen to the radio a lot. I know I should have listened to Morrissey and gone vegetarian, but I took solace in *The News Huddlines*.'

Even on family trips, Debs maintained her solitary existence, travelling in the back of the car listening to her comedy tapes through earphones on her cassette player. Whether she realized it or not, she had absorbed the essential ingredients for satire and had learned by instinct the structure and subtleties of gags – the nuance of language, timing, the juxtaposition of events, reverses, set-ups and subsequent punch lines.

It wasn't long before she was dreaming up jokes of her own and sending them off to the BBC under the name of D. A. Barham. Because of the formal, initialled appellation, the producers assumed they were dealing with some retired country gentleman, rather than a schoolgirl. The first gag of hers ever used by the BBC was for an edition of *Week Ending* on Radio 4 on 13 September 1991, when she was 14. The mix of celebrity, politics, and spite was to become a D. A. Barham trademark.

After it is revealed that Marilyn Monroe had an extra toe removed in case it ruined her popularity, we ask Neil Kinnock if he'll have his tongue cut out.

The thrill of the BBC using her gag inspired her to send more. She would lie in bed, listening in the dark, waiting to hear if her material had been used. Two weeks after the *Week Ending* breakthrough, *The News Huddlines* ran this timely offering of hers about the ageing rock band Status Quo:

> *Roy Hudd:* How about Status Quo travelling eight hundred miles in twelve hours to play four different concerts – amazing the value you can get from a Senior Citizen's Railcard.

Buoyed by her success with gags, she submitted her first ever sketch to a classical music comedy show called *Miles and Millner*. It was about school music exams, was pre-recorded in February 1992, and eventually used on the 16th of June that year.

She was credited in the 1992 *News Huddlines Election Special*, which was broadcast live on 9 April, with 'additional lines by D. A. Barham'. Debs sat proudly in the audience, having gone to London especially for the programme.

So, at 15, she already had three shows on her CV. She penned a regular supply of one-liners and end-of-pier gags that were used with increasing regularity. This she did without telling a soul.

Caroline Leddy was one of the *Week Ending* team who read through unsolicited submissions. By an amazing coincidence, Leddy also grew up in Sheffield and had even gone to the same school as Debs, albeit several years earlier. The Sheffield postcode caught her attention – and so did the material. She told a newspaper after Debs died:

> Her early work was exceptional. It was mature, spiky, wise, all the things that you would not have expected someone of that age to have a grasp of yet. She was simply unignorable. She knew the kind of stuff we wanted and she delivered it. She had a huge natural talent, but she also knew the field extremely well. It was clear that she had been listening and watching comedy all her young life.

Debs may have resented being bred as some sort of super pupil. The irony was that, alone in her room, she was creating her own version of a super child. The difference was, this was on *her* terms, rather than anyone else's. She was naturally proud of her breakthrough, but never boastful; and along with the secret thrill of success came the royalties – envelopes began arriving to her semi-detached home in Hastings Road, Sheffield addressed to D. A. Barham and embossed with the BBC logo. Her mother was naturally curious and Debs finally confessed all. 'She told us in a matter-of-fact way that she was writing for the BBC. It was more to explain the letters than boasting about her achievement,' recalls Ann.

The whole family were now listening out for the D. A. Barham name check. By coincidence, Debs' stepfather's brother, Robert, was a frequent voice on the shows and was a superb mimic of the defeated Labour leader Neil Kinnock. So the family had two credits!

She had decided on the career she wanted to pursue and entered a readers' competition in a magazine for budding writers, which she duly won. The prize was to attend a comedy writers' workshop given by Lawrence Marks and Maurice Gran at the Edinburgh Festival. Debs attended the workshop with a relative.

With one of the world's biggest broadcasting organizations interested in her work, and paying her for the privilege, Debs must have managed a wry smile at a teacher's remarks on one of her school essays about life in the fourth form: 'Another piece of good writing to complete an excellent year's work, although I don't like the very end. The tone is impertinent. The last sentence is ill-judged.' The last sentence was in fact: 'I can't be bothered to write any more.'

As more cheques came rolling in, Debs felt bold enough to want to attend script meetings, rather than simply sending her comedy contributions by post. She persuaded everyone that she should be allowed to go on day trips to the BBC in London, her train fares being paid for out of her royalties.

So, still 15, Debs travelled to the capital, a girl entering a male-dominated adult world. The courage she showed was simply remarkable. Indeed she later confessed in a letter to a boyfriend just how scared she'd been, stepping into this daunting environment for the first time: 'How can you make anything of your life if you don't take advantage of all the opportunities going? Nothing ventured, nothing gained. I was shit scared of going to my first *Hudds/Week Ending* meeting. I never expected to get stuff on, but if you don't try, then you never will.'

Of course, the cover was well and truly blown about the true identity of D. A. Barham. Like an under-age recruit signing up for the First World War, she lied about her age, fearing she might be shown the door if the BBC knew she was only 15.

She invented some cock and bull story that she was a working-class 19-year-old employed in a Sheffield green-grocer's who had left school at 15 to pursue a career in comedy. The romance of the story appealed to the coterie of older Oxbridge types at the BBC, who could not do enough to welcome this spiky northern lass into their midst.

Given her natural academic prowess, everyone assumed that she would sail through the sixth form and follow the family tradition by going to Cambridge. Everyone, that is, except Debs herself. In a private meeting with her Aunt Melanie in London, she confided that she hated school and wanted to leave. 'Having to plod slowly through the GCSE years at school really got Deborah down because she had already discovered that she could study much more effectively on her own,' recalls Melanie.

Her aunt advised her that, if she felt so strongly about it, she should investigate all the options, including studying A levels by correspondence course, and present Ann with a case. Starting with the Citizen's Advice Bureau, Debs began a round of furtive enquiries, including chatting to one local authority education official who erroneously told her that what she was planning was 'illegal'.

Soon after, she came home from school sobbing and stomped up to her room. Ann thought there had been a disaster. In fact Debs had just received the results of the school scholarship exam for free entry into the sixth form. Despite being the youngest in the year, she had won the only place. But these were not tears of joy. She blurted out that she had no intention of doing A levels at school and wanted to leave that summer.

As her family calmed down from the shock, Debs explained that she wanted to try her luck with the BBC and study for A levels by correspondence courses instead. She shrewdly argued that, under her plan, if the BBC work came to nothing, she could still go to university later. We were all stunned by the news, including Debs' headmistress, who, at a showdown meeting, exclaimed that no one in the school's proud history had ever turned down a scholarship. Ann in particular was distraught that she was throwing away her good start to life.

That summer, Debs came to stay at our home at Waddesdon, near Aylesbury. She wrote to Melanie, saying she was hoping to do voluntary work in the next few years, in hospital and community radio, and had joined Friends of the Earth, even getting a reply from a cat shelter offering to allow her to come in on Saturday mornings to clean out and feed the cats. But there was no mention of the BBC.

Shortly after, Ann and John came to collect Debs. But there was an added purpose – a family crisis summit. While Debs was distracted by an afternoon with her grandparents, who had moved from Surrey into my previous house just fifty yards away, we all met secretly at the other end of the village in the small rented cottage where my cousin Judith lived.

Huddled in her tiny front room, I, my wife Sally, Ann, John, and Judith talked through Debs' future and the implications of her request to leave school. The mood was serious and businesslike, but with very little real disagreement. Ann was understandably concerned, and so was I, as the details of Debs' secret life were revealed. But I think we all recognized that she had a plan and that nothing would stop her achieving it. She had properly researched the courses available, and put forward a reasonably convincing argument. I figured that if anyone could be focused enough to do A levels by correspondence course, it was her.

We discussed the various alternatives, but they meant very little: if Debs was not in favour we knew that forcing her was pointless. In fact, it was only talking to her Aunt Melanie a year after her death that I learned that they had talked a lot that summer about her future. Debs had made it clear to Melanie that if we'd have forced her to stay at school, she would have run away. And I believe she would have done.

So, with reservations all round, we made the decision expected of us, and Debs got her way. At the leaving service in St Marks Church, Sheffield, the sixth formers bid their farewells. Debs, who had sailed through ten GCSEs, was one of a handful of fifth-form leavers.

Jane Brocklebank, her classmate for the whole of secondary school, thought she had made a friend for life. Saying goodbye at the church, she promised to ring Debs the following week. However, when she called, Debs just hung up the phone without saying a single word. She literally cut her off for good. It was almost as if Jane represented the past and Debs wanted a clean break from her unhappy school life. It was a sad ending to a friendship.

Debs duly kept her side of the bargain by studying for A levels, enrolling at evening class for German, and learning Physics by correspondence course. However, it wasn't long before the inevitable request came – she wanted to leave Sheffield for good. She had found her calling and was determined to go through with it. There wasn't much any of us could do. Ann insisted Debs stay with her Aunt Melanie and phone home every day – an arrangement that was to last precisely a week.

I believe now that this had been Debs' plan all along. She knew there was no way any of us would have allowed her to give up her education and move to the capital, which was no place for a teenage girl on her own. But she had skilfully manoeuvred us into first letting her go to London on a daily basis whilst continuing her studies, and then putting all her efforts into her new career.

So with her belongings contained in three luggage bags,

including her beloved comedy cassettes, Debs was dropped off at Sheffield station to catch the train to St Pancras, a starry-eyed girl fleeing her birthplace for the Big City. It is a scenario that has been played out thousands of times in novels and in real life. Many hopefuls vanish into thin air, and are never seen by their families again. At least we knew where Debs was; and, in some respects, we were a party to the decision. However, within weeks, the phone calls home dried up, the A levels went out of the window, and Debs had moved out of her aunt's home into a place of her own.

She had got what she had yearned for – freedom. Freedom from the misery of school; freedom from the torture of home; freedom to go to the capital and write. A final escape from her 'unmitigated hell'.

She never went home again.

Twelve

I start to try to find out more about the enemy we are all fighting by trawling the Internet. Just typing in 'anorexia' or 'eating disorders' opens up a wealth of information.

I already know that anorexia nervosa is a psychological illness that strikes mostly girls and young women. I suppose I first became aware of it when one of my favourite singers, Karen Carpenter, died from the condition in 1983. In recent years, the press have called it the slimming disease, because for many of its victims the condition starts with a perfectly normal weight-reducing diet that results in them virtually giving up eating altogether. There has been debate that the media, and its emphasis on super-thin models, may be influencing the way girls see themselves. But I discover it is far more complex than that. Nobody knows for certain all of its causes, and no two cases are the same.

I discover that around 5 per cent of girls in the UK are estimated to have anorexia and that they are mostly white and from middle-class homes. For some reason, boys and children from ethnic minorities are much less likely to be affected. I shiver as I read that 20 per cent of victims will die after twenty years of onset of the illness, but I take comfort and hope from the statistic that 60 per cent do recover.

I find that Debs has many of the traits of 'typical' victims: a dominant, over-protective and critical mother; a passive or withdrawn father; a tendency to perfectionism; a strong desire for social approval, and a need for order and control in their lives. Sufferers tend to be conformist, compliant, and hard working. They are often popular with teachers and may have given little cause for worry over the years. They tend to be mildly obsessional, organized, and tidy. These traits may be quite marked before the onset of anorexia but they are usually accentuated by the disorder. Some doctors say anorexia is born out of the struggle to grow up or through a childhood trauma, such as parental divorce or a sexual assault.

The families of anorexics are often high achievers with similar expectations of their children. Both Ann and I went to Cambridge University. The anorexic seems excessively willing to accept this value structure, setting standards for herself that seem extreme. Other experts point to an underlying vulnerability in the victims themselves, with emerging evidence that it may run in families, and to a possible biological explanation – some sufferers have been shown to have unusually high levels of the chemical seraton, which controls mood and appetite. Dieting may be a way of lowering these levels to reduce anxiety. Victims starve themselves, but the body adapts by adding more receptors, leading to more dieting and a vicious circle of despair.

Next, I look for advice about coping and care. Again, it is plentiful.

Attempts to frustrate an anorexic's efforts are generally met with anger or deceit, or a combination of both. Confrontation, rational discussion, bullying or bribery will probably fail to cause more than a very brief change of eating behaviour.

I read that I should remember that Debs has the problem, and it is up to her to do the work. I need to make a pact of complete honesty; be patient; sympathetic; non-judgemental, and a good listener. 'Let your loved one know that you care and have her best interests at heart.' I must not try to control her life, and when her behaviour affects me I should express myself without placing guilt or blame.

Whatever happens, I must not take her actions personally. I learn that I must show compassion because Debs may be overwhelmed as she gets in touch with painful issues underlying the behaviour. I should keep in mind that an eating disorder is a way of Debs feeling in control of her life. However, I must try not to be manipulated or lied to for the sake of her illness. As a parent I may or may not be the cause of the disorder, but I might have contributed to it in some way and I need to acknowledge that. I will need to re-evaluate my values, ways of communicating, rules about food, ways of handling feelings like guilt, anger, frustration, denial and cynicism.

This is proving to be quite a lesson.

And what about actually tackling this illness? Advice is

plentiful. Since anorexia is a form of intentional starvation, weight gain is a crucial first step. But this will be difficult because sufferers often deny they have a problem. I must accept that recovery is a process and will not happen quickly, and I must encourage Debs to be patient too.

I download and print off as much information as I can.

Thirteen

Gag writers are often the unsung heroes of comedy, particularly in radio. As Clive Anderson observed in a radio tribute to Debs:

> What sort of person wants to be a gag writer? There is an obvious appeal to the fame and glory of telling jokes and getting laughs in public. But it is a special sort of person whose ambition it is to come up with material and let someone else take all the credit. But that's what Debbie Barham wanted to do and did so from the age of 14.
>
> Gag writers come and gag writers go and often their names pass completely unnoticed by the watching or listening public. Who now knows who wrote all those jokes for Bob Hope? Who cares who wrote jokes for Bob Monkhouse? As a rule, reviewers only mention the writers when they want someone to blame if their favourite comedian doesn't seem to be on form.

It's certainly true that the success or failure of comedy depends on the wit of its writers. Coming up with a good gag offers not only a buzz, but underlines the very purpose of the writer's professional existence. Nigel Smith, a writer and producer of ITV comedy shows, says: 'There is triumph in a good joke; there is an element of puzzle too, putting the words in precisely the right place and order; there is power in a joke, a sense of winning against the world because you are making people laugh.'

But it's a stressful, precarious profession, and not as funny or romantic as one might imagine. Comedians use the language of life and death. They talk of dying on stage if the material is bad, killing the audience if it's good. Write boring drama and you might get away with it. Write bad comedy and you are hated – just witness the reaction to an unfunny stand-up at an open comedy night.

Writing can be a cruel, cut-throat, and lonely business, not one for faint hearts or for an insecure young girl from the provinces. Yet this was the world that Debs entered as she walked through the swing doors of the BBC offices near Broadcasting House in London's West End to launch her writing career at the age of 15.

I can only imagine what must have been going through her mind as she traipsed the stairs to the BBC radio comedy department. Fear, trepidation, excitement? Probably a mix of all three. She certainly wasn't daunted by the history or heritage of this British institution. She probably hardly gave a thought to the great names in whose footsteps she was following. She had proved to herself she could write – and that's all that mattered. Comedy was to be her stepping-stone to much greater heights. And Debs had fled her home and her family to gamble her skills as a writer.

Number 16 Langham Street was a joke factory for

thousands of hours of comedy over the years. The Writers' Room was on the second floor right at the end of the Radio Light Entertainment corridor. On the left were bound copies of the *Radio Times* going back to the 1940s, a living, if dusty, archive of every name, every programme in British radio and TV comedy.

Debs must have been surprised to see a piano in the corner of the room, used not for parties or sing-a-longs, but for musical sketches – one of the many genres in which she was to excel. Less appealing were the abandoned polystyrene coffee cups, chocolate wrappers, well-thumbed newspapers and screwed-up bits of paper with already disposed of gag or sketch ideas on them.

There was not much to write with. The place was littered with cannibalized machines – an elephant's graveyard for typewriters, as one wag commented. Only a couple of old manuals actually worked and sometimes the odd electric one. The only way to guarantee having something to work on was to bring your own equipment.

Sure enough, it wasn't long before Debs turned up with a laptop computer *and* a printer, which she had bought from her royalties. They weighed a ton, but she lugged them around with her from meeting to meeting. She received envious glances from the other writers, most of whom were still grappling with pencils and pieces of scrap paper. And she was also one of the earliest to get a mobile phone. It was the size of a brick, not like the compact models of today.

Debs started out on *The News Huddlines*, fronted by

the chirpy Roy Hudd, a stalwart of variety and radio, who first came to listeners' attention during the final years of *Workers' Playtime*. Hudd's constant fellow-performers were Chris Emmett, a comic and impressionist, and June Whitfield (successor to Alison Steadman), who had gained numerous radio, television, and film credits over the years.

The show was thrown together at immense speed. Scripts were written from Monday to Thursday, which was recording day. The actors saw the script at 10 a.m., did a run-through, and then faced the Paris Theatre audience in Lower Regent Street for the recording at 1 p.m.

It was good old end-of-pier variety and concert-party format. Roy Hudd came on with a bang-bang-bang monologue and then the cast performed sketches and ended on a song. Each show contained a string of 'news items' and sketches about the week's events. The material was openly willing to appeal to an older audience, with every gag ending on a recognizable punch line. Roy rarely wrote any of the show – that was the job of the team of scriptwriters. Debs, of course, knew the score. She had already had material accepted for the show as a schoolgirl. Now she was part of the regular writing circle.

Roy Hudd recalls: 'First it was D. A. Barham, then we eventually found out it was Debbie Barham. She thought we would reject her because it was a girl writing! I remember it made a terrific impact, a *girl* writing one-liners for a broadminded comedy show! But she certainly could write marvellous one-liners.'

Soon Debs felt assured enough to attend meetings for *Week Ending*, Radio 4's flagship topical comedy series. *Huddlines* was its downmarket cousin on Radio 2 and, rather snobbily, pooh-poohed by some of the more pretentious writers. *Week Ending* also consisted of gags and sketches, but was more clever and satirical.

The shows formed the main topical weekly radio comedy output for the BBC. They were separate entities with their own staff teams. But the routines were similar. Both shows were fast turnaround, recorded at the last minute to be fresh and up with the news. Even the producers were changed regularly to prevent formats becoming stale. Each show had commissioned writers who got the pick of the ideas to develop and were supplemented by a small army of non-commissioned writers who fed from the scraps left on the table, aiming at more 'off-beat' material. If you were lucky, and the producer liked your stuff, you got on the show and were paid accordingly. A one-liner was worth £8. A sketch paid £18.85 per minute or part thereof, plus 65 per cent extra for repeat transmissions.

Both shows encouraged accessibility for scriptwriters and were a nursery for the Corporation's talent. People just turned up off the street. There were no forms to fill in, except to give your address for payments, and nobody asked any questions about your age or status. The non-commissioned writers were a mix of two distinct groups – supremely confident Oxbridge types, who'd cut their teeth on university amateur dramatics and already had a track record of sorts – and plumbers, teachers, car mechanics trying desperately to start a new career. One of the few women who attended these meetings was writer Kay Stonham, who followed in the footsteps of Debs: '*Week Ending* was almost an unofficial school for writers. Anyone could go. In many ways it was a very open forum but having said that it was (a) mainly male, (b) mainly white and (c) mainly university educated. So although it appeared to be open, in some ways it was a secret society. The people who knew about it, knew about it.'

The programme was served up to viewers at 11 p.m. every Friday. Each Wednesday the team of non-commissioned writers would assemble, clutching their newspaper cuttings, ready to pitch their ideas. After the meeting, they had twenty-four hours to come up with one-liners or a script. Unlike *The News Huddlines, Week Ending* was not recorded before an audience.

Hugh Rycroft, who went to public school and who wrote for the *Oxford University Review* before trying his hand at the BBC, met Debs on *Week Ending* and vividly recalls her among the cast of fifteen to thirty-odd hopefuls who came in each week.

Into this lion's den of competitive male egos, there suddenly appeared a pretty, fresh-faced and clearly rather younger woman dressed in black and wearing clumpy Doc Marten boots, a sort of English Rose meets Goth. On appearance alone, she certainly stood out. She seemed incredibly shy and for a while I suppose most of us had her down as just another comedy hopeful about to have her dreams cruelly dashed by the whims of a Radio 4 producer.

But then, as the weeks went by, some of us began to notice a strange correlation between the presence of this girl at the meetings and the appearance of the name D. A. Barham in the end credits. A rumour began to circulate that this girl, and the mysterious DA, were indeed one and the same. And so it proved. She was taking on the blokes at their own game and was winning hands down. It was extraordinary that she was accepted, yet she was.

The fact that she was female merely made her unusual. That she was so young – much younger than any of us knew at the time – was totally unprecedented. With such breadth of knowledge and such sharpness of intellect she couldn't surely be younger than 21.

Initially it was hard for anyone to get much sense out of Debs. She kept her own counsel during meetings, preferring her written work to do the talking. Her stock response to any approach was to make a joke of it almost as if it was a reflex, a sort of comedy Tourette's Syndrome, or maybe just a defence mechanism. As Hugh Rycroft remembered:

You rarely got a straight answer. You got a joke rather than her risk any revelation about herself or her inner feelings. But whatever she was feeling inside, there was nothing childish about her. Yes, she was nervous and shy, but then so was I – and I was ten years older than her. More than anything else, I remember how incredibly poised and calm she seemed.

On Thursday afternoons, as the writers waited for news of their ideas, most sat in huddled cliques, looking terrifyingly self-confident. Debs and Hugh Rycroft would quietly settle down and devour as many crosswords as they could lay their hands on. Crosswords and Scrabble, indeed all word games, were her specialities. As she established herself as a writer to be reckoned with, her shyness began to disappear. One of the commissioned writers at the time was Nick R. Thomas, who added an initial to his name after one of his cheques went to a different Nick Thomas at the BBC.

I first heard the name D. A. Barham in the credits of *Week Ending* early in 1992. The name stood out because I always use an initial when I write. I assumed this was some retired university professor. One day I noticed this tall, young girl sat typing with her back to me. She got up and went out of the room and another writer, Ben Francis, said: 'That's D. A. Barham!' I said: 'What, that punky girl?'

I didn't see her again that series but she got a fair amount of material on and there was a bit of a buzz about her. Everyone believed she was 19, but we now know different. The time I first saw her would have been just before her 16th birthday and she probably should have been at school, not writing gags at Broadcasting House.

She came out of her shell a bit as the series went on. I remember someone asked her why she'd started writing and she replied that she'd heard comedy shows on the radio and thought she could do it better. I think that ruffled a few feathers.

Another of the former Oxbridge set was fellow writer Paul Powell: 'We were all very competitive, all fighting to establish ourselves, yet we were genuinely pleased when someone like Debs got stuff on. None of us ever knew her real age. She had a dry sense of humour, confident without being arrogant or sarcastic.' Hugh Rycroft says: 'She knew how a joke worked. She was not a warrior for truth or social change. She was never driven by social or political correctness. Script writing is fairly mercenary. If it gets a laugh, we get paid. That's it.'

As a producer in BBC Radio's entertainment department for many years, Carol Smith read thousands of gags. On *The News Huddlines*, she received literally a thousand unsolicited jokes a week. But she says Debs was in the highest echelon of gag writers, developing her craft to an absolute art form, knowing instinctively where the weight of a gag should be and so how to structure it most effectively, not to overload it with words and ruin the impact, and how to tailor it to its performer. 'She might submit twenty variations on jokes about someone in the public eye and would always be in direct competition with many other writers going for the same subject. But whilst they would go for one joke, and usually the most obvious one at that, Debs would put her subject under the microscope, examining every aspect of it, making sure that she had wrung every atom of comic potential out of that subject. Only when she was confident that she had done so, would she move on to the next subject.' Debs would fire off hundreds of gags, like an automated joke factory, each subject explored to the full. An example of this almost mechanical approach is her offering to an ITV variety show after David Beckham had dramatically re-styled his hair. The quality is mixed, and was probably dreamed up in one session at the computer. But no one can say the producer was not given a choice!

The director wanted some severe cuts this week. But I said – no, I'm not having a David Beckham haircut for anyone.

The director asked me to do some jokes off the top of my head. But I thought I'd leave that to David Beckham.

I was going to do some gags about David Beckham's head – but it's a bit of an empty subject.

I was going to do some gags about David Beckham's head – but there's nothing in it.

David Beckham had his hair shaved off. The barber had to be ever so careful. One wrong move and he could have let all the air out of Beckham's head.

David Beckham has had all his hair shaved off. He didn't really want a skinhead but he couldn't count up any further than Number One.

Did you see the football highlights last week? No, neither did I. I think they're still on the floor in David Beckham's hair salon.

David Beckham has a new skinhead cut. He never was much good at being able to keep his hair on ...

David Beckham has had a skinhead haircut. He always was number two in his household.

David Beckham has had a skinhead haircut. It's the nearest he'll *ever* get to being Number One at Manchester United.

David Beckham has had a skinhead haircut. What's the big deal? We *know* he's never had much Up Top.

David Beckham has had a skinhead haircut. He looks so much like a neo-Nazi thug he's been offered a 5-year contract with Leeds United.

David Beckham has had a skinhead haircut. It fits
perfectly with his image – nothing between the ears.

And so on . . .

During his time at the BBC, Nick Thomas met hundreds
of writers, but none like Debs. He says three things made
her special. First, the sheer quantity of her output; second
her gags were instant perfection – they came out fully
formed and rarely needed tweaking. Finally, her ability to
adapt – she got the style of everything she tackled.

> All topical writers came up with basic joke ideas. But what
> we COULDN'T do is produce such endless streams of
> them, writing for a huge number of topical markets, week
> after week, regardless of whether the news that week
> inspired ideas or not, and spoiling those markets for choice.
>
> She also had this incredible chameleon-like ability to
> adapt her ideas to different formats. She could sense the
> style required instantly. Her jokes were written with
> perfect economy, everything in its right place for
> maximum effect.
>
> Sometimes when you have an idea, you have to keep
> tweaking, chopping and changing, does this work better
> than that? You may even realize *after* something's been
> accepted and broadcast that it would have worked better
> another way. But her jokes arrived perfectly formed and
> her sketches flowed seamlessly from one big laugh to the
> next and seemed to be written effortlessly.

Another member of the writing team, posting an anonymous tribute to Debs on the web, says:

Genius is a word used far too loosely. It shouldn't mean very good, it should mean possessed of a transcendental, almost supernatural, quality of almost perfection. Which is precisely what her writing had.

I was lucky: I was writing for *Week Ending* at the same time she worked both there and on *The News Huddlines*, and in addition to hearing the words performed I had the opportunity to look at the scripts. What made Debbie's contributions stand out to me was that there was an inexorable quality to them: once they had started there was only one punchline, and they got there via a series of very funny jokes, never a line wasted.

She was clearly the best writer there, as well as the youngest, though most of us thought she was several years older than her real age. Which raises one question: should someone, even one as precociously talented as Debbie, be allowed to earn their living by their talent when still really a child? Perhaps not, but she was no Michael Jackson, pushed into it. She rejected childhood, preferring to live as an adult, competing with and surpassing adults from her mid teens. If someone can do that, should they be held back? Play with wax crayons, when they can use oils like Turner?

Debs became very much part of the gang. The pub was a great place for networking. She loved talking shop and was particularly encouraging to any new writers who arrived on the scene. She was a regular at the 'BBC pub' – the Yorkshire Grey near Broadcasting House, boozing and telling filthy jokes, two activities that contradicted her sheltered upbringing. Once she collapsed paralytic on the floor and was bundled off home in a taxi. Someone even nicknamed her D. A. Bar-room. Another time, the worse for wear, she wrote a rather tasteless remark on an appeal poster for a disabled child, along the lines of how much she approved of people raising money for someone who was legless.

Hugh Rycroft says: 'She thrived on what was – and is still – a fairly macho and chauvinistic world. In fact she became a sort of honorary bloke, such was the esteem she was held by her peers. It's the kind of world where male writers do still occasionally moderate their language when a woman enters the room. Debbie of course was the exception. Whenever she entered any room the jokes inevitably got a lot filthier.'

Nick Thomas recalls: 'Despite being so young, she seemed to know every slang expression for sex, bodily functions, etc. References would crop up in her sketches that I had not heard since I was at primary school. I once said to her: "How come you are so *rude*?" and she just said: "Well, thanks very much." But I think she was pleased. She saw it as a compliment.'

How the innocent blue-eyed Brownie metamorphosed into a crude, foul-mouthed drunk, I'll never know.

Within a few months, Debs was made a commissioned writer for *The News Huddlines*, which meant she was guaranteed at least one minute's pay whether her work was used or not. She also started to write for 'Stop Press' on *Huddlines*. Tony Hare, one of the script editors, and a group of around half a dozen invited writers, would sit in a cramped dressing room at the BBC's Paris studios writing last-minute one-liners about that day's news while the cast read through and rehearsed the sketches and songs in the studio itself. The monologue was typed up and handed to Roy Hudd just before the recording. Debs and the rest of the writers would have a chat and a coffee and watch the recording, before charging back to Langham Street for the *Week Ending* deadline.

One writer recalls: 'We'd handwrite each gag as we thought of it, tear off the strip of paper and put it down for Tony, who was typing up the monologue as he compiled it. Every fourth gag or so would be something filthy/tasteless/legally dubious – certainly not for broadcast. Tony would stop typing every so often, read the latest strips, including the 'Badlines', as they were known, and sometimes read these out. Tony picked up her gag, gave a mock gasp of horror and said, in a rather camp way, "*Deborah*!" It was something about people smuggling drugs up their rectums being the reason it's called crack cocaine.'

During one show, Roy Hudd mentioned Debs by name on air, which was highly unusual. She was an expert at puns, some brilliant, others somewhat corny. One of her early 'Stop Press' efforts went: 'And finally Stop Press. A club has been set up for people whose hobby is spotting agricultural machinery. [pause] I suppose all the members are ex-tractor fans!' This drew light-hearted groans from the audience, which led to Roy Hudd telling them: 'A girl wrote that, Debbie Barham. I want you to know where the blame rests for that one.' Confirmation that when material stinks, it's all the writer's fault!

Debs began extending her gag skills into sketches (although Roy Hudd thought her early attempts were not sketches at all, merely an assembly of one-liners). One, broadcast on the last *News Huddlines* of the summer 1993 series, when she was 16, made a huge impact. It was centred on the collapse of the Holbeck Hall Hotel on the East Coast. The hotel was situated high on Scarborough's South Cliff. Over several days, after a number of landslips, much of the building disappeared into the sea. The catastrophe received wide exposure over several days in the print media and on national TV news.

Roy Hudd and June Whitfield played a couple checking into the hotel for a sly weekend away amid the crashing of masonry. Debs's sketch went:

Manager:	Good afternoon, sir, madam. Welcome to Holbeck Hall Hotel. Have you reserved a room?
Female Guest:	No, we just decided to slip away over the weekend.
Manager:	Unfortunately so did our foundations. [much laughter]
Manager:	Can I have your names, please.
Male Guest:	Yes, of course. Mr and Mrs, erm, Smith. Yes,

that's right, Smith.

[sound of loud crashing noise]

Male guest: What on earth was that?

Manager: Nothing to worry about sir, just a couple more slates falling off the roof.

Female Guest   [aside to man]: 'Ere, I thought you said this was the best hotel in town, darling?

Male Guest: I must admit it's certainly gone downhill since I was here last time … [pause] About 300 yards downhill by the look of it. [more laughter]

Manager: I'll take it you'll be wanting a double room, will you, Mr and Mrs, er Smith?

Male Guest: Yes please, yes …

Manager: How about number 66? That's on the third floor.

Female Guest   [nudge and wink]: Oh, I don't know. I expect we'll be too tired to walk up all those stairs, don't you, Bernard?

Male Guest: I certainly hope so, Mildred.

Female Guest: Have you a room free on the ground floor? [Sound of a much bigger crashing noise of rubble falling]

Manager: Certainly sir… How about number 66?

The sketch barnstormed and received fantastic audience response. Being the last show, there were a few celebrities in the audience, a buffet afterwards, and a speech by Jonathan James-Moore, Head of Radio Light Entertainment. Unfortunately, Debs had a little too much to drink and displayed one of the few signs of her real age. James-Moore in his speech singled out her hotel sketch. He was so impressed that he'd asked who the author was; he said he 'didn't know we had a bloke writing called Deborah' (a reference to there being so few female comedy writers).

Debs found this all rather embarrassing and tried to hide behind her colleagues while her boss was talking about her. She hated compliments, especially in public, and usually told the blokes who congratulated her to 'fuck off'. After some more wine, she started to make loud rude remarks about some of the cast, in particular June Whitfield's age.

In the end, she left in the care of one of the producer's assistants and apparently fell over, threw up, and crashed out in his office.

She was making her mark in more ways than one.

Fourteen

Holed out at my home for three weeks now, Debs feels her
crisis is only a temporary blip and that in a matter of weeks
all will be well. She is convinced that the major reason for
her decline is not the state of her mind, but the state of her
flat. She grumbles that a pile of newspapers fell over and
she simply hadn't the strength to pick them up. To her, this
is the cause, rather than the effect, of her problems, a physical barrier to her recovery, rather than anything deeper.
This had made it impossible for her to work – the one driving force that keeps her going.

Sue and I look at each other. We know in our hearts that
Debs' assessment is extremely optimistic, even delusional, but we go along with this notion anyway. To put her
mind at rest, Sue and I will visit the flat to pick up the newspapers and generally tidy up.

We drive down together from Aylesbury to clear up Debs'
home and pick up one or two bits she left behind. The two-
bedroom flat is on the second floor of a former council
block at Church Path, half a mile from Chiswick Park
Underground station. Debs has been living there for three
years, buying it when she was 18 for just under £67,000,

with help from some money left in trust by her great grandmother.

We are greeted by a soulless redbrick building. It is noisy and the aroma of cannabis fills the air. There is no lift. We wonder how, in her physical state, Debs has managed to negotiate these stairs day after day. Access is via an open staircase at the rear, which is exposed to the elements. The staircase is dirty, dank, and smells strongly of urine. Debs had warned us that the communal rubbish chute is often blocked. Now, in the height of summer, we can smell the evidence.

Her flat is at the end of the block on the second floor. We locate the lock on the peeling green-painted door, turn the key and enter. We get the shock of our lives. It is a picture of utter squalor and in a disgusting state. The sickening stench of Debs' cremated cooking pervades the air. Everything is filthy.

The first room we enter is Debs' darkened bedroom. The curtains are drawn, but there is just enough light to make out that her clothes are scattered everywhere. The bedding looks as if it has not been changed for months. Computer and TV cables are everywhere. Opening the curtains sheds light on Debs' 'wardrobe'. There is a huge collection of expensive designer clothes ranging in size from 6 to 16, all her own stuff, bought over the years to fit her fluctuating figure.

The kitchen is in a revolting state. As we walk across the lino floor, our shoes stick to the surface. The work surfaces are covered in crusted, congealed food and the washing machine has a residue of black, putrid water. On the sides are a number of appliances – blenders, juice-makers, etc – all filthy.

Having witnessed the state of the flat so far, we should have been prepared for the sitting room. But this leaves us stunned. The room is a decent size – 15 by 12 feet – but the floor is virtually covered in a newspaper pyramid, the peak about a metre high and the edges almost touching the sides of the room. The papers almost cover Debs' exercise bike. So much for Debs's assertion that some newspapers had 'fallen over'! There are literally hundreds of newspapers, going back years.

On a small round table just inside the door is the most extraordinary computer I have ever seen. A small black laptop, the screen-surround is painted with a halo of gold brushstrokes and every part of the case daubed with splodges of red, green, and gold. A psychedelic laptop! Half of the keys are missing, revealing biscuit crumbs congealed into the general stickiness of the contacts beneath. The roller ball at the front still turns, but is hindered by crumbs. The screen is only just still attached, with cables exposed and the hinge joints fractured.

This computer, in almost this condition, outputs much of the work she produces for Rory Bremner, Graham Norton, and others. I will come to treasure this laptop because it sums up the mix of absurdity and creativity that is her life.

A small area around this table is the only part of the room that is accessible. Looking around at this devastation it seems impossible that anyone could work creatively in this environment. Yet clearly, for some weeks or months, Debs has struggled on, still writing as inventively and profusely as ever, blocking out the worsening problems surrounding her.

Elsewhere, the bathroom is beyond description and the floors of the whole flat are littered with droppings from Debs' former pet Chinchilla. The animal's cage is open but Debs had in fact got rid of it, no doubt reasoning that she could not even look after herself, let alone a pet.

I am both upset and puzzled by the state of Debs' life. I had stayed here with her soon after she had moved in. At the time I was training as an aerobics instructor in London and she had put me up, after some persuasion, for two weeks. She had been extremely house proud, always cleaning and insisting that I put the futon away every morning and tidy the room, even though she never entertained visitors.

The contrast now is enormous. This visit teaches us the shocking scale of Debs' problems. Afflicted by her eating disorder, she became obsessed by work, to the exclusion of everything. Then, weakened by her lack of food, it was physically impossible for her to sort things out. She had quite simply given up.

On the way back to Aylesbury, I decide to be understanding of Debs' plight rather than reproachful. Now that she knows what we have seen, she need not have to explain or excuse the state of her home. Besides, she has already decided she wants nothing more to do with it. She wants to erase the whole painful memory. The plan is for me to clear it and she will put it on the market.

A week later

Sue and I have enlisted the help of my 18-year-old son Sam to make the return journey to clear Debs' flat. I have hired a van and the three of us will spend the whole of Saturday removing every trace of her life from Church Path, Chiswick.

I have thought through carefully how we are going to achieve this. I had originally planned for a skip, but hadn't realized that in London you have to have a permit, and I hadn't left time to arrange one. We would have needed several anyway. With no lift and being two storeys up, I decide on an extendable ladder to reach up to her second-floor window.

Sue and I pack everything into black plastic bags and use the ladder as a ramp to roll them down to Sam, who loads the van. Many burst and we have to collect newspapers from all over the pavement. It takes three hours just to bag and remove the pile of papers from the lounge. Everything is going out of that window – cupboards, tables, chairs, steel four-poster bed, hamster cages, computers, printers – the lot. And none of the neighbours bat an eyelid. It is backbreaking, hard work, but we can't help but laugh at how ridiculous it must look. It takes numerous visits to the refuse dump at Kew to clear everything, and the workmen there can't believe what is being thrown out. We have been instructed to dump everything – her expensive clothes, shoes, furniture, even her trainers, but we cannot bear to throw away her expensive designer clothes. We smuggle them back to the house without Debs realizing and pass them on to charity shops in Aylesbury. But there is one possession that she is determined to rescue – the library of comedy audiotapes she collected as a kid. They are one of her few joyful memories of her unhappy teenage upbringing and inspired her early dream to become a future writing queen of comedy.

The following morning we awake to this note:

Thanks. The word is completely inadequate, but it's the only one I have at 3.30 am. You are both superhumanly wonderful huggable individuals. (Flat-clearing will get you nowhere, but by God will it help me.) An overwhelmed Debs.

Debs doesn't ask about, or offer to pay for, the cost of the van or other materials. I don't think it even occurs to her what we might have spent, such was her lack of interest in financial matters. But she does offer to pay for the flat to be professionally cleaned at a cost of £700. Even the professionals failed to completely get to grips with the state of the kitchen. It was that bad. The flat has been a huge burden, and now that is lifted Debs immediately sets about the task of selling. It goes on the market for £149,950, a potential profit of £83,000 – not bad for what had become a pigsty. It has proved a shrewd investment, if a source of painful memories.

Fifteen

As Debs took root at the BBC, her confidence gradually grew and her ambitions began to expand. She was having more and more success with her material on live national radio. Next stop was live, topical theatre.

Nick Thomas had told her about *Newsrevue*, a successful weekly satire stage show, which enjoyed a cult following in comedy circles. There had been a tradition of young writers from BBC comedy trying their hand on the revue. Indeed, in the 1980s, David Hatch, then head of BBC Radio Light Entertainment, and the writing team of *Week Ending*, generously allowed the show to use rejected scripts originally submitted to the radio programme.

The show helped launch the careers of people who went on to become stars on TV, such as Rory Bremner, *EastEnders* actress Michelle Collins, the actress and comedienne Josie Lawrence, Reece Sheersmith, of *The League of Gentlemen*, and comedy actor Bill Bailey. It had a variety of venues over the years but settled at the Canal Café in the heart of London's fashionable Little Venice district in Paddington. The sixty-seater theatre was above a pub called the Bridge House. The format had remained largely unchanged since two writers from a London University revue group – Mike Hodd and Jack Thorington – had the idea in 1979.

Newsrevue was a fast-paced show of sketches and songs based on anything in the news – particularly politics, sport, and celebrities. It was performed four nights a week by two men, two women, and a musical director, backed up by a director and a team of writers, and served up around forty sketches and songs, updated by up to 40 per cent each week. When it celebrated its twenty-fifth birthday in 2004, it was officially listed in *The Guinness Book of Records* as the world's longest-running live comedy show. By then, there had been nearly 7,000 shows containing 10,000 sketches performed to a total audience of 350,000 people. It has used over 1,000 actors, musical directors and directors and more than 500 writers, but none as young as 16-year-old D. A. Barham.

The need for fast, funny, and topical material was right up Debs' street and before long she was writing huge chunks of the show. Debs and the rest of the writers would meet in the bar one night a week, discuss the following week's show, and then go upstairs to see how their material was received by the largely middle-class audience. Nigel Smith, who went on to become a sitcom writer for ITV, remembers the petite girl in black sitting alongside him: 'On Thursday all the writers would gather in a room and discuss the latest news stories. They would have a big sheet of ideas which everyone would discuss. We would go away and write our sketches for the following week. I would get one or two on but D. A. Barham would write half the bloody show! We would get a sheet with whose stuff had been accepted and her initials would be everywhere.' What's more, Debs always trumped his punchlines. 'In the writers' meetings I'd offer a nervy gag, and this little thing in black would quietly, politely, *immediately*, improve it, not to show off, or to get one over on you, but because she was just naturally funnier than the rest of us.'

The pay was poor but with the volume of material Debs was getting on the show, it was proving quite lucrative. It was a tremendous outlet for her emerging creative talent, and Debs had great fun penning songs and music about scandals and gossip in the news. One of her offerings was a barbed number on the death of the magnate Robert Maxwell, who, it turned out, had been plundering his employees' pension funds.

John Random recalls meeting Debs when he was writing for the show. Like her, he was a former writer for *Week Ending*, although their paths never crossed at the BBC.

She was a modest, self-effacing presence, always dressed in black, not one to boast about her success; not one to be snooty about others who couldn't match it. We didn't have her brilliance long enough at *Newsrevue*.

She was the dominant force at that time and probably one of its classiest writers despite her tender age, which is amazing in its own right. None of us guessed just how young she was. And she was better at 16 and 17 than most of us ever get to be. I can still remember her version of Abba's 'Fernando', where she talked about the rumoured relationship between Peter Lilley and Michael Portillo – 'Pleasure me/At the Treasury/Portillo or 'The sight of your neat quiff/Gives me a stiff, Portillo'.

And sticking with stiffs, she wrote a new version of 'English Country Garden' relating to the mass murderer Fred West. 'How many stiffs can you hide without a whiff in an English country garden?/Fingers and tendons/In the rhododendrons in an English country garden'.

Sixteen

Debs has been with us for a month. Sorting out the mess in her flat has given her a degree of contentment. Not only that, she is lining up a new home – in London's Docklands. Everything is lovey-dovey, with many spontaneous three-way hugs with Debs leaning on my shoulder, displaying a level of physical intimacy I have never previously experienced from her.

Sometimes, at the table, I reach across and hold her hand. She does not pull away. I believe she is beginning to welcome this physical contact rather than do her usual retreat. Today she decides to break cover and send a long e-mail to Rachel Swann, her agent, probably the one person she trusts above everyone else, finally revealing where she is holed out. It is clear her spirits are improving, although physically there has been little progress. She is still extremely frail and emaciated. Her W. H. Smith ring-bound notebook reads;

Notes for mail to Rachel
Re. meeting up. Blacks? Next week?
What I've done.

Advs. Family will watch eating, help sleeping, support, out of London flat. Lots to catch up on. Converse non work.

Work – please etc. Will get scared that I can't.

Alternative to therapy (which didn't work). Cheaper!

Someone to make sure I'm OK.

Flanders and Swann album

7 years of shit. He's sorted – been through it all etc

Take it slowly

Turning up out of the blue. Unrecognised. Never talked.

Fresh start (flat-bed stuff)

Still physical problems. Bowels. Uck.

Near enough to London to commute.

More regular hours. Guilty about inconveniencing. Hope to be accepted.

Must meet kid – Charlotte. And Frances?

One bit of family. Low profile still.

Provided can find coffee shop.

Flat – throw out most of possessions. Docklands?

Sue and I feel confident enough about Debs' mental state to take a planned weekend away with Sue's family in Scotland. Debs is not very practical and we return in some trepidation. Indeed, in our absence there have been one or two minor disasters in the kitchen. We are welcomed home with a small gift and the following note:

Welcome Home! Debs's Disaster List (oops)
Minor cockup with some oats – will give you gory
details later. Have bought replacement bag. Ditto the
sultana cereal in larder, you may find bits lurking in
your crevices. Stuck lump of broccoli thru lid of one of
your mousses. Couldn't find replacement – you have a
pot of cream as compensation. Have thrown out/eaten
most of mouldy stuff, I think. Your post is on the big
box of tax stuff. The hamster is in the hamster cage
and bunnies in hutch, I hope, not vice versa. The
bathroom is in a reasonable state. The crap freebie
book from crap magazine is yours if you want it. The
gin is v. restrainedly unopened.
Debs.

Seventeen

Whatever her childhood hang-ups and problems at home and school, Debs certainly seemed more content with herself as she settled into her new life in London. There was no concern from anyone about her weight or her self-esteem. She seemed to have left any troubles behind in Sheffield. She was, as she put it years later, 'having a ball'.

She even had the confidence to treat herself to high tea at the Ritz – not an inexpensive venue – but something she had promised herself she would do when she could afford it (although what the waiting staff made of this girl sitting alone scoffing scones in her Doc Martens is anyone's guess).

Her boozing sessions and fast-food lifestyle had increased her weight to around 11 stone. Photographs reveal a beautiful 16-year-old elegant brunette, with shoulder-length hair, a full face, and piercing eyes, and looking much older than she was.

She was already self sufficient, making several hundred pounds a week from *The News Huddlines*, *Week Ending* and *Newsrevue*. The unpredictable, freelance nature of the work did not faze her. As she said to one of the team, who was at least ten years her senior: 'When you depend on writing for a living, you'll find the ideas will come.'

She had a reputation for being good with money. In fact,

some writers used to joke about how careful she was. She made two investments when she came to London: her laptop, printer, case, etc., which came to under £500 (she compared prices in *Computer Shopper* magazine), and a season ticket for the Tube and buses – around £350. When she got her mobile phone (something of a novelty then), she managed the best deal after negotiating the minefield of choices about phones and rates.

Her lodging arrangement with her Aunt Melanie lasted precisely a week, during which Melanie was actually away! She rented a bedsit in Chiswick – a basement studio in Acton Lane, which cost her £75 a week, including council tax. She wrote to *Huddlines* producer Richard Wilson saying she'd now 'found a garret to starve in', horribly ironic in view of what was to happen in her life.

She used to enjoy visiting the Hammersmith shopping mall, where she had business cards printed saying 'All work considered' and wrote while sitting in the Lyric Theatre café. To help pay her rent, she used her IT skills to research and learn how to predict biorhythms. She printed off some leaflets offering to do predictions for a year for a fiver and gave them out to people outside Tube stations, even getting the odd order.

Being a woman was both an advantage and disadvantage. Certainly Debs was noticed more. The BBC was keen to attract more women writers, even staging women-only writers' workshops. Consequently, *Week Ending* was beginning to get more female writers – and more female names in the credits, which often stretched to 40-odd writers, read out in double-quick time – almost a joke in its own right! Without consultation, one producer changed her credit to 'Deborah Barham' to give the illusion that the workshops had attracted a new woman on the team. Debs was furious. She had already been writing for the show for more than a year. After a word with the producer, she reverted to D. A. Barham.

At the beginning she had instinctively guessed it would not be in her interests to reveal her sex. In fact, she did encounter some chauvinism and sometimes felt her work came under greater scrutiny simply because she was female. She hated not being taken seriously, particularly by the male-dominated industry. She tried to take her sexuality out of the equation, dressing demurely, almost boyishly, to be accepted for what she could do rather than for her looks.

Nevertheless, she attracted many admirers. In those early days she had at least three secret boyfriends, or should I say man friends. They were all fellow BBC scriptwriters, all bespectacled, in their thirties – almost twice her age – and none knew that Debs was just 16 or 17 at the time they dated her. All the relationships lasted just a few months before Debs ended them. One partner describes her as being 'bulimic' with relationships. She loved the challenge of courting her men, but then spat them out soon after when she found she could not cope with the physical demands and level of commitment.

She was witty and attractive, but despite a fulsome

figure, she had a low opinion of her body. Perhaps this dated back to her severe eczema as a child or some other deep-rooted psychological problem. She hated to be seen naked and found intimacy with men difficult.

The most serious liaison was with fellow writer Nick Thomas, who enjoyed a four-month romance with her at the beginning of 1994 when she was 17. Nick and Debs were soul mates from similar backgrounds. Both came from outside London, were from broken homes, and did not particularly like their stepfathers. They were bullied at school, had under-achieved academically, but had come through personal difficulties to succeed as writers.

Nick was born and brought up in Bournemouth on the south coast. He dropped out of grammar school at the beginning of his O levels because he suffered from agoraphobia, which he eventually conquered with the help of therapy, only to contract Crohn's Disease. His early work consisted of a series of dead-end jobs. He used to write as a hobby, entering competitions and sending off ideas to magazines. At the age of 21 he won a *Punch* caption competition, which gave him the confidence to try his luck at the BBC on *Huddlines* and *Week Ending*. It was five months before he got anything used.

By the time he met Debs he was 33 and a commissioned writer on the *Huddlines*, but his courting of her was almost doomed before it began due to an embarrassing episode.

He'd been working with a couple of amateur writer-performers in Bournemouth and had made a rather cheap and nasty 'Review of 1992' tape consisting mainly of material that had been rejected by the BBC. They ran off about fifty copies, which were mostly sold to pub customers by the female in the group, who was very attractive and worked as a barmaid.

Nick decided to sell his quota by mail order and duly placed an ad in the *Viz* comedy comic and in *Private Eye*, '60-minute satirical tape, £3.95'. He got just one reply, a very formal word-processed letter, which read: I enclose a cheque for £3.95. Please forward one satirical tape. Yours faithfully D. A. Barham.'

Nick was horrified. First he didn't think the cassette was very good. Second, and worse, he was getting his only order from another BBC writer, one with a growing reputation, who would find out he was responsible! Despite his discomfort, he posted the tape off and banked the cheque.

Scared of a critical reception from his attractive BBC colleague, he successfully avoided speaking to her for about a month but once, at the *Huddlines* recording studio, there were just the two of them left in a room. She frowned at him and said: 'Did you do a tape?'

'I sheepishly admitted that I had and that it wasn't up to much and she said: "Was it just a lot of stuff you had rejected by *Week Ending* and the *Huddlines*?" Then I pointed out that some of it had even been rejected by *Newsrevue* as well.'

They travelled back to Broadcasting House together on the Tube and chatted meaningfully for the first time.

'I remember she seemed very serious,' said Nick. Their friendship blossomed in the rather unromantic setting of the BBC canteen. Over the years, Debs was to spend many hours there and eventually grew to despise it. She was later to offer this colourful description in an e-mail to a friend:

```
Anyway, yes, let's do the coffee/bevvy thing
sometime. Anywhere other than the BBC canteen, which
still insists on dispensing cups of lukewarm piss
avec someone's beard trimmings in the bottom,
despite its recent delusions of grandeur. (I was in
there for the first time in ages, t'other week, and
the only nearest I could get to a soft drink was
something called 'Sparkling Hemp and Apricot'. I
mean, what the fuck? This is the bloody Beeb
canteen, for gawdsake. The place where one can quite
conceivably end up paying for a plate full of mashed
parsnip under the misapprehension that it is sponge
pud. And where once a year it's Caribbean Day,
meaning the staff wear silly hats and bunting and
you get a raisin in your salad. Or it might be a
mouse turd. The Beeb canteen! Not some fucking
swanky juice bar. I blame that Naked Chef. Then
again, it is all funded by the licence payers, so I
s'pose we can't complain.)
```

But it was a great place for social intercourse. Debs and Nick sat for hours chatting, bouncing ideas off each other, reviewing each other's work, even writing together. Nick had a sketch on the *Huddlines* about rogue minicab drivers.

The sketch went very well, but it was the two gags Debs added that got the applause from the audience. Her pun punchline, from the boss of the firm, mimicking President Bush's famous election mantra, was: 'Read my lips. No new taxis'.

But it was while working with her on the 1993 *News Huddlines* that Nick realized he was falling for her. One day they were travelling on the Tube together – Nick to go to Waterloo for the train to Bournemouth, Debs to her bedsit in Chiswick. She got off at Piccadilly to change lines and was closely followed by two youths whom Nick was convinced were planning to rob her of her laptop. The train pulled away with him frantically – and unsuccessfully – trying to attract her attention through the window. Without any contact numbers for her, he spent the next few days worrying that she had been mugged.

On the Sunday evening she turned up at the BBC studios to write last-minute lines for the Hudds Christmas show. She was about 5 feet 8 and was very pretty. She had probably the palest blue eyes I'd ever seen – one slightly lazy – nice teeth, very pale skin and never wore make-up. Her hair was often pulled back off her face and scrunched, revealing her favourite earrings. Her natural colour was mousey so she dyed it darker, sometimes almost black. Her voice was sometimes slightly husky, educated, but every so often the odd word would slip through that was broad Yorkshire (ak-choo-ah-lay for actually) but she always furiously denied having a North Country accent. She nearly always wore a jacket, white blouse and a waistcoat to hide her figure. She had three – burgundy, dark green and, I think blue. This night she had a long black coat on and it was about the most feminine-looking thing I'd ever seen her wear (very Scottish Widows TV commercial).

I told her I'd worried she'd been mugged and she thought this was hilarious. I think it was the first time I'd ever heard her laugh out loud – she always used to laugh a lot, but silently – she called it 'hysterical grinning'. I guess this was when I realized I was really becoming attracted to her. In the end I think I got more on the show than she did, the last time *that* ever happened.

Soon after, this amazing Christmas card arrived from her. She'd taken everything, the cartoon, the greeting, even the cartoonist's biography on the back, and altered words, added her own gags, and the odd unflattering drawing of other writers. It was covered with BBC in-jokes and must have taken ages to do. Her message wished me 'A Merry Christmas and a Happy "News" Year'.

Back at work in the beginning of 1994, Nick told her he had been knocked out by her Christmas card, which she said had taken her the best part of an hour to do.

I told her I was going up to the eighth-floor canteen at BH and she said she'd see me when I came back. But I was waiting in the queue and she suddenly appeared alongside me. She just threw anything onto a plate. When we sat down it turned out that what she'd dished up for herself was just two types of potato, mashed and boiled.

It was just that having something on her plate seemed to give her an excuse to be in the canteen and therefore with me. It was pretty obvious that she felt something for me too. One or two writers had even started to refer to us as an item, though we weren't at that stage.

I held back from getting involved, but she was so attractive and funny and was making all the running and I found it very hard to resist.

There was another worry too. One of the *Week Ending* writers had asked me at the Canal Café Theatre if I thought he should have an affair with Debbie Barham. I was a bit gobsmacked and I think I'd mumbled something about not thinking she was very big on relationships – anything to try and put him off – but it had shaken me as I realized I didn't like the idea of anyone else being involved with her, so I felt I didn't have much time.

In the first *Week Ending* of 1994, Debs wrote a sketch that was well received. The debate in the news at the time was about Sunday trading. She converted the Lord's Prayer into the Sunday Trading Law's Prayer, which was broadcast complete with church music and delivered by the 'vicar' and his congregation.

Our cashier

Who art in Tesco

Sharon be thy name

Thy customers come

Thy tills be rung

On Sundays and in the week

Give us this day our daily bread

(Only 35p for one large loaf down in price for all this
  month)

And forgive us our pushing past a pensioner to grab the
  last cream horn

As we forgive those who leave a jar of fishpaste on the
  cake shelf just to annoy us

Lead us not into temptation

(Although chocolate Hobnobs do have 15 per cent extra
  free and after all are too good to resist)

But deliver us the six-piece patio set we bought on impulse
  within 28 days or our money back

For thine is an open shop, the deli and in-store bakery

For six hours each Sunday

Amen.

Nick, listening at home in Bournemouth, chuckled along
with the rest of the nation. The programme even received
requests from vicars for copies of the sermon. To everyone's delight we included this prayer in Debs' memorial
service.

The following week, Debs heard that she had been made

a commissioned sketch writer for *Week Ending*. Again, Nick and Debs chatted for ages in the BBC canteen – for so long, that he almost missed the last train back to Bournemouth. 'I remember mentioning to her that a writer friend of mine, Roderick Millar, had had a sketch broadcast which mentioned the children's game "What's the Time, Mr Wolf?" and I didn't know what this was. And she proceeded to give me a giggly demonstration of the rules, using the cruet and everything else on the table as props.'

At the end of the evening, Debs made her move. She suggested he stay over at her place. What she didn't know was that he was already in a relationship and was having a battle of conscience. He later kicked himself for missing the opportunity to cement their friendship.

Eighteen

Relieved that the house has not burned down, we have decided to go ahead with our annual holiday in the Canaries, which we had booked in advance of Debs' unexpected invasion of our home. She is still eating very little, although well into her work/London routine. Frankly, we need a release from the stress of the house, so we are jetting off to Gran Canaria, leaving Debs to fend for herself. Relaxing in the sunshine will give us time to assess the situation.

We return from our one-week break to another note, attached to another gift.

Welcome home, O Ye Weary Travellers! I hope – no, – I'm sure you had a wonderful time. Me – I'm bushed and will probably have gone to bed by the time you get back … I think I've chucked out everything that's gone off, except for your bread. There is however something sinister and ectoplasmic lurking in the bowl in the back of the fridge – I didn't like to pursue closer acquaintance with it but I think it may once have been a beetroot. Your call.

Please Help the Blind! Specifically the one in the bathroom – it unrolled rather enthusiastically and I've had to jam it open with a bottle. I'm afraid I also borrowed the phone from your bedroom and plugged extension into the socket. Have left it on the bed. Apologies for the disruption. Also for commandeering your Savlon.

I haven't moved out just yet. It's still subject to contract (yup, I've made an offer – and accepted one on my place; cash buyer, no chain, which is good). Fingers crossed from now on, but the main hold up will be the other vendor finding somewhere. Eek. Did you by any chance come across the DEEDS to Church Path in that awful box of tax stuff? Financial bits – somewhere there's a remittance thingy from the Sun for £900 and invoice for £500 which can be added to the file.

Errrrrrrrrrrrrrrrrrrrrrrr.

That's it? Probably not, but if you come across any other mess-ups, it's probably my fault. If you are putting any washing on, there's a skirt/tights etc on clotheshorse. Follow your nose (nothing too ghastly. I just managed to spill hot coffee all over myself on the sodding train tonight. Ouch.)

Apologies for the green wheelie thing which isn't in the garage.

I remembered to put it out on Monday but couldn't get it back in (as The Clash *once sang ... 'I fought the door and the door won').*

More effusive apologies for the other *green, wheelie*
thing, which is in the garage. Explanation tomorrow.

Debs xxxx

We know of course that the green wheelie thing outside the
garage is the dustbin. But we haven't a clue about the other green wheelie thing *inside* the garage – and are too tired
to find out. Our lie-in next morning is rudely disturbed by
a strange noise from the road outside. I look out of the window to see Debs – dressed in a black nylon jumpsuit – astride
this green electric scooter. She'd bought it via the Internet
from a dealer in Edinburgh while we were away. Green
politics appealed to Debs and apparently she has scoured
various websites searching for a non-polluting mode
of transport to ride around London on. All the rage in
Beijing, I gather, but not here!

It is great to see her so positive, but surely her frail frame
can't handle this metallic monster. I am horrified to see that
she is about to try to ride it. I grab some clothes and race
downstairs. Too late! She is already off down the hill in a
wibbly wobbly line. She has no control, no helmet, and, as
far as I know, no tax and no insurance. I chase her, like a
father pursuing a 5-year-old learning to ride a bicycle. Not
only is she breaking the law, she is risking serious injury –
with a busy T-junction looming fast at the bottom of the
cul-de-sac.

Somehow, at the junction, she turns right – narrowly

avoiding a row of parked cars. Thank goodness there are no moving vehicles. With that, she disappears up the road. I wait, panting for breath and wondering what to do next. Suddenly the distant buzz of the electric motor grows louder and Debs comes down the hill towards me. She comes to a skidding halt beside me, grinning from ear to ear. No sooner have I begun my lecture about no tax and no insurance than she is off again. Rather than risk a coronary by chasing her, this time I decide to rush for the car.

By the time I find the keys Debs has gone AWOL. I start the car and go in hot pursuit. After just two corners I'm concerned to see a group of people huddled around a heap in the road. My worst fears are quickly confirmed. The heap is the green scooter and the figure in black lying in the road is Debs. As I arrive, she is being helped to her feet. Blood is pouring from a wound on her head. She has misjudged a bend and fallen off. I explain to the concerned bystanders that she belongs to me and am just about to suggest that I drive her home when she is off on the scooter again, this time thankfully heading straight back to the house.

Fortunately, the injury is not serious. More than anything else her pride has been dented. As for the scooter, she is banned from riding it again until she has registered it, arranged insurance, and bought a crash helmet.

Two days later

Debs arrives home with a helmet but, despite lengthy enquiries, has failed to get guidance on what vehicle category the scooter belongs to, or how to insure it. Even with her ingenuity, she cannot give me a convincing answer as to how she will charge an electric scooter with flat batteries in the centre of London. Pop into a café maybe and order 'one cappuccino, must be hot, and 10 amps to take away please'. For someone so technically brilliant, Debs can be so impractical.

Nineteen

Thursday night in the BBC canteen was becoming a regular date for Nick and Debs. The following week they again talked long into the night. By now Nick was smitten. He lied that he'd missed his train and asked to stay at her flat. She agreed, and in a giggly and flirty mood, they took the 94 bus home together.

Debs' bedsit was in a house divided into a number of smaller studios. She occupied the basement flat, which looked out onto a shabby little garden where she would wave at the cat every day. Her home was clean and tidy and Nick found it virtually a shrine to writing, with little that was not connected to her trade, including reference books (*Brewer's Phrase and Fable* and the *Radio Active Year Book* were prominent) and videos from the two duos who'd made up the Mary Whitehouse Experience (she preferred Punt and Dennis to Newman and Baddiel).

There wasn't much in there that wasn't connected with the business of being a comedy writer, except albums by her favourite band, the Doors. Above the bed was a wacky-looking toy parrot, which ensured, she said, that she could at least wake up to a laugh every day.

We sat and talked all night and told each other our life stories. I was amazed to learn that she had eczema because she had the most glorious, smooth skin but she said she sometimes had outbreaks and constantly used steroid creams. She really worried about it returning.

She said she'd never got into the same things as girls at school, like 'shagging boys', and thought the whole scene of people going out to clubs and picking up strangers to have sex with was 'tacky'. She talked a little about the bullying and teasing at school. She said she used to wear a coat with a hood and that the other girls would drop things in the hood.

She told me that on her first date with a *Huddlines* writer her eczema had broken out and she'd had this big pus-filled spot on her lip, which made kissing him goodnight difficult. No one had ever known about this relationship and it took a while for her to tell me who it was with.

Myself and the two before me were all about the same age: I was 33, and the others were 34 and 32. None of us exactly looked like Brad Pitt. The others wore glasses and I'd started wearing them for reading. Debbie said 'I do like men with glasses.' She was forever taking my specs off and trying them on.

It was about 6 a.m. when I finally kissed her. I pointed out that the trains would be running again by now but she said 'You're not going anywhere!'

Nick was worried she might regard their night together as a one-off, but she said the relationship was something she'd wanted for months and when he boasted that he regarded himself as being perceptive, she replied: 'Well, you couldn't tell when someone fancied you, could you?'

Although their friendship was common knowledge at the BBC, Debs was adamant their affair should be kept secret. It meant arriving and leaving work at different times and using separate entrances and exits. They had their own lovers' code. If they wanted to go up to the canteen together they'd leave the Writers' Room at staggered times. Nick would signal he was leaving by loudly jingling coins in his pocket and she would follow him upstairs shortly afterwards.

Her life was extremely compartmentalized and she didn't like acknowledging her relationships. In the Writers' Room, we'd try and act the way we had before we got involved. Away from Broadcasting House it was different: she was happy to walk arm in arm and had no embarrassment about standing next to me while I paid for condoms in a 7-11.

Despite her cynical approach to life, it could all be romantic. There was a softer side to her. We sent each other Valentine's cards (she signed hers but then I don't think she'd ever sent one before!). I'd sometimes buy her flowers (I don't think anyone had ever done that, either) but never chocolates because of her skin problems. And we once went into one of those Photo-Me booths and had pictures done, the only shots of the two of us together. Debbie mucked about, laughing and doing 'rabbit's ears' behind my head with her fingers.

They lived virtually half the week together. He would stay over Thursday and Friday nights and go back to Bournemouth late on Saturday. She actually thanked him for getting her out of the BBC drinking scene. She was no longer getting drunk, waking up feeling ill the next day and not remembering what she'd done the night before and if she'd embarrassed herself.

Nick recalls Debs drunk with her head down on the table. Someone was talking about some sort of psychological trauma and, almost in comic-sketch fashion, she suddenly lifted her head and slurred: 'Hypnotherapy. It worked for me. I was in a terrible state.' But before anyone could ask what she was talking about, she crashed out on the table again. 'We used to laugh a lot,' said Nick. 'Sometimes I'd tease her and she'd say, "Right, you've done it now!" and chase me around her flat. That could have been frightening – she was very strong physically, probably from lugging all that heavy computer equipment around all the time.'

Everything in Debs' life was connected to comedy – and Nick was happy to become part of her fixation. Friday nights they would go out. Their first proper date was to a cinema in Swiss Cottage to see her hero, Woody Allen, in the comedy *Manhattan Murder Mystery*, about a couple who suspect their neighbour has been bumped off.

Debs would record the 11 o'clock edition of *Week Ending* and they would come home and listen to the tape, often laughing together and hoping their stuff had made the show. Once, more as a joke between themselves than anything else, they submitted a 'stiff line' about the death of a famous female greyhound racing trainer:

'As a mark of respect at her funeral the coffin will be towed along on a piece of string while six mourners run along a few feet behind.' They were amazed to get home and discover the line had been used in the show, giggling and celebrating after it went out. Other Friday trips were to comedy clubs, one-man shows, and listening to comedy tapes.

Debs had borrowed a bicycle from her aunt (although she told Nick she'd bought it off someone second-hand for a tenner) and on Saturday mornings she'd pedal down to Sainsbury's, coming back with the *Daily Mail* and the *Guardian* in a carrier bag. In the afternoon, she would polish off the *Guardian* crossword and then it was off to Hammersmith library to get out cassettes of songs that she could parody for *Newsrevue*.

Nick says Debs never seemed to avoid food, either eating at home, using her microwave oven, in the BBC canteen, or at the various bars dotted around the BBC buildings. They often joked about a place on the fourth floor of 16 Langham Street that served hot drinks, sandwiches or biscuits.

It was always an adventure going up there because the woman who served in there was absolutely terrifying. She'd tilt her head on one side, eye you suspiciously, bellow 'WHADDYA WANT?' and then hold out her hand about an inch under your nose for the money. Debbie often liked to joke about the famous 'Minty Lamb' which seemed to be slices of congealed lambs' fat in bread. There were usually piles of these left over even if every other type had sold out.

She seemed to eat a pretty healthy low-fat diet: During the week she'd have soup and pitta bread, for example. She'd snack on wholemeal bread in between. When we went out, we might have, say, a salad in a restaurant but at other times we might have takeaway burgers.

We stayed in one Friday night and I did us some sort of pasta bake which she was very impressed with but it was something very simple. Before we went out, she would always fill an Evian bottle with tap water and take this with her in her duffel bag (the top came off once and soaked everything). Coffee was very important to her, even then, spending some gift money from her grandparents on an Espresso machine. She'd have all manner of flavours, vanilla, nut, etc.

Work took a lot out of her, and she'd often write until two in the morning. She survived on little sleep during the week, but made up for it on Saturdays, sometimes sleeping through until well into Sunday afternoon. Whilst Nick only wrote when he had something specific to write for, Debs was always writing, ready for when new markets appeared. They once went to the Ideal Home Exhibition, where Nick wanted to look around the gardening section because he grew organic vegetables. She was horrified at the thought of anyone 'wasting their time' gardening. 'You should be writing!' she told him.

'A few weeks after we started seeing each other, she put in a proposal for a Radio 4 series called *Slice of Life*. She'd planned out the whole thing, the characters, a synopsis of the plot of each 15-minute episode, how it would develop. It revolved around corporate team building, company staff being sent off into the woods on exercises, all very popular at the time. My phone rang one lunchtime and she yelled "I've gotta pilot!", although I don't think the programme ever did get made.'

Debs was still enjoying working for *Newsrevue* and even contributed to an unsuccessful TV pilot of the show. Fellow writer John Random's diary for 1994 reads:

February 6th
Debbie Barham writing great stuff.

February 10th
Debbie Barham is the current star.

March 12th
Newsrevue was duff with few highlights except for Debbie

Barham's song called 25 Cromwell Road (address of mass murderer Fred West sung to the tune of 'English Country Garden').

March 25th
Debbie Barham continues to dazzle.

April 21st
Debbie Barham's scintillating filth spoilt by dull cast.

May 12th
Debbie Barham's Ronnie Knight song is a classic.

A later entry in John's diary reads: 'Debbie Barham looked like a tall, wet seal in her tight, black clothes. She was relaxed, witty and perceptive – and we had a good, old bitch about *Week Ending* weirdoes.'

Twenty

By the spring of 1994, Nick was aware that they'd passed what had previously been her time limit for relationships. He had put up with the secrecy, but was not happy that a previous boyfriend was still ringing her up for dates but she was refusing to explain to him that there was someone else in her life. The former lover had even written a sketch for *Week Ending* featuring two Conservative MPs discussing future sleaze scandals that included the line: 'What about Nick Thomas? He got off with a couple of sixth-formers last week' – an obvious and somewhat hypocritical dig at their romance.

Going out suddenly wasn't so much fun. One rainy Friday afternoon they went for a riverside stroll near Kew Gardens and they hardly walked together. Later that day they got up to get off a bus at the same time and ended up squashed in the aisle. Debs said loudly, almost shouted, 'You're in my way!' Nick didn't feel she was just talking about him blocking a gangway.

She had arrived at a major crossroad in her career – applying for a BBC contract writer's award. This was a bursary given to four Radio Light Entertainment writers each year. They were paid £6,000 each to write whatever the department wanted them to and also encouraged to come up with new sketch shows, sitcoms and panel games. This money was a minimum and they were able to keep anything else they earned once they had done £6,000 worth of work. Repeat fees were also paid on top. The award was very prestigious within the BBC, being seen as official recognition of a writer's talent and a passport to more lucrative TV work.

In all, thirty-three people applied for four positions. These included both Nick and Debs – her application was sponsored by *Huddlines* producer Richard Wilson. The general feeling was that even if there had only been *one* position available, not four, it would have gone to Debbie, such was her reputation by now.

The post obviously meant a lot to her. She complained to Nick that she was missing the industry gossip and wanted to get back to the gang at the Yorkshire Grey. She began to belittle him, particularly in drink. He found it difficult to take. It made it worse that he was teetotal and had to endure her insults as she got progressively more intoxicated. 'She could be sulky and moody but wouldn't usually say what was wrong (although she'd sometimes say her skin was irritating her). She'd never want to have any long talks about the relationship. If I ever suggested that we could end it if she was unhappy, she'd say, fiercely, "You'd better not!" And I certainly didn't want to.'

The News Huddlines was about to become the longest-running audience radio comedy show in broadcasting history and on the 31 March 1994 one of the new series was transmitted live to mark the occasion. As part of the pre-publicity, the *Sunday Times* and the *Independent* both ran features about the programme. The *ST* piece, written by Jonathan Margolis, provides a colourful assessment of the status of the show and its writers.

With a glowering, arms-crossed grimness that suggests they are probably comedy writers but might also be axe murderers, the men in anoraks stand at the back of the BBC's Paris Theatre in Lower Regent Street. The lunchtime audience, mostly pensioners, settle down to another recording of Roy Hudd's Radio 2 show, *The News Huddline*s. The anorak men remain standing, making it clear they are writers rather than punters; perhaps this Thursday will be the one when Roy uses one of their sketches. Or one-liners.

Anything would be a triumph for them; the 20-odd quid a writer receives for getting a line on Hudd's show is beside the point. Anybody involved in comedy will tell you that it is *The News Huddlines* and no other show in which gag writers get their wings. Most big names – such as Grant and Naylor of *Red Dwarf*, David Renwick of *One Foot in the Grav*e, Andy Hamilton of *Drop the Dead Donkey* – have done their stint on *Huddlines*.

But Roy Hudd? Isn't he a bit ...? Passé? Don't even think about it. Roy Hudd is universally acknowledged head boy of British comedy. Yet, as Hudd is the first to admit, he doesn't write his own stuff. 'If like me, you're not clever, you need people to write material for you. We do insist on proper jokes. We don't go in for comments on things like "Isn't it funny when you put your finger through the toilet paper?" Well it isn't funny unless there's a joke connected with it, an old-fashioned joke with a feedline and a tag.'

For the write-ups, Debs gave her first press interviews. It was to be a rare occurrence. She much preferred staying out of the spotlight. The articles were accurate enough about her lifelong dream but she still felt the need to keep up the pretence about her age and her mythical 'working-class' background. At the time of the articles she was 17 but told the writers she was 20. The *ST* piece went on:

If Roy Hudd had not been allowed to carry on for 18 years and 334 episodes, Debbie Barham, for one, would still be working in a greengrocer's shop in Sheffield.

Barham is just 20, and regarded as one of the brightest new comedy writers around.

She left school in Sheffield at 16 with no idea of what she wanted to do. She had, however, been obsessed with radio comedy since the age of 12, building up a reference library of 350 cassettes recorded off-air and now stacked in the West London bedsit where she lives and works.

Does she not find Hudd's style a little old fashioned for her? Not at all.

'There are certain subjects that fit the formula,' she says diplomatically. 'Pot noodles, Jeremy Beadle, Germans and

British Rail are perennials. But you write differently for different shows,' she says.

The *Independent* feature actually opened with a quote from Debs.

'If you did go to see a recording of the show, you'd probably find you were the only person there with their own teeth and hair,' says D. A. Barham, one of the writers of *The News Huddlines*. Barham is 20 and was thus a babe-in-arms when Roy Hudd launched his weekly programme on Radio 2, 18 years ago. This week, this aural temple to what another of its writers calls 'good honest vulgarity' starts a new season ... Deborah (she uses the initials because she thinks comedy writers cut more mustard if people think they're blokes) is a slight, spiky sort of woman. Shy to a degree, she was working in a Sheffield greengrocers and living with mum and dad when she decided she would send in a few one-liners to the BBC Radio Light Entertainment department. She now has a flat and a mobile phone in London, so the chances are that sooner or later she will transmogrify into a writer for television. That seems to be the standard trajectory.

The *Huddlines* style of comedy is wholly un-PC. Barham had something of a shock when she started writing for the show. 'I set out never to make gags about gays and so on; but you end up doing it,' she says.

The articles caused quite a stir in the department. One producer remarked to Debs at the coffee machine: 'Who's a little Miss Media, then?'

Debs felt the press attention put her under intense pressure, particularly with the contract award in the air. She felt she had to have a lot of material on the show to justify the attention, but she could not devote all her time to it as she was now commissioned for *Week Ending* as well. Worse still, the show had a new producer who did not seem to accept her stuff so readily, demanding rewrites.

The night before the record-breaking show, Debs' ears perked up when the pub discussion centred on a radio duo who earned £50,000 a year writing sketches for TV. It was probably her first realization of the sort of money that beckoned. As the night wore on, she drank more and started being quite offhand and bitchy with Nick. He left and got the train home to Bournemouth. She got very drunk and crawled into bed in the early hours.

The following day she rang him at the unusual hour of 7.30 a.m., apologizing 'for being such a cunt'. She'd been up since 6 a.m. writing her *Week Ending* material. Nick asked her if she still wanted him to stay that night and she replied: 'You'd better!' The show went well. Debs had several sketches used, although she still put Nick down at the celebration party afterwards. Maybe she thought the success of the show had improved her chances of the contract job, in which case she would have no time for a relationship.

Certainly the tension of the award was getting to her. At

a later show at the Paris studios, she was among *Huddlines* writers watching the recordings through the doors rather than sitting among the audience so they could beat the audience rush and get back to Broadcasting House for the *Week Ending* deadline. The cast were performing a sketch of Debs' which, unusually, wasn't getting laughs and would obviously get edited out before the broadcast that evening. Nick looked at her and she was brushing away a tear, the only time he ever saw her cry. Her reaction to the setback was to go out and get drunk.

Several days later, a shortlist for the contract award was posted on the notice board. There were eight names, including Debs. But Nick was not among them. The following day, the candidates were called in for interviews. A nervous Debs hovered outside the office until they called her in, worried in case she entered too soon. When they did call her, she stood there, hesitantly, saying, 'What, shall I come in? Shall I come in now?' She didn't want to put a foot wrong.

The day after the interview, Debs was told that she was one of the successful four. She was thrilled. But her success marked the beginning of the end of her relationship with Nick.

Many *Huddlines* writers were struggling to get sketches on with the new producer. The dreaded blue pencil was put through many of his offerings. By now, it was the fourth show in a run of ten, and Nick had not had one sketch used, his worst run since he had started on the programme three years earlier. At the recording that week, a long sketch by him went down well with the audience, but was edited out. Other, less successful sketches, stayed in. It was beginning to look as if his sketch commission was under threat. To make matters worse, he'd gone self-employed only that day. Nick went to see the producer in his office, which led to an angry argument.

'I said quite politely that I thought he was editing out some good stuff but he just flew into a rage. He said: "This is not a charity, Nick." I foolishly replied: "It must be, if they've made you a producer."'

Nick knew he'd broken the cardinal rule: 'You just do not have a blazing row with a producer. The row reverberated around the BBC and everyone was talking about me, saying I had blown it. I was suddenly notorious and being sent to Coventry. Debbie supported me, but I am sure she was worried the row might affect her career. It certainly drew attention to her as more and more people were gradually realizing we were in a relationship.'

Debs was also beginning to get more secretive about her work. At one time they'd showed each other everything. But not now. She had even developed a new sitcom without breathing a word to her boyfriend. It was called *The Elephant Man*, set in a zoo, and was eventually broadcast in 1996. She shrewdly submitted the proposal days before her contract writer's job began, so that she would be entitled to any royalties.

By the end of April, Debs had made up her mind. On the way to *Newsrevue* one night she admitted she really didn't want him to stay. They rowed in full view of colleagues.

'I went to her flat, although she really didn't want me to, and the row carried on inside. I was beside myself. I didn't want to lose her and I seemed to be losing all dignity trying to keep her. She didn't say much, just kept looking furiously off to one side. When she did speak, the North Country accent was coming through: "Yeah, we had some laffs" and "Ah've never looved anybo-day". But then she said "It's going nowhere", the one expression I didn't want to hear because it was what she'd said about the previous two relationships.'

The following day she attended a meeting of writers at the BBC. Nick spent the day walking around Chiswick until he got bored and went back to the flat. She left her mobile phone with Nick at the flat. Instead of coming home after the meeting, she went out to a comedy club with some of the producers and got extremely drunk. She arrived home at 2 a.m. and crashed out on the bed fully clothed. Nick was furious and felt humiliated.

> I just thought I'd been treated with utter contempt. Maybe she was just so caught up in the excitement of the year ahead that she'd forgotten to call but it seemed to me then that after reluctantly agreeing for us to limp along on in some way, she'd regretted it and engineered a situation that would make me want to stop seeing her – so I told her that's what I was doing. She must have felt pretty rough after the night before. She looked really pale and

probably younger than I'd ever seen her look before, almost child-like.

I walked out of her flat feeling a great sense of relief. It was a bright, sunny morning and I felt I'd made a positive decision. But the journey to Embankment was about forty minutes and by that time I was already regretting it.

Nick was so hurt, he could not face going to the BBC and submitted material from home for two weeks. He wrote to Debs expressing his sadness and received a long letter in reply saying how guilty she felt at their parting. 'She said she <u>had</u> fallen for me (her underlining) but that there was no chance of getting back together, that she didn't want steady relationships, they were something for many years down the line, and that she'd come to realize that she wasn't really comfortable having anyone else in her flat. She said the contract was everything she'd been focusing on for the past year and was such an opportunity that she had to devote herself to it 100 per cent.'

Debs admitted she had been 'shit scared' going to her first *Huddlines/Week Ending* meeting, never expecting to get stuff on; now she was obsessed by her writing. An intensely private person, that letter to Nick stands as probably the most revealing record available of her inner thoughts and insecurities.

Although I'm horribly self-centred a lot of the time, I do have a bit of an inferiority complex: I couldn't comprehend why anyone would want to spend time with me, like me even, although I desperately want people to. That's why I go down the pub, I suppose, I want to get to know people outside the corridor.

The writing was the first thing I ever did that made people notice me or compliment me so I hung onto it for dear life. I do have a self-destructive streak, too, but I'm trying to control that by not drinking so much, etc, and not worrying like fuck over my Hudds sketches like I was at the beginning of the series, because that only makes things more difficult. The crashing out never helped, but that's purely to do with lack of sleep. I know from past experience. I do get depressed, less so nowadays, on the whole I'm very contented with my life.

I felt like shit when you left on Saturday morning, and not just because of the alcohol the night before, but that's a feeling of guilt not loneliness. I mean fuck, I've spent almost 19 years alone, travelling on my own, at school on my own, shopping, going to see films, watching TV on my own, and I have to admit, I rather like it. That's not a slur on you, or my family, or anyone else, it's just the way it is.

I'm just not ready for a relationship right now. Sorry, but it's true. I'm desperate to succeed in this career, it's what I've aimed at, been totally focused on (for longer than even I realize, judging by the tape collection). I'm happy doing what I do, but fuck it, I'm only young, I've got my whole life ahead of me to get involved with people, and right now I don't want to. It's taken a while, and a couple of failed involvements before you, for that to dawn on me. Like thermal knickers and knitting. I don't really want them, I don't really enjoy them much right now, but in later life I'll probably grow to love and depend on them.

I suppose it's a bit of a territorial thing too. I've only just started to realize this, but I'm not wild about having other people in my flat. (No, not in the physical sense, you know what I mean. People staying in my flat.) Does that sound weird? It's all to do with insecurity, I suppose, the way I don't really open up to people. Letting someone in my house is like allowing them to see all the private things about me. I just feel uncomfortable with it.

I wish I could have told you my feelings. I tried, but as I say I've been alone for so long that I think things rather than saying them. I talk to myself. I think I am learning, slowly – I shared more with you than with either of the other two.

I was so pleased when you wanted to be with me. I *had* fallen for you, like I'd never fallen for anyone else. I *had* never fallen for anyone else …That first Thursday night was very romantic, you're right. And deep down I was flattered by all the compliments – however misguided you might think now. I'm crap at accepting compliments. I'm crap at lots of things: conversation, thinking about other people, shagging, acting, map-reading. I get pissed off at things like (LATE) trains when I really shouldn't, and I know that worried and irritated you. Sorry, I couldn't understand that what you wanted out of the relationship was different to what I wanted – Hell, I didn't even *know* what I wanted.

Their relationship had lasted four months. Nick says she gave him great happiness and some of the best laughs of his life. Although they were very close during their time together, Nick did not realize until he read her obituary that she was 17 when they dated and not 20. And it was not until the day of the funeral that he discovered that Debs' 'friend' Melanie, whom she saw most Sundays, was in fact her aunt.

After the split, he never went near the BBC comedy department for over a year. He couldn't, he said, bear the thought of seeing her with anyone else.

As for Debs, she had realized that men were obstacles in the way of developing her career. She had got what she wanted – a hugely successful start as a writer, independence, including her own place in London, even a mention in the national press. She'd made it in radio, and on the stage. Next stop was Fleet Street – and the glamorous world of television.

Twenty-one

September 1999

It is 9 p.m. Debs is in London. Even though her food intake is minimal – mostly fluids and nibbles – she still finds the strength to continue her London routine. Debs calls me, but she is not ringing from the train but from Notting Hill police station. Can I pick her up? She has been mugged.

A woman alone in cafés or bars is a relatively easy target for thieves and her frail state emphasizes her vulnerability. She has been robbed before, ending the practice of carrying large amounts of cash in her purse. This means visiting cash points two or three times a day to pay for her not inconsiderable cab fares.

She'd been sitting in a café in Ladbroke Grove having coffee and typing on her hand-held and some lads had grabbed her bag. They'd tried to take her computer, but she'd managed to hold on. In the bag were her purse, some personal possessions, and the keys to her home in Chiswick. Her account was typical Debs:

```
It wasn't a particularly interesting incident.
Bloody cheeky though - I was sat in a coffee shop
working on my Psion, one of the bastards came up
```

behind me and pulled my stool backwards, his mate
yanked the phone (which was connected to the Psion -
Psion began sliding across table, I grabbed it out
of blind deadline-induced panic, which fortunately
caused the cable to break - along with modem, which
shattered on tiled floor). Whilst I was distracted,
the first little shit got my purse - this I didn't
actually notice (being so fucking relieved not to
have lost the Psion) until about ten minutes later.
The pair of 'em legged it, a couple of blokes tried
to chase them, gave up and that was all. Nothing
exciting. But all in broad neon light in full view
of approx 20 people, which I thought was the really
bloody cheeky bit. Felt thoroughly crap today, but I
suspect that was the effects of having procured
vodka as well as cash from friend the night before.
In a way I was quite lucky - I could have lost (a)
keys, (b) computer - containing approx two years
worth of vital data. I guess they were after that,
when they tried to pull it across the table - thank
God for shoddy manufactured cables … or (c)
blood/limbs/life, etc, not quite so disastrous as
losing (b) but still a bummer. As it is, they've
just really fucking inconvenienced me, re loss of
cards, money, access to money etc. They are not
going to get much cash for the phone handset, they
failed to get the modem (just broke it - cheers),
there wasn't a lot of ready cash in the purse and
they can't actually do anything with my cancelled
cards, other than chop their lines of coke up,
perhaps. And a couple of hours in a police station

was moderately more entertaining than some ways I've
spent my Saturday nights. I think the desk sergeant-
type woman was quite pleased to have someone to chat
to. And the beat bobbies were quite chirpy too, one
of 'em came in with a massively bruised face - not
injured in the line of duty, it just turned out the
poor chap had had his wisdom teeth out. Added
helpfully that he'd actually been in the coffee shop
buying coffee 15 mins before my stuff got nicked.
Bloody comedy timing again …
Cheers Debs

On getting her call I go into practical mode again! Leaving for London I grab a replacement barrel for the lock on her front door (I tend to have a lot of things like this lying around!) because it seems that they might have got the old flat keys and her address. So, after picking Debs up from the police station, we go to her flat in Chiswick and I change the lock to protect it from squatters. Debs sits in the car. It is her first – and last – visit back, but she does not want to go in. She spends the rest of the evening at home, backing up data on the Psion in case something similar happens again.

Twenty-two

Winning the BBC contract writer's award was a major career breakthrough. The name D. A. Barham was even painted on the BBC honours board in Langham Street. Paul Powell, who had won the award a year before Debs, says: 'It was always a good break. Everyone thought you had made it. It automatically guaranteed you six thousand pounds, which was a degree of financial security, but also meant that more opportunities opened up. Effectively you were a staff writer and asked to do special projects and pilots, etc.'

Sure enough, within hours of getting the award, Debs was offered a massive chance to leap from radio into the more prestigious and lucrative world of television. But it was not from the BBC.

Debs was celebrating in the Yorkshire Grey pub with many of her fellow writers. In the bar was former *Week Ending* writer Georgia Pritchett, a previous contract writer herself, but at that time a script editor on the ITV satire series *Spitting Image*. She invited Debs to send in material to the show. 'I was delighted she had won the award. It was great to have a young talent coming through, particularly that she was a woman. I knew just how talented and prolific Debbie was, so I suggested she began contributing to *Spitting Image*.'

Spitting Image was one of the funniest and satirically savage shows ever to be shown on British television. It was built around a team of rubber puppets which mimicked figures in the news, mostly politicians, the Royal family, actors and TV personalities. The premiere in 1984 opened with a puppet caricature of Israel's prime minister Menachem Begin wearing a magician's outfit. With a flourish, he produced a dove of peace from his top hat, then announced, 'For my first trick…' – and then wrung its neck. The sketch set the tone for eighteen series on ITV on Sunday nights. In its prime it attracted 12 million viewers a week and featured the voices of Harry Enfield, Rory Bremner, and Jan Stephenson.

The Queen was portrayed as a harried housewife, beset by randy, dullard children and screaming grandkids. Britain's most cherished figure, the Queen Mother, appeared as a pleasant, if somewhat boozy great-grandma, whilst Margaret Thatcher's puppet was a needle-nosed Reagan groupie who consulted with Hitler on immigration policy and sold off England's infrastructure to baying packs of yuppies. Her eventual successor, John Major, was portrayed as a dull, totally grey man who ate nothing but peas. The opposition Labour leaders, including Neil Kinnock, caricatured as 'Kinnochio', were pilloried for their inability to challenge decades of Tory rule.

The show thrived on its topicality – and was tailor-made for Debs' fast and cutting wit. Her job was to provide topical jokes for the 'news', as delivered by latex versions of

ITV newscaster Trevor McDonald and comedian Ronnie Corbett. The show was recorded on Saturday and edited that night ready for Sunday night transmission. 'We only needed four or five topical gags, but with Debs you got twenty pages of fax every Saturday, she was so prolific,' says Pritchett.

With a growing reputation, Debs attracted the attention of one of the biggest talent agencies in town. Casarotto Ramsay Associates had long been an established agency for film and theatre writers and directors. But in 1994 it decided to expand its client list into comedy writers. The agency poached Rachel Swann, the daughter of Donald Swann, half of the famous double act of Flanders and Swann. Rachel had been working for a production company called Tiger Aspect, which had been responsible for a number of TV comedy hits. Her brief at Casarotto Ramsay was to build a stable of new, young writing talent.

Rachel trawled her contacts and friends. One of these, Caroline Leddy, who had worked with Debs at the BBC and went on to become Head of Comedy at Channel 4, recommended the young Deborah Barham. Debs, now 17, duly became one of Rachel's first clients. Rachel remembers their first meeting. She recalls a tall, striking, good-looking girl, with a chubby face, dark long hair, with loose, flowing clothes. She had a confident air but was quite shy and socially awkward. 'Debs brought some of her work for me to see and I was immediately impressed. She already had some national newspaper cuttings about her role on

Huddlines. I thought her work was very witty and the jokes spot on.'

Agents traditionally seek opportunities for their clients, handle the negotiations over rates, and look after all the invoicing and payments. But a representative in the entertainment industry is often more than a mere business brain. Sometimes an agent feels more like a social worker, coping with the highs and lows of often frail egos. By taking Debs on, Rachel could not know what she was letting herself in for. Over the coming years Rachel became almost a mother figure, always there for Debs during her health crises. But in those early months, Rachel hardly saw her new client. 'She wasn't the type to drop into the office like some of my clients liked to do.'

The arrangement was that Debs would handle her own affairs regarding her writing for newspapers and other media; Rachel would look after opportunities in radio and television. Debs had already shown a skill for nurturing contacts among editors in the print and Internet world. Her growing track record and sweet personality, allied to her chatty and witty e-mails, charmed executives into giving her work – often without their ever meeting her.

After breaking into the world of TV comedy with *Spitting Image*, Debs looked around for her next opportunity. It came through the comedian/impressionist Rory Bremner, who discovered at school how to become popular – doing impersonations of teachers.

After a number of years with the BBC, Bremner had

moved to Channel 4, where the emphasis of his show switched from light entertainment to topical satire. For the BBC he had done send-ups of Sean Connery, Peter Allis, even Sooty. For Channel 4, the targets were more the deeds of politicians. An article in the *Independent on Sunday* described the new offering as 'probably the most biting satire on British television or radio'. This was some going, considering *Spitting Image* was in full savagery, along with *Week Ending* on Radio 4.

The show format was basically an opening and closing monologue with sketches in between, including an improvised routine between the two Johns – John Bird and John Fortune. The rest of the show was written by Bremner, John Langdon, and the producer Geoff Atkinson, backed up by a fine team of researchers who lunched lobby correspondents and cultivated moles in the various political parties. It was 'investigative satire' – a new genre in programming, with material such as a spoof documentary on the seedy underworld of Labour's 'rent-an-idea' boys.

The problem for Debs was that Bremner already had a core team of trusted writers – including, of course, himself. There was little room for outsiders. Anyone who wanted to write for the show would have to force their way in through the quality of their unsolicited material.

The series was run by a production company called Vera, set up by Rory and his agent Vivienne Clore, along with the producer Geoff Atkinson and another executive, Elaine Morris. Their offices were in a scruffy building in Soho, described by one observer as having too many second-hand desks crammed into not quite enough space, with crates of Jacob's Creek and Beck's piled into the tiny kitchen. In the corner of the main office was the fax machine. Here, several times a week, the team would be greeted by pages and pages of unsolicited material from Debs. Elaine Morris says: 'I was always in early and there would be this pile of paper full of material. It would be timed at 4.20 a.m. We just assumed the timer on her fax was wrong.'

The script editor was John Langdon, a former advertising executive and Russian folk guitarist who had cut his teeth on *Week Ending* and went on to become one of the elite comedy writers in the business. He had met Bremner in 1984 when the young comedian was doing stand-up at the Edinburgh Festival. He told him his act was brilliant but needed more jokes and fewer puns.

Bremner heeded the advice and was chosen to present Radio 4's *The Fringe* programme. Terry Wogan, who was about to start his television career, heard the show and invited Rory to perform on his first programme. The rest, as they say, is history. Bremner and Langdon have been together since, winning countless awards, including a BAFTA for *Rory Bremner…Who Else?*

It was John's job to 'taste' any new offering. He is a great encourager of new talent, but in the pressurized atmosphere of a fast turnaround, topical show, he regarded unsolicited stuff more like 'a virus'. But Debs was unignorable. 'She was prodigious – far more fluent and funnier than the other writers and her hit rate was exceptional. She literally forced herself on to the team,' he says.

Before long, Debs was getting four or five jokes on a show, which at £75 a gag was proving quite lucrative. Eventually, Vera thought it in their best interests to contract Debs for a guaranteed three minutes per show.

Part of the success of moving from BBC to Channel 4, was that the new broadcaster gave Bremner the freedom to record the night before transmission. This meant he could, say, listen to John Major's conference speech on a Friday afternoon, write his own version and record it that evening. But the downside of such topicality is a sometimes impossible work routine. Inserts have to be pieced together early in the week, with sketches filmed on Thursday during the day and the monologues written Thursday night ready for the audience recording next day. Often the writers worked throughout the night.

Debs, still just 17 (though still pretending she was 20) was invited to join the inner circle for the ideas and monologue sessions and to the recording sessions. Elaine Morris says she was great to have around. She remembers a tall girl with dark, wavy hair, engaging and witty, mixing with the production team and sitting quietly in the Green Room smiling as the channel's lawyer winced at some of the material being served up. 'I was surprised she was so shy,' says Elaine. 'I did not know her age, but having seen her stuff, I expected a loud, full-on sassy, personality. Instead she was softly spoken and nervous about looking you in the eyes.'

John Langdon says: 'It is very intimidating for writers to come in. They are working with household names and some people might either hold back or try to impress by taking over. Debs was completely at ease from the word go. There is always a natural desire to top someone's jokes. With her, you would say, "What do you think, Debbie?", and she would say something along the lines of, "Well, it could be…" and she would come up with a stunner. She was good at having the last word.'

After her first visit to the show, John took Debs out for an Indian meal near the Molinaire editing facility in Brewer Street. He explained that he'd also started out writing unsolicited material for *Week Ending*. He was thirty years her senior and she was keen to learn from his experience. They became great mates, down to, he jokes, their addictive personalities. 'Her knowledge of comedy was such that she could quote some of my stuff back at me that I could not remember writing. She was always quick to take on board advice about how to make her stuff even funnier, although to be honest most of the time it was already polished. Her craft was second nature. Radio producer Bruce Hyman described her as Mozartian, which is an ideal description. I would describe her work like a Picasso painting – it was just spot on.'

Rory Bremner says: 'There is an old line in this business: "Do you want it funny or do you want it tomorrow?" With Debbie invariably you got both. She was head and shoulders above other non-commissioned writers and forced her way in. She had a phenomenal work rate and extraordinary speed. She was excellent at writing for what the programme needed, slipping into the character of the person being impersonated. She was utterly dependable and would get the idea very quickly.'

Scripts were not just broadly political, but intensely, topically so. They dealt in scathing detail with quangos, government policy, and sleaze, although there was still room for Bremner to morph into a popular celebrity. Among Debs' early offerings was for Rory to become Bruce Forsyth for a new version of the game show *The Generation Game* called *Brucie's Re-Generation Game*, in which all those old actors you thought you'd seen the last of suddenly turn up in popular early-evening game shows. 'So let's meet the eight who we're going to resuscitate. Nice to see, to see you yet again.'

Debs was fast making a name for herself on the comedy circuit, adding Bob Monkhouse to the likes of Rory Bremner and *Spitting Image* to her CV. Monkhouse, who died in December 2003, was a comedian's comedian, widely admired for his joke-making and joke-telling ability. In his autobiography (*Over the Limit*, 1998), he gratefully singled out Debs amongst those who shared his own knack of turning news items into comedy.

Twenty-three

A few months before her eighteenth birthday, Debs began her first serious foray into the professional written media by writing for a weekly magazine. *Ms London* was for the Girl About Town and was given away free on the Tube, buses, and cafés in the capital. The editorial team were virtually all women and the magazine carried features on fashion, careers, cinema, travel, and dining out.

Debs' column was called 'First Off' and was the main welcoming feature on page three. The six hundred words were designed to be absorbed between Piccadilly Circus and Charing Cross. Each column carried a picture byline of Debs portraying a full face, long dark hair and make-up, a slightly wistful smile, and those piercing blue eyes. A footnote said: 'Debbie Barham writes for BBC Radio, *Spitting Image* and is a past winner of the BBC/Witzend TV scriptwriting competition.'

She was brilliant at turning everyday living into bright, engaging copy.

OK, so I am hoping to have unwashed dishes valued by Hugh Scully next time *Antiques Roadshow* comes to Chiswick, and the term 'bomb site' does spring to mind whenever one walks through the door. (I wouldn't be surprised if Kate Adie emerged from my loo in her flak jacket, organizing a safe haven for refugee cockroaches.)

Other topics included the sexual allure of politicians, school reunions, trying to master the mysteries of computers, cyber-cafés, even celibacy.

> A recent survey revealed that more women in this country would prefer to abstain from sexual activity than from chocolate. I can understand that. For one thing, a bar of chocolate usually lasts longer. It is also unlikely to stay snoring flatulently in your bed until lunchtime. And after having the female orgasm forced down our throats, as it were, by Desmond Morris in his latest TV series, it's difficult to enjoy a passionate liaison when you keep remembering that your moment of ecstasy looks disconcertingly like someone wringing out a soggy pink swimsuit.

The column also showed her ability to write for a market – in effect to give readers what she thought they wanted to hear. It didn't have to be based on any real semblance of truth. Like an actress playing a role, Debs simply made up stuff for the audience. For example, her piece called 'Old School Daze' contained references to her school as the 'Everton' of educational league tables, but with a poorer attendance record. 'The young ladies who did bother to attend generally concentrated on just the two GCSEs –

Smoking and Graffiti ...' She went on to describe the hell of attending that ultimate of torture, the school reunion. The truth was, of course, that not only did Debs attend a highly academic school, she never went anywhere near the place or met her classmates after she left. It was the same with a piece on computers. The editor obviously required her to pander to the stereotype of young secretaries struggling to come to grips with modern technology in the workplace.

I like to consider myself an independent, intelligent career woman. I am in favour of sexual equality in the workplace. I am as likely as the next woman, particularly if the next woman is Germaine Greer, to knee any male chauvinist pig in the pork balls. But I admit I still have to get a man in to show me how to work my computer. 'You go to your Sys Ops menu, right click on option 3, yeah, then format your document and initialize the printer. Okay, love?'

Fine, I say, feeling my way round the back of the screen in search of an On switch. He asks whether I have already installed Windows, and flashes me a patronizing smirk when I insist that, really, I don't need double glazing. I am informed that the blinking square in my top left-hand corner is referred to by the computer literate as a 'cursor'. This is, I discover, because I will spend the next few weeks screaming obscenities at it.

This from a woman with qualifications in computer studies and who programmed her own website!

Meanwhile, her radio writing was extending beyond gags. She used her expertise in crosswords by developing a Radio 4 quiz with former *Week Ending* colleague Hugh Rycroft. In April 1996, she inserted the following invitation on various comedy websites:

```
DO MARRIAGE ROMP? Not *another* sex-line spam posted
to several hundred inappropriate Usenet groups?

No. Merely an anagram of two words - RADIO
PROGRAMME.

Yes, FREE TICKETS are now available for recordings
of a new BBC Radio 4 quiz programme based on the
wonderful world of crossword puzzles. 'Cross
Questioned' - the show that jumbles up more words
than a Guardian sub-editor.

Exciting, stimulating, star-studded and hilarious -
are just some of the words our panel might be using.

Chaired by the lovely Caroline Quentin (of 'Men
Behaving Badly' fame) and featuring panellists from
the worlds of entertainment, journalism and stand-up
comedy, these recordings are taking place VERY SOON
at the BBC Radio Theatre in Broadcasting House.
```

Easily as much fun as a West End film, and a damn
sight cheaper at just £0.00 per ticket (YES, that's
right - FREE, GRATIS, ON THE HOUSE, WE'RE GIVING 'EM
AWAY FOLKS).

Recordings of CROSS QUESTIONED are taking place at
7.30 p.m. (doors open 7.15 p.m.) on:
Wednesday 17th April 1996
Saturday 20th April 1996
Saturday 11th May 1996

To ensure your place in the audience - and hear your
laughter (and/or boos and hisses) on national radio
- just e-mail crossq@skcollob.win-uk.net or apply
directly to Radio.Ticket.Unit@bbc.co.uk

Thanks
D. A. BARHAM

Hugh Rycroft remembers her mood at that time: 'This was
the only time I really worked closely with Debbie and
it was an absolute delight. She was constantly good-
humoured, self-deprecating, generous in her praise and
hilariously sceptical about the world in general. In short,
brilliant company.'

Cross Questioned coincided with the airing on Radio 4
of Debs' first sitcom, which she had dreamed up at the age
of 16, shortly before she was awarded the BBC writing contract award. It was called *The Elephant Man* and revolved
around the life of Terry (Peter Serafinowicz), an elephant

keeper at his local zoo. The regular cast also included Chris Emmett, Joanna Monro and Richard Pearce.

One day she was contacted by a radio producer who was to have an important role in her life. Bruce Hyman was an experienced theatre operator, responsible for more than 150 plays, musicals, and comedy shows in the West End, Europe, and on Broadway. Television had already undergone a revolution in which terrestrial broadcasters were required to commission a guaranteed percentage of programmes from the independent sector. Hoping that radio would follow suit, Hyman formed his own company called Above the Title to specialize in radio comedy, factual programmes, drama, music, and arts. The BBC was obviously his main market and he needed talented writers. He approached an old friend, Rory Bremner's script editor John Langdon, for advice.

John said I should definitely speak to Debbie Barham. He gave me her phone number and almost immediately she was sending me pages of ideas of an extremely high standard. These were not just gags, but what I would call social comedy too. We talked a lot about ideas. She used to have so many.

She was brilliant at extended puns, parody or satire and had she lived longer I believe she would have started writing character comedy too. Those of us who write comedy know it's hard to get the rhythm of the line just right, to tune it so that it hits the spot. Debs did this with the most extraordinary facility.

In print she could be brutal, savage and razor sharp. In conversation she was kind, sweet and rather lovely. But she had a rage which manifested itself in the volume and savagery of some of her work and which was rather good for writing comedy.

Debs was to play a key role in delivering commissions for the comedy arm of the fledgeling company. In four years she was to work on a number of productions for Radio 4 alongside more seasoned writers. But she more than held her own. So much so, that when Above the Title was commissioned to produce Christmas pantomime specials for Radio 4 – first *Cinderella* and then *Aladdin* – Bruce turned to Debs to write the topical, satirical lyrics to the songs. Both shows starred the cream of British radio comedy and were a hit with the critics. The *Daily Mail* said: 'Cinderella is taut, wickedly funny, fast-paced and beautifully performed.'

With John Langdon she wrote a six-part radio comedy series called *I'm Glad You Asked Me That*, presented by Gordon Kennedy; *The April Fool Story*, in which Anna Ford presented an illuminating – but utterly false – history of the traditions and customs of *April Foolery*; and *I Can Do That*, described by Sue Arnold in the *Observer* as the funniest spoof on radio for years. Presenter Valerie Singleton gave 'ordinary Joes and Joannas the chance to do something meaningful with their lives'. Subjects included a Yorkshire grandmother who had always wanted to solve the Middle East peace crisis, and an unemployed spot-welder from

Tyneside whose lifelong ambition had been to remove a gallstone. In one episode, sheep farmer Murray McCluskie, who had phoned the BBC to complain about poor reception in his remote Scottish hamlet, is invited to London to try for the post of Director General of the Corporation.

One scene written by Debs involved acting head of development Gavin Tucker sifting through various programme ideas. Tucker explains that hundreds of proposals roll in every day and are sorted into four categories – Very Good/OK/Awful/and Paul Daniels. Tucker is desperate for a new cop show. On his desk are ideas for *Cole's Law*, a cop who is also a vegetarian, and who uses poisonous genetically modified potatoes as ammo for his spud gun; *Bill and Coup* – he's a cop, she's a pigeon fancier, 'a sort of rozzers in the north'; *Law and Order*, a female cop who is also a nun; and *The Long Arm of the Lawn* – 'yes, he's a cop, but also Charlie Dimmock from *Ground Force*'.

The script included other Debs gems: *One Man and His Ewe* – a change of emphasis to impress Murray McCluskie; *Cherie and Tracie's Bunch of Old Aunts* – high-brow culture for the *Loaded* generation, rejected because Tucker wanted 'something more Billy Bragg than Melvin Bragg'; and a series for disabled listeners called *Address the Chair*, an idea turned down because Tucker said he wasn't sure the idea had legs. When the bemused farmer complains he'd been stuck in a lift with Valerie Singleton the room explodes with joy. What a great idea for a series!

One sparkling idea from Debs made it to air after she

died. *About a Dog* was a three-part radio comedy conceived by Debs but written by Graeme Garden. It was about
a dog's life seen from the point of view of the family pet. It
aired on Radio 4 in 2004, with a second series in summer
2005, and starred Alan Davies and Kate Ashfield. Debs
would have been proud of the reaction from critics. The
Sunday Telegraph nominated the first show Programme
of the Week and the *Sunday Times* made it Pick of the Day.
Susan Jeffreys in the *Mail* said: 'A lovely bit of work here
from Alan Davies, a nice idea from the much-missed writer
Debbie Barham and a perfect script from Graeme Garden.'

Another major breakthrough for Debs was teaming up
with Clive Anderson, hailed as the best of the new breed
of television chat show hosts. Anderson acquired a love
for comedy at Cambridge University and was a former
President of its Footlights Dramatic Club. He went on to
practise law whilst writing scripts in his spare time, contributing to various shows, including those by his old Footlights chums, Mel Smith and Griff Rhys Jones, *Not the
Nine O'Clock News*, and *The Frankie Howerd Variety
Show*. A former stand-up comedian, eventually he was
invited to host *Whose Line Is It Anyway?* on BBC Radio
4, which later transferred to television. His quick-witted,
teasing style appealed to Channel 4 bosses and in 1989 he
was asked to front his own chat show, *Clive Anderson All
Talk*, which ran for seven years before transferring to the
BBC and being renamed *Clive Anderson Talks Back*. Debs
began sending in unsolicited material.

Anderson recalls:

We decided we might want to put lots of different features in the BBC show so the producer rushed out to hire six or seven different writers to write monologues, sketches, bits and pieces, prop gags, all the sort of things we were going to do in this Brave New World of the BBC.

And then, by the time we started, we decided to do just interviews with maybe two or three written jokes at the beginning, so an extremely unpromising environment for a new writer as Debs was, coming into this group of shabby old men with plastic bags, stubble and jumpers – she an elegantly dressed young woman.

We noticed if there were two or three jokes getting on, she would be getting one or two of them on, so she became one of the writing team.

The show will probably be remembered for the infamous walkout by the Bee Gees rather than for the quality of the jokes. During the show, the brothers revealed they were formally known as Les Tosseurs. Anderson quipped that they would always be 'tosseurs' to him. At which point Barry Gibb unclipped his microphone and stormed off stage, saying: 'You're the tosser, pal', his brothers following suit. On another occasion, Richard Branson poured a glass of water over his head. Clive replied: 'I'm used to that. I've flown Virgin.'

Debs and Clive became great mates. They shared a passion for comedy, the same spiky humour, and a fondness for the zany style of Douglas Adams. Over the years she produced reams of gags for Clive's TV shows and for various speeches and awards dinners, including the Olivier Awards. 'Words and jokes just poured out of her,' he says.

All I wanted her to do was to come up with two jokes about pre-stressed concrete or a couple of jokes about the week's news. She would write hundreds, absolutely fantastic, huge copious amounts, quite impossible to work into an evening of handing out best Concrete Mixer of the Year, or whatever.

She could do all sorts – rude, political, topical. I once had to replace Lenny Henry on something when he was having problems with his marital life. She seriously imagined I would do a joke which had the punch line about being up at the crack of Dawn.

She was particularly sharp at topical political jokes. I remember there was a problem with the transport minister hanging on to his job. Her line went something like 'Stephen Byers is still refusing to go... he got the idea from the trains.'

She always included for my benefit jokes about me. I often am teased about looking like William Hague, the former Conservative Party leader. She seemed obsessed with the idea that in addition to having no hair, no eyes and no neck, I was also extremely short. She could not come to my fiftieth birthday party, but sent an e-mail saying, 'Congratulations on reaching 50, or was it 5ft 0 inches? I forget.'

Twenty-four

15 September 1999

Sue and I decide the best strategy is to make the necessary adjustments in our own lifestyle to fit in with Debs' chaotic routine. At least we will have some semblance of control and influence on her actions. We'll try to involve Debs in meals without making any issue out if it. From now on, our main evening meal will be at 11.30 p.m., so we can all sit down together after she returns from London. She will have her menu, we will have ours.

19 September 1999

This is not working as we had hoped. While we might be eating, say pasta, or a salad, she sips Covent Garden soups and picks at her brittle broccoli and a few frazzled carrots. Meal times are difficult at the best of times in the cramped space. Most of the dining-room table is covered by Debs' work debris and we all occupy what little space there is between piles of notebooks, scripts, newspapers, and computer equipment. Also, the narrow layout of the room dictates that in order to all sit at the table, Sue and I have to eat immediately opposite Debs, in almost confrontational mode. It makes it more difficult for meals to be 'normal' – I'm sure Debs feels we are ganging up on her.

Despite the fact that both Sue and I have demanding jobs and need a good night's sleep, we try to extend this ritual for as long as possible – often way past midnight – in the hope that Debs might actually eat something. Instead she plays with her food with her fork, like a cat toying with a doomed mouse. And, infuriatingly, when her food gets cold, because she has barely touched it, she puts it back in the microwave again. Everything *has* to be piping hot – until, of course, she allows it to go cold again and the whole absurd farce continues over again.

Last night, in the hope that more adventurous fare might encourage Debs to consume rather than pick and nibble, Sue introduced fish, buying some prawns from the supermarket. Surprisingly for someone supposedly sophisticated, Debs had never had prawns before. But instead of giving them a go, she merely pushed them around her plate, repeatedly microwaving them until they were hard and rubbery – and inedible.

'I don't think I like prawns,' she said. 'In fact, I fucking *hate* them!'

With that, she threw the lot up in the air.

Debs' presence in our home is beginning to affect our relationship. We both have full-time jobs and, after little sleep because of the late meals, we leave the house just as she is turning in, often after a restless night punctuated by the constant beeping of the microwave or the sound of her struggling up the stairs to the one bathroom.

She doesn't make any particular effort to be quiet. Tact and consideration are not her strong points. The strain is taking its toll on Sue and me. When we aren't talking through the situation late into the night before going to sleep we are sniping at each other, probably because we don't feel we can take our irritation out on Debs.

Because the ground floor of the house is essentially open-plan, our bedroom is our only refuge. Weekends are particularly difficult. Debs' nocturnal regime means we have to tiptoe around the house for half the day in case we wake her up, and this is particularly difficult for Sue's lively 11-year-old daughter Sophie. This Saturday note from Debs is typical.

> *Folks. Am turning in now – 8.55 am – work a bit in bed then zzzzz. If no sign of intelligent human life by approx 1.30 pm, kindly hurl obscenities or practise darts against door. Will set alarm anyway. Have a good day, will see you later (than now, but not as late as yesterday) Beds xxx I mean, sorry Debs xxx zzzzz (why, why, why...) etc*

It is clear our tactics are just not working. Whilst they may suit Debs – and her London routine – if she, indeed our marriage, are to survive, urgent changes are needed.

Twenty-five

In the days and weeks following Debs' death, I found myself wondering what part the Internet played in her demise. The World Wide Web is, of course, one of the great inventions of modern times, and Debs was one of its children.

The breakthrough came in 1969, seven years before her birth, when scientists in America discovered they could transfer data between computer networks via phone lines. By the mid 1970s, when she was born, ten nodes spanned various academic institutions across the States, linking just sixty-four computers on one single network.

By the late 80s, when Debs first began to show an interest in computer technology, the 'Net' had spread to businesses and homes. Electronic mail (e-mail) was an ad hoc 'add on' – nobody predicted in those early days how 'people-to-people' interaction would transform our lives. Today there are millions of computers across the globe, with hundreds of thousands of different networks, enabling transfer of data and one-to-one communication across the world.

Debs latched on early to the potential and wonderment of this new technology. For someone so precociously bright, the information 'super highway' was a route to much treasure – but for an addictive personality it was also the road to compulsion. She did almost everything online – she chatted, communicated, researched, played, shopped, ordered food, medication, even met at least one boyfriend.

It fuelled her addiction to writing. The Web gave her access to an infinite well of news, information, and gossip, which she processed and communicated via e-mail in a way she could never have done even a few years before. It was like a powerful drug – 'e-speed'. And the faster she produced, the more fuel was needed.

Professionally, it was not just an access to her market. Thanks to the dot-com revolution, it *was* her market, as sites sprang up everywhere demanding entertaining and thought-provoking content. Along with the radio (also accessed via the Internet), it was her link to the world during those long virtual nights. Is it any wonder, with so much information buzzing around in her head, that sleep became nigh on impossible and had to be chemically induced?

As a teenager, Debs admitted that she was 'hooked' on the Internet. One of the plethora of newsgroups she subscribed to asked her, along with several other 'star' contributors, to explain what they actually did on the Internet. This was her reply:

```
What do I *do*? I get withdrawal symptoms if I
haven't checked my e-mail for 90 minutes. I have a
telephone line more frequently engaged than Liz
Taylor. Each time I leave the house, the chairman of
National Power sees his profit forecasts drop by at
least 50%.
```

Yes, I admit it. I'm an Internet Addict. It's not so bad - a bit like being a drug addict or an alcoholic, only not so socially acceptable and you don't get to meet such interesting people.

Professionally, though - what do I do? Well, I work as a scriptwriter for the likes of Rory Bremner, Clive Anderson, (the now defunct) Spitting Image, and so forth. And that's where being on the Internet really comes in handy.

Currently, I'm Programme Associate on Bob Monkhouse's new TV series, which means constantly scouring the newspapers for new topical material. But now, thanks to the marvels of technology, I can dispense with the long hours of inky-fingered tabloid thumbing in the BBC canteen and simply hop across to http://www.the-times.co.uk, or http://www.telegraph.co.uk. A quick net search for key words and phrases - 'Hugh Grant', 'Hurley', 'Fergie', 'disgraced Tory MP in sex-n-sleaze scandal', and so forth - and I've got the stories there at my fingertips in an instant. It also works out cheaper than buying all the papers in Dead Tree form, and - in the case of the Sunday Times - a desktop PC, modem and laser printer bundle is far less weighty to lug around.

Of course, the Net can't replace newspapers completely. Lining the cat-litter tray with my old 486 laptop resulted in a comprehensively corrupted hard drive. Although on the up side, I now own the only moggy in the neighbourhood with a 240V-induced Mohican hairstyle. What else? I also like to contribute to the massive surge of irritating adverts currently engulfing the Internet. Having recently developed a Radio 4 panel game (hosted by Caroline 'Men Behaving Badly' Quentin), I posted brief messages in uk.media and uk.radio to try and drum up some audience members. Internet users are obviously completely devoid of proper social lives, since quite a few people expressed an interest in tickets. Some even mailed afterwards to say how much they'd enjoyed the show; not that you should believe everything you're told on the Internet.

And thanks to Auntie Beeb now dragging herself into the Nineteenth Century and upgrading Broadcasting House's computers from the original Slide Rules to the more advanced 'Abacus 95', I can even deliver scripts via e-mail. This is also useful, since a missed deadline can now be explained as a 'flaw in the BBC's Internet Gateway' rather than (as previously) a 'hangover'.

Sometimes I try to justify my geekiness (and recoup the cost of my extortionate phone bill, which is now so large it has to be delivered in a fleet of large articulated lorries with a police escort) by writing about the Internet for various magazines, the likes of Wired UK and .net Directory, or talking about Net related issues on the radio. This gives me a chance

```
to (a) educate the Great British Public about the
wonders of cyberspace and - far more importantly -
(b) get my mitts on a load of free stuff, plus
complimentary Internet accounts from those charming,
lovely and devastatingly attractive people at CIX
and AOL (that's enough brown-nosing - Ed).

I most certainly do not use the Internet for trivial
time-wasting purposes. My interest in the UseNET
group alt.sex.binaries.pictures.david-mellor is
*purely* academic.
```

Debs used her supreme computer knowledge to create her own website at the age of 17, laboriously hand-coded, being long before the days of web page creation software packages. D. A. Barham's Brand Spanking New Homepage, as it was titled, boasted more than 20,000 hits and was, according to her, 'officially one of the Top 5 Per Cent Least Frequently Updated Sites on the WWW'. The small print read: 'This site does not in any way advocate the unseemly practice of spanking. That title was chosen purely to annoy sad pervy types who use the WWW search engines to locate pages with the highest occurrence of the word. Spanking, Spanking, Spanking, Spanking.'

The site featured a picture of Debs looking like an English rose, albeit with slightly chubby cheeks, and carried the following message: 'This web page has been optimized for people who downloaded Netscape about 6 months ago and can't now be bothered with upgrading to the latest version.'

The content gives us a real picture of her personality. The home page carried this 'Blatantly Egotistical Personal Biog', written by her but in the third person and still lying about her age!

```
D. A. Barham was born in 1973. This was probably
her first major mistake, and one which she has not
managed to rectify. She attended a number of schools,
at which she totally failed to shine. In a vote for
the 'Pupil Most Likely Not to Succeed', she came a
disappointing third. D.A. left school with no
ambition whatsoever, and now claims to write for
various British TV and radio programmes. She says she
likes being self-employed, because it pisses off the
Inland Revenue and gives them more forms to fill in.

During the past year, D.A. has written for Rory
Bremner, Clive Anderson, Bob Monkhouse, David Frost,
Spitting Image, The Guardian newspaper, and a lot of
radio programmes which nobody listens to. She has
even worked for Celebrity Squares, which just goes to
show what some people will do for money (although she
hasn't admitted that to her parents yet. They still
think she's earning a living through prostitution and
porno movie bit-parts). Her main claim to fame is
having once been in a lift with Sue Lawley. As a
self-confessed nerd, she has recently extended her
not very considerable talents to writing for Wired
magazine and The.net Directory and mumbling
incoherently about computers and stuff on London
Radio. Well, at least I don't do it in public.
```

```
BBC Radio also seem to believe that she is writing
an 8-part sitcom for transmission in autumn 1999.
This, she finds slightly worrying. The rest of her
life is frankly too dull to mention. So stop reading
this bit and go check out some of my neat links…
```

```
And if you don't want the stuff on here to look
utterly shite, turn on your Image function PRONTO!
```

Visitors were directed to various witty audio links, including 'EXCLUSIVE to this Webpage – a frank and open confession from the frankly open Divine Brown, famed Hollywood prostitute who always gives good headlines.' Another text link was to a list of Hugh Grant jokes, 'an actor who's on everyone's lips in Hollywood. Allegedly.'

Other links included a website called ANORAK, Swedish stand-up comedy ('My name's Sven Elton, goodnight'); NASA research into shagging on space shuttles ('Did the earth move for you, dear?'); and the UK Sitcom Database, to track down the entire works of Bernard Cribbins.

Her listed top five movies were *The Usual Suspects, Trainspotting, Pulp Fiction, Short Cuts,* and *Monty Python's Meaning of Life.*

```
AND 5 films I'd sooner fellate the entire Government
than see.
```

```
· Mission Impossible (packed so full of shit, it
  should be called Motion Impassable)
```

- *Mad Dogs and Englishmen* (Liz Hurley in THAT dress)
- *The Cable Guy* (aka the Straight-to-Video Guy)
- *Tank Girl* (Zzzzzzzzzzzz ... more like Trank Girl)
- Anything with Jean-Claude Van Damme in it (twat).

The five most popular items on her CD rack were *Drugstore, Divine Comedy, The Cardigans*, the soundtrack from *Pulp Fiction*, plus the PC Pro Cover CD Dec 1995 – 'only kidding. It's October 1995 actually.'

There were links to hacking sites, online newspapers, plus this guide to whether or not you are an Anorak:

Do you possess any or all of the following?
- The name Kevin
- More than four Biros in your pocket?
- A cagoule, wind-cheater, zip-up jerkin, Pac-a-Mac or any other proprietary brand of hooded, weatherproof outerwear?
- No friends?
- Halitosis, poor eyesight and questionable personal hygiene?
- A Blake's Seven Video, which you still watch and/or fantasize over?
- A tattoo of your favourite URL?

One of her first cyber friends was Yoz Grahame, one of a breed of super-bright computer 'geeks' who grew out of the dot-com boom. 'I first saw the name D. A. Barham in 1994. She was one of the first customers at Delphi UK, the tiny offshoot of the then huge US online service, and I was doing phone support in my spare time from university. She was funny, smart and wild and had a lot of knowledge, making a big difference to the otherwise dull forums. After that, I started seeing her name in lots of other places; not just online, but in the credits of almost every topical comedy show on TV.' ·

Several years later they were to meet by chance 'offline', as it were, when Yoz was being shown around the offices where Debs was working in Camden. 'She recognized my name and pulled me out in the hallway for a chat. We ended up working on the same game. Although we were never particularly close, we did meet up for coffee over the years.' He was surprised to find almost two different personalities. It was almost as if the Internet allowed her to cast aside her inhibitions and insecurities. 'There were two separate persona – a human and a cyber person. The human was shy and quiet, the e-person was extrovert, feisty, loud and wickedly funny.'

Debs invented numerous e-mail accounts and belonged to a range of newsgroups covering music, the arts, and comedy. She would work and 'chat' online for hours, both as D. A. Barham and, if she wanted to hide her identity, under a plethora of pseudonyms.

She was a great believer in the Internet as a forum for comedy writing and encouraged many community groups. One online contributor says: 'Debs was the first professional comedy writer I know who told me the stuff I wrote was funny. For that alone I owe her more than I'll be ever to repay now.' This memory, posted on a website by Matthew, reveals her nocturnal search for companionship:

I used to chat to Debbie Barham via IRC. She'd moved to London and gotten a regular gig writing for the Rory Bremner show, and would often while away time on IRC at odd hours as she came down from a writing binge. I think we got chatting because there was a discussion of Bond movies, and we both thought On Her Majesty's Secret Service would have been the best Bond movie ever, if it wasn't for George Lazenby.

We'd mostly chat about radio and comedy, and try to make each other laugh, though she was also interested in geekier topics. I particularly remember her telling me how incredibly thrilled she was when they had The Stranglers guest on the Bremner show, and she got to meet them. I always felt bad that I didn't get to meet her in person before I left for the US. Another time we got the whole channel swapping ideas for ridiculous phobias after she'd just finished an article on the subject.

She could be sharp, yes. To be funny, you often have to be. But at the same time, she was a good person, and always friendly to me. She seemed to need to write the way other people need to breathe; she wrote for everyone on every subject, yet never wanted to be in the spotlight, in spite of how much she deserved it.

Among her first paid online work was writing for the 'e' version of the computer magazine *Wired*, specializing in news and features about technology and innovation. Her reviews of new gadgets made interesting reading:

HEY BIG SENDER

The most eye-catching thing about the Video Sender is not its stunning use of the latest Japanese flat-screen technology, nor its sculpted, ergonomic design, or even its magnificent CD-quality surround sound. The Video Sender has none of these. It does, though, have a small sticker on the base saying, 'Illegal For Use In The UK'. For the purposes of the following review, therefore, product testing was undertaken on Sark.

Feel like an early night? What could be more decadent than snuggling up in bed with your loved one and a video of *Casablanca*? If the VCR happens to be downstairs in the living room, this may present a problem. 'You lie there and relax, darling. I'm just dashing out for 50 metres of coaxial cable and some drill bits' – it does rather kill the moment.

With the Video Sender – no problemo. It cordlessly relays a signal from any audio-visual appliance to any TV within a given radius. The possibilities are endless. Got kids? Worried that the poppets are surfing the Net or playing Quake when they purport to be doing homework? Just hook up their PC to the Video Sender and monitor their exploits on the family 24-inch. Dinner-table conversation will never be the same. 'Oh look, dear! Young Tommy's viewing the goat-fucking.gif again.'

Given thin enough walls, neighbours too can enjoy the benefits of your cable subscription. So next time that git next door refuses to loan you his lawn-mower, you can emulate Jim Carrey and thrust your face up against his window, screaming, 'I gave YOU free cable TV!'

Alternatively, should he have cable already, you could sneak into his property, connect the Video Sender to his telly and enjoy Premier League matches on your own small screen. Dammit, what's one conviction for breaking and entering when you're already using illegal equipment?

Despite minor niggles (the signal could be a tad stronger), the versatility of this device far outweighs any criticisms. Buy one today. Just don't tell the bizzies I said so.

D. A. Barham

Her online work expanded into all areas. She was a master of debunking highly technical and dry subjects with her unique brand of popular, witty writing. Here she uses a predictive formula to review the explosion of Personal Digital Assistants (PDAs).

A PSION OF THINGS TO COME

Ten years ago, if you'd suggested that a computer no bigger than a Kellogg's Individual Variety Coco Pops packet could be surfing the net with – look, ma! No wires, you would have been laughed out of town. 'Mad, completely mad ...' the nurses would sigh ruefully, confiscating your green-screened Psion Organiser II and replacing it with a nice wax crayon, of similar hue.

But PDAs have come a long way in the past decade. And now it's crunch time for the clamshell. With more platforms than a Spice Girl's wardrobe, we've reached a crossroads – sooner or later, the jostling crowd of rival operating systems (EPOC, Palm OS, Pocket PC, etc.) will have to evolve towards a more universal standard. To make things even more confusing, Ol' Bluetooth is back, poised to bite through all those clumsy cables and render the mobile office truly mobile. The PDA is mutating with a speed that puts even the most rampant of genetically modified salmon to shame. So where will it be, in another ten years' time? Scrolling forward to 2010, we checked out those crucial Agenda entries along the way.

June 2000

Desperate to consign Windows CE (aptly known as 'WINCE') to history's great Recycle Bin, Bill Gates launches a new cutdown operating system. Sadly for Bill, his 'Small Windows Edition' becomes universally dubbed 'SWINE'.

September 2000

Trying to name their latest models, palmtop manufacturers realize they're running out of four letter words ending in 'o' (Revo, Velo, Nino, Aero, etc.). Nokia launch the unimpressive 'So-So' and the 'Dodo', which is immediately rendered obsolete.

April 2001

At the Ideal Home Show, Philips unveil a palmtop with an inbuilt fridge-freezer. Computer magazines describe its dimensions as 'a little on the bulky side'. Millions of gadget freaks rush to buy it, however, on the basis that having a little light come on when you open the case is 'really cool' and you can stick magnets on the front to keep your Tesco Online shopping list handy.

August 2003

Wearable technology becomes the latest must-have. Communication devices are implanted in shoes, leading to coachloads of irritating yuppies declaring, 'Yah, hi! I'm on the trainers'. Donna Karan unveils her Don-an-anorak range on the catwalks of Milan, including combat trousers with a pocket organizer to help you work out how many pockets you've got in your combat trousers. Posh Spice refuses to model a new stylus on the grounds that it makes her look fat.

December 2003

The first ultra-mobile office hits the streets, comprising a palmtop PC, folding keyboard, roll-up 14-inch screen, micro-mini printer, wireless phone and 20GB of flash memory. The entire set-up weighs less than a bag of sugar.

The battery, however, is the size and weight of a small family car.

January 2004

HP's retro-style 'Yoko' is criticized for being ugly and tuneless and causing a rift between other members of the PDA family. Psion abandon plans to develop the 'Ringo' when they can't get the clock to stay in time.

March 2006

Genetic engineers create a human being with extra large hands and 15 fingers, Palmtop developers heave a sigh of relief, and add yet more unnecessary features.

September 2006

Psion unveil the 'Pseudo', a sleek, chromium-plated empty case for swanky young executives to show off in meetings, without having the hassle of typing all their contact details into it only to find they can't make it work.

October 2007

In recognition of the new religion of PDA usage, a new National Holiday is declared 'Palm Sunday'.

July 2008

In recognition of the reliability of such machines, Palm Sunday is immediately followed by another holiday: Crash Wednesday.

February 2009

A major breakthrough for text recognition software:
the first system actually capable of decoding doctors'
handwriting.

October 2010

Industry bigwigs agree to drop the term 'Pocket
Computer' in favour of the more accurate 'Backpack or
Large Suitcase PC'. Rival manufacturers stop competing
to make the smallest and begin boasting about whose is
the biggest. Women sigh: 'So what's new?'

January 247548

The first PDA with integrated cappuccino machine,
bagless vacuum cleaner, nasal hair trimmer, cruise missile
launcher, rotary clothes-airer, sunbed, sauna-and-solarium
is launched. In their enthusiasm, engineers fail to notice
that a bug has sent the date function completely haywire.
The tiny minority of purchasers who actually notice this
return their defective models, but are politely informed
that the 12-month guarantee expired 24,500 years ago.

*Debbie Barham is a TV scriptwriter, columnist and
writer for magazines ranging from *Computeractive* to
Cosmopolitan. She owns more handheld PCs than she
has hands and is currently working on a major piece
of humorous fiction: her tax return.

Twenty-six

22 September 1999

There has been a gradual decline in Debs' well being. We noticed a change on returning from the Canary Islands. Her cheekbones had got even more pronounced. God knows, she was pathetically thin when she arrived. And we have failed to get her to improve her eating habits.

I go back to my research.

The symptoms are very familiar. I discover that during a period of weight loss the body tries to conserve energy as best it can and so inessential functions become gradually lost. The menstrual cycle stops as the weight falls below about seven stones four pounds, and may stop earlier if the eating pattern is very abnormal. The circulation diminishes with coldness of the hands and feet, which often become reddened. The heart rate slows and the blood pressure falls. Danger from a failing heart becomes a risk at very low weights, below around five stone, if the weight loss is extremely rapid, or if the chemistry is distorted by an extreme of vomiting, purging, or diuretic (water tablet) abuse. It is hard to assess a dangerously low weight, but sudden death will more frequently occur once the weight has fallen by 40 per cent of normal.

For Debs, this is somewhere near five stone, the weight she is now.

I read on. The successful regaining of a normal weight is an essential component in the process of recovery but not the only element of it. The course of the illness is closely linked with development and maturation. Recovery is often associated with the continuation of maturation after a period of emotional regression and therefore involves several stages.

Regaining normal weight with a normal eating pattern is the first priority and may require admission to hospital for its achievement. The return to normal eating unmasks the underlying psychological issues so that these may be explored. These issues will need to be managed according to what problems arise in practice, a task that varies from one patient to another. Only by eating can Debs begin to lead a normal life again, a task that may be slow and tentative as a result of the profound loss of confidence that is so characteristic of the illness. But she is still determinedly stubborn about eating properly, and about seeking any specialist medical help.

Sue and I know that time is running out. But there is little we can do to turn things round. My daughter is slowly wasting away before my eyes, and I am absolutely powerless.

Sue and I constantly go over the best way to encourage her to eat. Sue wants us to seek professional help. But although Debs refuses to reveal any of the detail, I know she's already tried that and it failed. I also fear that if she feels pressured by us in any way, she will simply flee. I try to jolly her along with pathetic notes of my own.

Dearest Debs

I have gone to the rubbish dump (where I belong!) and to see Granny. Sue and Sophie are down at school fete. Didn't like to wake you, although it would probably have done more good if I had (so that you sleep later). Call if you need me. I'll be back about 4pm. Have something to <u>eat</u> when you get up – especially if you go out, or I'll smack your bottom (what there is left of it!) See you later,

Peter

xx

She replies:

Daddy Dearest

Have departed replete with yoghurt drink. Should be back about 7pm? I think I took too many sleeping pills last night ... or took them too late in the day. Ah, well. I doubt if you could have woken me (unless your friend from the Mermaid could have loaned you his 3ft pneumatic drill) – the only thing which did was my plumbing at 7am this morning, but I hope I didn't leave any messy evidence in your bathroom.

Debs

Well rested but feeling a bit wobbly. Did you say you had a spare clock-radio-alarm? If so I may take advantage of it for tomorrow ...

Twenty-seven

In the spring of 1995, Debs got on the property ladder, purchasing her own flat a few miles up the road from her rented bedsit in Chiswick. She was naturally proud of her new home, the purchase of which went through reasonably smoothly. She already had her independence and some degree of financial security. But this was hers, an investment not just in cash, but an emotional commitment too.

Soon after moving in, she met her first online boyfriend, via a comedy site. Scott Colvey was 25 and a self-confessed computer 'geek' and budding comedy writer based in Norwich. They had spent many hours e-mailing each other. He expressed an interest in writing for *Week Ending* and she was able to offer advice and support. After several months of correspondence they agreed to meet up and he came down from Norfolk to stay at her new flat. Again, she lied about her age, telling him she was 21, rather than 18.

Scott describes the romance as one of his less conventional relationships, with lots of drinking, and not a lot of eating. In four months they seldom went out for a meal and made love just twice. 'She was never a great love of my life but was a great friend. I would travel down at weekends and we would have a great time but she was always focused very much on her work.'

By the summer it was over. The relationship had reached the crucial cut-off point for Debs with her men – three to four months. But Scott was among the first to see the worrying signs of weight loss. 'The Debbie I knew was a rather thin person. I do recall her fridge always being empty, except for black coffee and orange juice. I asked her once why she never had food in and she replied: "Sainsbury's is just down the road and I can get all the ready meals I want from there."'

They parted on friendly terms. What he could not have known is that, from a health point of view, it was to be downhill for Debs from here. She was gradually sinking into her all-night work routine with progressively less sleep and food. The first stages of her illness had set in. She had lost the full face and figure of her early teens. In the months ahead she was to become more and more reclusive and her weight was to plummet.

NEVER SAY DIET

A friend once told me an exceedingly politically incorrect joke about the unsuccessful entrepreneur who opened a Weight Watchers clinic in Ethiopia. Sick, isn't it? Or is it? Is it not simply illustrative of our current obsession with attaining the perfect figure? The diet and fitness industry is a multi-billion-pound market – are that many of us really unhappy with the way we look?

The answer, probably, is yes. Just look at the number of slimming magazines currently available. I propose that such publications be banished to the top shelf along with *Penthouse*, *Big Jugs* monthly and the like. Not only are they just as unsavoury, but stretching up to reach them, we would burn off at least a calorie.

I myself cannot claim complete abstinence from all exercise-related activities. A year ago, I was shocked to discover an abnormally large lump growing out of my chest. This was soon identified as my stomach. Having no regular sporting pastimes (apart from watching *Match of the Day* when I get in from the pub), I literally took the plunge and began an energetic, but sadly short-lived rowing career.

There are two types of rowing; the first involves arguing with another person. The second rhymes with snowing and involves arguing violently with another person while you balance precariously in a small boat in the middle of the Thames. In four weeks, I expended a laudable amount of energy shouting abuse at my fellow oarswoman. I even purchased a rowing machine for use at home.

If there is one section of the human species I would dearly love to see become extinct, it's skinny dieters. We all know at least one of these miserable specimens. She is nearly always a woman – men are too preoccupied crediting themselves with EXTRA inches – is 5ft 8in, a size ten, weighs nine stone and still refuses to lick a stamp because the adhesive contains 4.6 calories.

She looks permanently depressed, except when she is

doggedly smiling 50 times over in succession to lose weight from her cheeks. It's infuriating to watch and I would like to advocate that all public places display 'No slimming' signs (symbolized by a Ryvita with a red line through it) to protect us from passive dieting.

And to the girl who told me that she was having fat cells transplanted from her posterior to her lips 'to make me much more attractive', I have just one thing to say.

You're talking out of your arse, love.

[*Guardian*, 3 May 1995]

This article was written shortly after Debs ended her relationship with Scott Colvey. She had been asked by the *Guardian* to review a new book on dieting and used the occasion to attack the whole culture of slimming and exercise fads. Truth was, she was slowly becoming involved in a serious dietary battle of her own. Not a diet as such, more the eating disorder anorexia nervosa.

Seemingly, Debs had it all. Her career had taken off in a style few dreamed possible. She was writing for virtually every medium available – press, radio, television, magazines, and the Internet. Her reputation had soared and she was in big demand. She had an agent, her own flat, was extremely well off for a teenager, looked fantastic in her favoured designer clothes, and was courted many times in the male-dominated world in which she mixed.

On the face of it life was beautiful – except that whatever

demons were lurking in her psyche were starting to surface. Nobody really knows the reasons. In the year or so that precedes the start of anorexia, there is often an increase in the problems or pressures that create anxiety or unhappiness. The most usual trigger is weight loss, mostly from a normal weight-reducing diet to lose 'puppy' fat. She told different stories to various people over the years. She complained to some colleagues that she was really hurt when walking to the ladies' lavatory in a pub she heard some lads comment: 'Look at the arse on that.'

There is speculation too that a comedian had made a joke of her weight that had embarrassed her. Later she told a friend that a boyfriend had complained she was getting fat. She told me during her retreat to my house that it all started after getting food poisoning in Edinburgh, which put her off eating for life. She told a similar story to psychiatrists and others. But how much of any of these stories was totally or partly true, or provoked her condition, we will probably never know for certain.

At the outset, anorexia sufferers are single-minded in their determination to lose weight, and their weight loss is slowly progressive. It may be several months before it seems a cause for worry, usually because by then the weight loss is extreme. Then, as the illness takes hold, victims typically begin to lose contact with friends and may appear to lose interest in everything apart from food and work.

They tend to display increased obsessional behaviour, undergo a personality change, and become more serious and introverted. Serious? Less fun? Not good news for a comedy writer. But we are dealing with two people here. Debs the person was slowly withdrawing; but Debs the writer, fuelled by anger, was as sharp as ever.

The onset of the illness was gradual, with no cause for alarm until the late summer of 1996, when she was 19. I saw her at my father's funeral in June of that year. I thought she looked radiant, slim, rather than thin, and certainly not anorexic. What I did not know of course was the battle she was undergoing.

After that, her lifestyle changed. Calls and visits to family dried up. She worked through the night and caught up on sleep during the day. She retreated into a shell, going for weeks without physical contact, so few people noticed that she had stopped eating. And the thinner she got, the more reclusive she became. Nothing mattered except work.

Debs' agent, Rachel Swann, decided it was about time she touched base with her client. Career-wise, Debs was flying and both parties were more than happy with their business arrangement, but it had been a while since Rachel had actually seen her.

Rachel heard that Debs was going to make an appearance at a recording of one of the BBC shows to which she was contributing, so she went along especially to see her. Rachel was in for the shock of her life. 'After the show I went backstage looking for her. When I eventually met her I must say, I did a double-take. I did not recognize her at all.'

The chubby-faced girl Rachel had taken on two years previously had been transformed into a skinny, pathetically thin person. It was almost as if she had been given a new body. The flowing garments had been replaced by a miniskirt, thick tights, and knee-length boots. The shock transformation made it impossible for Rachel to hide her surprise. 'I seemed to say over and over, Oh my God, how you've changed.'

Over the following weeks, the episode preyed on Rachel. She replayed the incident over in her mind and reasoned that she might have overreacted to Debs' appearance. She figured that girls do change the way they look to suit the fashion of the day; and although she had lost weight, it did not enter Rachel's mind that Debs was anorexic.

However, the doubts surfaced when Rachel began to get calls from producers who were concerned about Debs' weight and the decline in her general health. The first employer to contact Rachel was Elaine Morris, one of the founders of the production company Vera, which produced Rory Bremner's show for Channel 4. There had been a ten-month gap between series, and when Debs turned up at the Fountain Studios in Wembley for the first recording of the new series, the production team were shocked.

'We all did a double take,' says Elaine. 'She had lost so much weight. We all commented on it. She told a girl on our team that a bloke in a pub had made a comment about the size of her backside and she had gone on a diet. I was cross because I never thought she was that big. She was gorgeous just as she was. At first we did not take in that she was ill, just that she had gone through a drastic and focused change. In fact, many complimented her on her new appearance.'

However, as the series went on, she became painfully thin. 'We said, hang on, this isn't a weight-controlled diet but something else. I remember saying to my colleagues that we ought to do something. I had never dealt with anorexia before and did not really know what to do. I felt I needed to discuss her condition with someone, so I rang her agent Rachel.' Rachel says: 'I told Debbie that she must start to prioritize more, to focus on a few main clients, and not just say yes to everything that came along. That way she could maybe get her lifestyle back on an even keel.'

Debs' close colleague from the Rory Bremner show, John Langdon, remembers seeing her walking through the West End one day. She was dressed in her customary black out-fit and looked gaunt. Their humour was black too. He called out: 'Oi, Karen Carpenter, where you off to?' She stopped, giggled, and they chatted about work, but there was no discussion about her illness.

Just before her twentieth birthday, Debs heard about the chance of a full-time job working for her childhood hero Douglas Adams, author of *The Hitchhiker's Guide to the Galaxy*. His London-based company, The Digital Village, wanted a writer to provide dialogue for a computer game called *Starship Titanic*. This was an extremely techni-cally advanced game that had a text engine whereby the characters could talk back at you. The company's chief executive, Robbie Stamp, recalls: 'We needed somebody highly intelligent to come in and write to Douglas's demanding standards.'

The prospect of working with Adams was a dream come true for Debs. As a child, she had spent many hours listening to a tape of the cult radio series. She loved the off-the-wall script, zany special effects and assortment of characters such as Ford Prefect, the roving reporter; Marvin, the very depressed paranoid android, and Hotblack Desiato, the intergalactic rock megastar who died for tax purposes. Perhaps it was how the comedy science fiction series was conceived that appealed to Debs: the idea that became *The Hitchhiker's Guide* came about while Douglas Adams was lying drunk in a field in Innsbruck (Adams himself died in 2001). But first, she had to get through the job interview. Debs was nervous and excited as she got the tube from Chiswick to Camden.

'There was this tall, very very thin, almost skeletal person wearing a floppy leopard-skin pill-box hat which looked so big on her because her face was so thin,' recalls chief executive Robbie Stamp. He liked her and her work well enough, but he told Rachel that he was inclined not to offer Debs the job because he considered her to be anorexic. Rachel agreed to raise the matter with her client.

A basic feature of any addictive or compulsive behaviour is the psychopathology of denial. The sufferer does not believe that she has the problem in the first place and therefore sees no reason why it should be treated. Patients with eating disorders do not see themselves as others see them and a feature that totally obsesses them is heard with total incredulity by other people. Debs was being told that she had something she did not believe she had. Other people's viewpoints therefore were totally distrusted.

Rachel says: 'I got Debbie in. She was looking far worse than before. I remember she was so pale and I noticed her little thin wrists. I told her what The Digital Village people had said. She was absolutely bristling with indignation. "Of course I am not anorexic. It is none of their business, anyhow."'

Despite misgivings over her condition, however, Robbie Stamp eventually agreed to take her on. 'I thought about it long and hard. In the end, I considered it inappropriate not to employ her simply because she did not look well.'

Working at The Digital Village was Debs' first 9–5 job and she immediately made an impression. Douglas Adams told colleagues that Debs was one of the few writers he trusted to mimic his own eccentric style. Robbie Stamp says: 'Her work was very good, brilliant in fact. She was a very bright person, spiky, funny and able to tap into the Douglas Adams' mindset.' Indeed, one review of 'Starship Titanic' read: 'A redeeming feature of the game is the jokes. They are quite different from what is usually seen but not at all unlike what you'd expect from Douglas Adams. Insulting and satiric, but very funny.'

But between the laughs, Debs was declining rapidly towards danger levels of weight.

The company had a caring culture and a vibrant social scene – evenings out, chocolate cake on birthdays; but when Debs did attend dinners, her colleagues watched in embarrassment as she just pushed her food around her plate.

At Christmas, Debs showed her face at the BBC Radio Light Entertainment party at the Radio Theatre. This was a popular bash among the cast of hundreds who contributed to the Corporation's comedy output. One of her former colleagues from *The News Huddlines*, Clive Coleman, remembers seeing Debs propped up against a wall, looking very much the worse for wear. 'It was quite a shock for me because I had not seen her for five years. She looked absolutely ghastly. I hardly recognized her. Her hair had obviously fallen out because she was wearing this blonde wig with an Alice band and her skin was grey and papery. I got the feeling that people who had seen this gradual decline were a bit blasé about her condition, but to me it was like seeing some concentration camp victim.'

Back from maternity leave in January of 1997, Rachel Swann was faced with a growing crisis over her client's health. There were more and more calls from concerned people in the media industry. She had no experience in dealing with anorexia and so needed to find out about the condition. A friend gave her a book by an American priest called Vernon Johnson, a former alcoholic, who had pioneered a form of compassionate treatment for all addicts. The central thesis was that anorexia is an addiction. You support it by tolerating it.

The book was designed for the relatives and friends of the 'chemically dependent', but it contains advice for confronting any addiction. Called *Intervention*, the front cover reads: 'How To Help Someone Who Doesn't Want Help'. Desperate for any strategy she could get, Rachel read the introduction with interest:

> You want to help. At the moment, though, you are not sure how to go about it. Furthermore, the person does not seem willing to accept help from you or anyone else. In fact, she may loudly deny that a problem exists ...
>
> If you are like most people, you may believe that there is nothing you can do except wait for the person to 'hit bottom' and then try to pick up the pieces. The opposite is true. Waiting is too dangerous. It is also cruel. It allows an already bad situation to get worse. If a friend wanted to jump off a bridge, would you let her do it before you reached out a hand to stop her? Of course not; and neither must you stand by and watch the chemically dependent person plumb the depths of suffering and despair before doing something about it ...

If Rachel had any doubts about intervening, these had now evaporated. The book explained that, like diabetes or the mumps, addiction is a disease; that the victim is not abusing herself deliberately but because she is sick. And that she is probably the *last* person to come to that awareness.

The main tactic is that 'meaningful' persons in the life

of the sick person gang up and directly confront her, explaining that her behaviour is unacceptable and is hurting the people who love her. All of the team write down specific data about the events and behaviour, arrange a surprise confrontation, and explain the evidence in a non-judgemental way. The sufferer is offered specific choices – this treatment centre, or that hospital, etc. The book even offered a suggested script: 'We've been getting together over the past few weeks because we all care about you and are deeply concerned about what's been happening to you. If you will hear us out, I'm sure you will understand why we feel as we do. We are here to talk about the fact that you are not eating and all we ask is that you will hear us out …'

Rachel duly set about assembling her intervention team, gathering evidence, lining up specialist support, even rehearsing the moment itself in her mind. Her first problem was gathering the team. The book specifically advised against someone confronting a dependent person single-handedly – 'The person's defence systems are far too highly developed to be breached by one person acting alone.' But there was nobody in Debs' life that Rachel could call on. Being freelance meant that those who knew her best were scattered over the whole industry. She had no real close friends, and her family were not in London: they could hardly cite appropriate evidence if they were not part of her life anymore. Asking Debs for their contact details would also arouse suspicion. Besides, there might have been issues with her family that were at the root of her problem. Rachel had no choice but to go it alone.

Next, she had to gather the data with which to confront Debs. This part was easy. There was a long list of producers who had contacted her expressing concern. And then, suddenly, there was a call from a very worried Robbie Stamp, Debs' employer at The Digital Village. He said she had become so weak, she was unable to open the front door to get into work. The female staff in particular were extremely distressed at her condition. As chief executive he felt he had an obligation to act.

Robbie recalls: 'I decided that the kindest and most supportive thing I could do for Debbie was to call her agent and terminate her contract. We knew deep down that if she did not face up to her illness she was going to die. Work was the only tool we had to make her stop starving herself to death.'

The following letter duly arrived by fax at Rachel's West End offices;

March 18th 1997

Dear Rachel,

I am writing to you on a matter of great concern to myself and other colleagues at The Digital Village, with respect to your client Debbie Barham.

I want to stress from the outset that we have been entirely happy with the work she has done on *Starship Titanic*. Douglas Adams, in particular is, I know, very grateful for the contribution she has made. She has more than delivered on what she was contracted to do.

However, her colleagues are now so seriously concerned about her health, that I cannot continue to allow her to come to work both for her own sake and for the sake of those around her. For the present situation to continue, would in effect be to ask the team to collude in her own denial, which I can no longer allow them to do. As of today, I believe that Debbie requires immediate support and help to enable her to confront her anorexia.

We will of course pay her for the full period of her contract and will return any personal items which she may have left in the office to you by courier on Wednesday.

It is with great reluctance that I am taking this step. Debbie is precisely the kind of person whose considerable abilities The Digital Village wants to work with. She must now confront an issue, which if not addressed will at some stage in the near future prevent her from employing those abilities at all.

Yours Sincerely

Robbie Stamp

Chief Executive

Debs had in effect been sacked to try to save her life.

Rachel decided it was time for her intervention and Robbie's letter was a perfect trigger. The final part of the strategy was to line up specialist medical support. She visited the Promis Counselling Centre in South Kensington and made an appointment for Debs to see a private specialist. They told her that anorexia was the hardest addiction to break and that Debs would almost certainly need in-patient treatment. 'Bring her along and we will do the rest,' they told Rachel.

With all parts of the plan in place, Rachel phoned Debs and concocted a story about an urgent issue that had cropped up, too important to discuss over the phone. She needed to see her urgently. Could she come to Wardour Street the following day? Debs agreed.

The trap was laid, but the prey did not show. As Rachel sat twiddling her thumbs, wondering where Debs was, she got a frantic phone call. It was from the Italian Graffiti Café down the road. Apparently Debs had tripped on a paving stone and had cut her face. They were waiting for an ambulance to take her to hospital.

Did Debs have some sort of sixth sense? Or was it a genuine accident? She was certainly very weak and could easily have tripped. In view of her fragile state, it was fortunate she'd suffered no more than a cut. By now, her bones were extremely brittle. Rachel is convinced her client had instinctively known that something was up and may have somehow contrived the fall.

She rushed to the café and, rather than wait for an ambulance, took Debs to hospital by taxi instead. The confrontation Rachel had stage-managed to take place in a quiet office took place instead in a London cab in a spring traffic jam.

'I told her the whole thing, how I had set up the meeting, how everyone was concerned about her and that I was marching her down to a clinic as soon as her cut was treated to seek "professional help."'

Debs sat silently, mopping blood from her face.

'I said: "You're anorexic, aren't you?" She just replied: "Yes."'

This was Debs' first ever admission of her illness. It was an important step. But there were many obstacles ahead if she was to be saved.

Twenty-eight

Debs and Rachel sat and waited in the Casualty Department of University College Hospital in Euston.

'She told me about her family. She said she was brought up by her mother and her partner and had not really seen her real father,' says Rachel. But Debs refused to give any explanation for her illness – 'I'm not going to tell you about it,' she said rather indignantly.

There were several moments of awkward silences as they waited for treatment, watching the busy daily drama of one of London's major Accident and Emergency departments. Rachel secretly hoped Debs would be sectioned then and there. Examining Debs' cut forehead, a nurse said: 'She's very thin, isn't she! Almost like treating a skeleton.'

After Debs was patched up, they took a taxi from Euston across town to South Kensington for the pre-arranged appointment at the Promis Centre. The centre was set up by Dr Robert Lefever, who himself suffers from an eating disorder, once losing two stone in three weeks. He believes that anorexia nervosa is probably a genetically inherited defect in the neurotransmission (brain chemistry) systems in the mood centres of the brain and is similar to other compulsive disorders such as alcoholism and drug addiction. Thus, addicts are responsible for their behaviour as it affects other people, but not responsible for having an addictive nature.

Arriving at the clinic in Pelham Street, Debs and Rachel went nervously inside. When Debs' name was called, Rachel was horrified that the doctor insisted she come in for the consultation too.

Debs stripped down and stood pathetically on the scales. She weighed just under five and a half stone, bordering on extreme danger. One of the staff said this was the worst case they'd seen. But if Debs was expecting tea and sympathy, or a shoulder to cry on, she was in for a shock. They sat for twenty minutes while Dr Lefever read the riot act.

'He absolutely laid into her. He said scratch the surface of an anorexic and you will find a ball of fury underneath. He said to her, "What the hell do you think you are playing at? Your agent will stop representing you unless you pull yourself together. You must be doing this for a purpose. I am anorexic too, you know, so I know what I'm talking about."'

Both Rachel and Debs sat in stunned silence. Neither had expected such a tough consultation.

The doctor made the following case notes:

PROBLEM: ANOREXIA

You are so thin that it would be dangerous to do anything other than take you into inpatient treatment so that this can be your total focus of attention. That way you can get the problem sorted out so that you can have a happy time in the long term. The alternative would be to go on having trouble indefinitely while you try to control it yourself.

Her height was noted as 5ft 6in., weight 5 st. 7 lb.

The doctor wanted Debs to volunteer for in-patient counselling. His treatment regime is based on an idea by an American professor that patients should be centrally involved in their own care and that treatment should involve active participation, rather than be something they receive passively. He explained to her that she would sit alongside other people with compulsive behavioural problems, such as drug addicts, gamblers and alcoholics. The premise is that you will not change an anorexic by telling her she is too thin and should eat something. But by putting a sufferer in a group where they openly discuss their addictions, she might gradually realize that many of their experiences, thought processes, and emotional patterns are similar to her own and that she has problems too.

But Debs refused point blank.

'I would rather die,' she told Rachel and the doctor.

The £25 assessment was over. With Debs declining in-patient treatment, there was little Rachel or anyone could do. They went to the Underground and made their separate ways home, Rachel to care for her family, Debs back to her punishing nocturnal work schedule.

A few days later, Rachel received the following e-mail from Debs:

```
Boy - what a day Wednesday turned out to be. I've
not been prematurely sacked, threatened with
imminent death (or worse, the forcible withdrawal of
everything that keeps me remotely sane), poured out
```

my life story to someone and left blood on the
streets of Soho all in one day since ...ooh, must've
been at least last week. Sorry I had to drag you
along for the ride. Agents have more than enough to
cope with as it is.

I hope I didn't worry you too much by not returning
your calls yesterday, by the way. I'd switched off
the bedroom phone when I got back on Wednesday night
- having written some gags for Clive's banker speech
I just went straight to bed and slept - ah the
bliss, etc, insert suitably poetic Shakespeare/
Wordsworth/Byron quote about the joys of sleep here
- pretty much right the way through the day until
you rang at 9 pm.

I suppose that's what they mean on the medical
card by 'May Cause Some Drowsiness'. Found myself
adequately entertained, though, by a succession of
exceedingly vivid, bizarre (and probably highly
significant if I believed that sort of thing, which
happily I don't) dreams. Better than anything
Carlton could come up with, anyway.

Oh, and I've developed an absolute prize of a
black eye now - could rival both Princess Diana and
Chi-Chi the Panda. Guess I could also give both a
run for their money when it comes to eating habits,
but that's beside the point. I think I'm going to
find a photo booth though, and capture this one for
posterity (also I suppose, as useful piccie to refer

to as I put on weight). Which I am, definitely, going
to do. My way. As outlined below – we come to that
part in a minute.

The Digital Village job was interesting though. I was
pushing myself work-wise, though the office
environment/9-5 type of thing had started to seem
quite attractive by the end of the first fortnight or
so. They're a very 'happy' company, I think, which
helped immensely – and obviously very concerned about
staff health. I even went for a complimentary company
massage one week – you certainly don't get that at
the BBC, unless broken springs poking out through
chair-backs qualify on any count. It's also very
beneficial, some of the time (though obviously not all
in the case of a writer, as I think they realized),
to work with other people around you. And hey, I
discovered daylight. Whoopeee.

But – I guess the thing I hadn't realized was the
amount of physical effort it was going to take out
of me. I have been getting much weaker recently than
I've allowed myself to admit. Suppose it really hit
home when I started having trouble opening the outer
door to my flat, although it is one mother****er of a
door and tough enough to open at 11-and-a-half
stone, never mind five stone 1. (That's what I was
yesterday morning – I've promised myself it'll never
go down any lower. Now that I've got a reference
point to work from, I can start seeing the
achievement.) Or when I ran for a bus and suddenly

discovered I couldn't. I can still function normally
on the whole, but stairs aren't a whole bundle of
fun now, and there really were an awful LOT of
stairs at Camden Road station.

I'm kind of sorry about the whole Digital Village
episode, particularly since it now makes it look
like I got the job under false pretences - claiming
health wouldn't affect me. Getting you to claim it
wouldn't affect me. I did try to make sure it didn't
affect the work, but perhaps that just meant I was
pushing myself even harder and ...(for the record, I
did enjoy it. Didn't realize I was seeming so
obviously incapacitated there, though.) And sorry if
it got you in any awkward situations having to
explain stuff to them.

I think I can beat this ... whatever it is, without
going to the PROMIS centre. For one thing, it's
totally against my principles to spend Local
Authority money sending some stupid, obsessive, and
entirely self-fucked-up individual on a six-week
holiday to Kent (and dammit, I must have written so
many sketches in the past denouncing exactly that
sort of 'funding').

Secondly, it would drive me crazy and the upshot of
that is more likely to be my discharging myself than
my getting anything under control, which'd be a dead
loss of time and money all round.

So what I'd prefer to do is take, for a start at least, a two-week 'holiday' whereby I can avoid as many actual meetings as possible and just work completely from home. That way I can concentrate on building up my strength again, getting into a proper sleeping/waking routine, sorting out all the stuff I've been putting off for the last six months or so (cleaning flat, doing accounts, putting flesh back on face and hip bones and growing breasts again etc). Not to mention rediscovering the charms of the local area, and indeed my tastebuds.

I reckon I'm actually a repressed foodie at heart, judging by the number of crap cookery shows I watch. Oh - and radio-wise, I really do need to at least sketch out some ideas - and find a producer - for the next series of Elephant Man. Thankfully they only want six, and not eight as before.

So basically, I don't want to take on too many commitments over that period, but I've got to keep working. Any jobs that require mainly faxable input are ideal - if you could tell people I was 'on holiday' but working whilst I was there, that'd be perfect - just so the phone wasn't going all the time and my life turning into a constant torment of answerphone messages on a million different answerphones (which it has rather been recently).
Cheerio
Debbie

Oh - by the way. Found the funniest thing on the back
of the PROMIS Centre brochure. More superstitious
individuals would call it an Omen. Fortunately, as
stated earlier, I am definitely NOT a superstitious
individual.

The map showed the name of a village near the country
clinic where they wanted to send Debs. It was called
Barham.

Twenty-nine

Having finally come clean to Rachel about her illness, Debs was suddenly receptive to more suggestions. Rachel arranged for them to go to see Debs' General Practitioner, Dr Fleur Navey, at the Bedford Park Surgery in Chiswick. The doctor congratulated Rachel on persuading Debs to come and immediately referred her to the eating disorder clinic at London's Gordon Hospital.

The clinic occupies a rather depressing building, tucked away in one corner of Vincent Square, close to Vauxhall Bridge. The double front doors are locked, reminding visitors that the patients are, in fact, detainees. You cannot leave without the doors being unlocked with a key. I was to pass through those doors eight years later as part of the research for this book. I was shocked to see rather ghostly, vacant, skeletal figures drifting down the corridors. I had forgotten how scarily thin Debs had been – but these sufferers were nowhere near as bad.

So, in the spring of 1997, Debs began a series of regular weekly out-patient appointments at the Peter Dalley Clinic under the charge of Dr Barbara Rooney, consultant psychiatrist. She was co-operative and a fairly regular visitor for most of that year. Her case notes offer an illuminating view of the world as Debs saw it, including the various family and childhood experiences that had obviously scarred her for life.

She was described as:

Emaciated ++ (skeletal)

Pale ++

Alert and vivacious

Weight 33.6 Kg; Height 5ft 6ins, Body Mass Index 11.9.

Psychiatrists considered that 'in her thought content she found she was thinking about food a great deal. In her perception she showed a distorted body image, her cognitive function was intact and insight was present'. They did, however, put her on a course of the anti-depressant drug Prozac.

Debs confessed that she started dieting after contracting gastroenteritis. She said she received several positive comments about the weight she lost from the stomach upset and hoped to get down to about eight stone. People had told her she looked more attractive, but the weight loss had got out of control and she continued to lose weight obsessively, even for a while using laxatives.

She said at one stage that she had weighed 11 stone, but was now just under 6 stone. She was recorded as 'extremely thin', although did not feel she was thin. However, this is contradicted by another entry which reads 'considers she looks ghastly and wishes to gain weight'.

The notes reveal she had been losing weight for eighteen

months, existing on a vegetarian and coffee diet of a packet of broccoli, a packet of spinach, a pot of cottage cheese, and 'lots of espresso'. She reported weakness and discomfort sitting and walking on prominent bones and of chest pains, palpitations, and dizziness getting out of the bath. She had not had a period for eight months.

She admitted she was socially isolated, was competitive and a perfectionist, had no close friends or contact with family, and that 'work is my reason for living'. Interestingly, from a work point of view, she told doctors that she was writing a sitcom, but it did not offer the same instant gratification that she received from her staple output of satirical one-liners and sketches.

Asked about her family background, she said: 'My whole family is screwed up.' She said that she had nothing in common with her mother, who filed boring reference books, was very boring herself, and jealous of her seeing her father. Debs told doctors she had more to talk about with me, but rarely saw me. She said that she found the break-up of my second marriage disturbing and blamed me for this. She didn't like her stepfather, who had two children of his own, but she comments that she had nothing to say to any of them.

She said that, as a teenager, days would go by without exchanging a word at home and that there had been loads of conflict with her mother, who had wanted her to go to Cambridge and was disgusted when she threw away her scholarship. She said she had been happy at primary school but had felt an outsider at secondary school because she started two weeks late due to chicken pox. She considered herself to be the 'most unfashionable girl at the school', with dowdy clothes and a pudding-basin haircut given to her by her mother 'without using a pudding basin'. She confessed she was teased about her appearance, even by the younger children. She suffered severe eczema between the ages of five and seven, and hot flushes during her teens.

She said she had come to London at 16 and 'had a ball'. As for boyfriends, she offered that she had six or seven sexual relationships since losing her virginity at 16 but found herself easily bored with partners and was adamant that work must come first. The men usually felt neglected and rejected. She said she ended her last relationship because she felt threatened by her boyfriend's 'excessive' eating habits.

The psychiatrist concluded that anorexia allowed Debs to avoid looking at her difficulty with personal relationships at an intimate level and allowed her to put all her drive into her work, which she enjoyed.

At this stage of her illness, Debs seemed to be doing the most she could to find a cure. Six months after she began attending the eating disorder unit, she arranged additional 'top-up' help from a private therapist in West London, whom she visited three times a week. She also agreed to a suggestion from Rachel to meet a former fellow sufferer to gain advice and moral support. Through her industry contacts, Rachel knew a stage, musical, and television actress named Carla Mendonca, who had beaten anorexia after a long struggle.

Carla was only too happy to help and agreed to meet Debs in a café near her Chiswick flat. Carla had in fact already briefly met Debs before – in the Writers' Room at the BBC – shortly after her arrival in London from Sheffield. At the time, Carla was working on some comedy ideas and Debs was bashing away at her computer keyboard dreaming up some gags for *Week Ending*. They were introduced by one of the producers, Caroline Leddy.

Carla remembers: 'I said to her, "So you're D. A. Barham. I always thought you were a bloke!" She was complimentary about my acting skills and I in turn was impressed by her work.'

But the figure who walked up to her table in Café Rouge in Chiswick High Road was a shadow of the girl she remembered from the BBC. Debs was dressed in her customary elegant style, head to toe in black with a matching hat. Carla recalls those huge amazing eyes and beautiful skin. There was, of course, now a crucial difference.

'The Debbie I first knew was a tall, sturdy girl, very shy, with a smile reminiscent of Princess Diana. To be frank, when we met in the café, I hardly recognized her, she had lost so much weight.'

At first, Debs said she didn't really want to talk to anyone about her illness, but she found Carla a supportive and knowing confidante and gradually opened up about her illness and her feelings. Debs said her anorexia started after going down with food poisoning. She had never been happy about herself and had been trying to lose weight all her life. Suddenly a miracle had occurred. She lost a stone in a week because of the bug and she liked what she saw. But it had all got out of hand and the slimming regime turned into an eating disorder.

She confessed to Carla the root of her troubles: her relationship with her mother and her stepfather. She had, she said, run away to London to escape.

Carla in turn told Debs her story. She had been brought up in Coventry, the eldest of four children to a Portuguese father and an English mother. As a child, she had dreamed of being an actress and studied drama at Warwick University. She was spotted playing piano and singing in a hotel bar during the Edinburgh Festival in the early 1980s, when Debs was still at primary school.

The comedian Jasper Carrott came in with his manager John Starkey, who was impressed with the talented, good-looking woman at the piano. He signed her up as a backing singer to a pop band called the Maisonettes. But acting was Carla's overriding ambition. Starkey found her a role in a post-student production of one-woman plays at a theatre in Kenilworth and brought TV executive Paul Jackson along to see her. Jackson was dazzled by her performance and invited her to take the lead role in a Channel 4 comedy called *Pushing Up Daisies*, starring Chris Barrie and Hale and Pace. So, at the age of 22, Carla had made it on TV.

Carla told how she had become anorexic at the age of 31, after the break-up of her four-year marriage to the music composer Howard Goodall. The structure of her life had gone, and the guilt of walking out on her husband turned to depression. Because of the stress, she had lost weight. But while feeling good about her body, like so many sufferers before her, she became immersed in a terrible downward spiral. In two years she was down to just under six stone. Although her friends were worried sick about her condition, she was in denial for over a year. The first time she acknowledged her illness was when she bumped into an old actress friend in the West End and they went for coffee.

The friend had asked: 'Are you anorexic?'

In a matter-of-fact way, and without any fuss or emotion, Carla had replied: 'Yes.'

Carla told Debs that the key to conquering the illness was to recognize that she was in fact suffering from depression. Whilst some turned to drink, or drugs, to try to deal with their problems, Debs' particular choice had been to stop eating. The route to survival was finding out what was making her so unhappy. But this was easier said than done. 'Victims are in a trap. We are in the grip of something and are too frightened to let go. If you do, you feel your whole world will fall apart.'

Over coffee, Debs listened intently as Carla spelled out the grip the disorder has on its victims. Anorexia imposed a distorted vision on Carla – and sparked a crisis if she began to lose control over her body.

'If you have eaten a big meal you feel huge the next day. You might actually look like a crow, but you feel fat. And then if you gain weight, you are furious, crying and panicking. You feel helpless, alone and afraid.' Debs empathized as her new friend confirmed how she herself had compartmentalized her friends to stop them ganging up.

'Anorexics are the best liars in the world. You do anything to keep control. You place people into separate categories, those you trust, those you don't, those you can confide in and those whom you lie to. But of course the reality is that underneath it all, you are lying to yourself all the time.'

Carla met Debs a number of times and kept up regular e-mail correspondence. Over the weeks, she explained the three crucial events that led to her own recovery.

The first was while shopping in Marks & Spencer. Carla was trying on a cardigan and, in a fleeting glance, witnessed the look of disgust from two girls who could not disguise their horror at the state of her emaciated frame. That image, reflected in their eyes for a split second, stayed with her. In that one moment she was able somehow to step outside the distorted fantasy world she had been living in and see herself as those girls had – a pathetic, sick person.

The second wake-up call came after dinner with friends. They had long accepted her for what she was and were used to making their choice from the menu while Carla ordered just a bowl of ice – to chill her wine. 'I used to joke, Bon Appetit! as I downed my drink.' But the more they tolerated their sick friend, the more odd it seemed to Carla. She wanted to be one of them again: 'I wanted to be my old self.'

Carla reached her nadir after organizing a celebratory dinner for two actress friends. She shared the same agent as one, but at the dinner everyone seemed to ignore her. She felt a non-person, totally worthless. She responded by going home and eating the entire contents of her kitchen in one enormous, sorrowful binge.

Afterwards, she was so disgusted with herself she contemplated suicide there and then. The only thing that stopped her was the thought of her flatmate, who had been so supportive during the whole ordeal, discovering her body and having to deal with the gruesome consequences. Her life in turmoil, she cried herself to sleep. Next morning she felt totally drained. But although she could not get out of bed, she felt a different person. It was as if the whole psychological nightmare had exploded in her head and the residue had been washed away by her tears. And though she was suffering emotional aftershock, she knew she was over the worst.

Carla had been in private treatment for a while but progress had been slow. With the support of her best friend, Melanie Jessop, she booked an appointment with her GP, who put her on a course of anti-depressants and sent her for psychoanalyst assessment under the NHS. Eventually she ended up under the care of anorexia expert Dr Janet Treasure's Registrar, Geoffrey Wolff, at the Maudsley Hospital in Camberwell, South London, who, in conjunction with her existing private therapy, saved her life.

Part of her treatment programme involved 'homework' – writing letters to an anorexic friend, expressing inner thoughts and feelings, and portraying the illness as a make-believe figure, such as a stick insect nestling on your shoulder. Sufferers are encouraged to control this demon, this little nobody, and flick it away. In time they realize that the demon is in fact themselves, but that it can be controlled, regarded with similar disdain, and eliminated in much the same way.

Carla and Debs met a number of times, sharing thoughts and experiences, even working up ideas together. Carla recalls meeting in a coffee bar in Carnaby Street in the height of summer. Debs turned up in a short skirt, black tights, or long socks, showing off her figure to the full.

'As she walked towards me, I was so shocked at how thin she was. She was getting the looks that I used to get. When you are anorexic you are proud of your achievement, you want to show off, you don't see yourself as a spider. It sort of depresses you if people say you are looking well. But it secretly pleases when people express concern, because the dramatic changes you have made to your body have been noticed.'

During one boozy session at London's Soho House club, Debs fell asleep at the table in mid sentence. In a scene reminiscent of the *Absolutely Fabulous* comedy series, Carla dragged her drunken accomplice across the street and into a cab. At first the driver refused to take them, but Carla assured him her friend was 'tired', rather than drunk.

They went to Debs' flat in Chiswick – Carla had to carry her up the stairs. Carla was about to be greeted by the same shocking squalor Sue and I were to witness a year or so later: dirty dishes, a mountain of newspapers, and pet droppings everywhere.

'She did not want me to see her flat, and no wonder. It was like walking onto the set of *The Young Ones*. Frankly, it was a health risk, particularly the kitchen, which was filthy. It was the classic habitat of someone in a serious crisis.'

Carla put Debs to bed and went home. She hardly slept a wink, worrying about Debs' general condition and fearing she might be sick and choke on her vomit. Next day, phone calls went unanswered and Carla contacted Debs' agent Rachel to express her concern. Finally, at 3 p.m., Debs called, saying she was fine and had been working all day. She also sent Carla a huge bouquet of flowers, thanking her for looking after her.

In November 1997, Carla was among a small group of friends, which included Rachel and Clive Anderson, who celebrated Debs' twenty-first birthday at a restaurant in Berwick Street. It was a warm, emotional occasion and Debs was touched by the gifts and their support.

But having seen the way Debs was living, it was clear in Carla's mind that her friend's treatment regime just wasn't working. Not only that, she judged that Debs had absorbed the weekly trips to the clinic into her destructive/compulsive behaviour. Carla took a huge gamble. She detected in Debs an interest in her own treatment at the

Maudsley. So six days after Debs' birthday, and behind her back, she wrote to the Gordon Square clinic suggesting Debs be referred to the care of Janet Treasure, the consultant who had helped her so much.

Dear Dr Rooney

You may think of me unethical for writing to you, but I don't know of any other way to approach this problem.

I am a close friend of Debbie Barham – a patient of yours who is suffering from anorexia nervosa. I am a recovered anorexic myself and eight months ago successfully completed a three-year combined psychotherapeutic and psychiatric treatment programme. Because I have experienced the disease, Debbie talks in depth to me about how she feels.

I am one of a small group of friends of hers who are extremely worried for her. She is 'out', as it were, to all of us, but she will only talk to me about the 'realities' of her depression and anorexia because she trusts me.

Whilst being completely empathetic towards her struggle with food, her massively distorted body-image and her slowly developing awareness of the link between her family history and her illness, I am understanding of her and not colluding with her.

She is terrified of being admitted to hospital. She has told me that you may admit her under Section 4 of the Mental Health Act before Christmas if she has not gained a certain amount of weight by that time.

As I would have expected, she is resisting this idea violently. She says she is trying to eat, but I know that it is an impossible mountain to climb and overcome in such a short time. I am also afraid that if she does achieve a significant weight-gain, she will have 'lost control' and the severity of her underlying depression will emerge during the holiday season when psychiatric back-up will not be available to her.

She lives alone (in quite appalling conditions – dirty and chaotic), has no real close friends and no contact with any family.

Out-patient care worked for me because I had a support network of close friends around me who helped me cope with the daily recover/destruct conflict. Also, I was never at as critically low a weight as Debbie is.

It seems to me that Debbie's out-patient hospital and thrice-weekly psychotherapy appointments have become *part* of her daily regimen. She has fitted these events into her obsessive-compulsive daily routines and made them *part* of her life. Therapy and hospital visits don't seem to be having the disturbing and provocative effects needed to penetrate the hard protective shell her anorexia gives her. She can come home after each session and get right back into her necessary routines.

She is an incredibly talented and successful writer. It has now reached a stage where her career is seriously threatened. People are becoming nervous of employing her. She lives to work. (Literally – she writes *instead* of eating.) Some of her professional contacts feel it might be the risk of her losing writing commissions and being dropped by her agent which will force her to agree to accepting in-patient care.

I was treated by Dr Geoffrey Wolff and Dr Janet Treasure at the Maudsley. Debbie knows this. She is violently opposed to admittance to the Gordon. However, I think she would (after a fight, certainly) agree to go into the Bethlem Maudsley.

I have not approached Debbie about this yet as I don't want to 'get her hopes up', should a referral not be practicable. I honestly believe this is her only chance. I am convinced it is the only scenario she would agree to and, if it is possible, I would be extremely grateful for your aid and support, as I'm sure will she – if not now, most certainly in the months to come.

Carla also wrote to Dr Janet Treasure along similar lines in the hope that the two specialists might collude. Shortly before Christmas, the clinic wrote back, thanking Carla for her concern, but assuring her they knew what they were doing.

Catastrophically, Debs somehow found out about the letters. She regarded Carla's intervention as a great betrayal. She cut Carla off dead – and stopped all her treatment. Her case notes at Gordon Square for 1998, read:

9/2/98	Did not attend
3/3/98	Left message on phone
10/3/98	DNA
14/3/98	Called on her mobile to make appointment
16/3/98	DNA
20/4/98	Called on mobile

So, after a year, the clinic sessions fizzled out. She made little progress in terms of gaining weight or finding a way to end her suffering. Halfway through her treatment, the dietician reported: 'We continue to meet but failing to make progress.' Debbie's weight stuck at 35/36kg (approx 5 st. 5 lb) and her Body Mass Index was approx 12.5.

The notes make it clear she had 'flatly refused in-patient treatment, was aggressive when it was suggested, and stated that she would deteriorate mentally and physically if this was undertaken'. Debs managed somehow to stave off detention under the Mental Health Act.

Carla, who had done so much to try to coax Debs back to health, had acted in what she had been convinced was Debs' best interests. Now she was left with a sense that she had betrayed her friend, albeit for the best reasons. She recalls: 'I felt an enormous amount of responsibility because I had been through it all and people were asking my advice. However, I was a trusted confidante and I should have realized the implications for Debs of losing control.'

It was two years before Debs spoke to her again. They kissed and made up at Debs' club, Blacks in Soho.

As it was, the clinic's verdict was that Debs should stop work immediately. It was fuelling her anorexia and slowly killing her. But, as everyone knew, work was all she lived for. And without it, she said she would kill herself.

The last entry in the case notes underlines just how accurate that prognosis was.

It is a report of Debs' death in the *Guardian*, spotted by her dietician five years later.

Thirty

Despite her failing health, the D. A. Barham bandwagon went rolling on. She felt comfortable enough to talk about – even exploit her illness – as in this piece for the *London Evening Standard*.

Ever wondered what it feels like being fattened up for Christmas? At least the turkey only ends up having to suffer the indignity of being slaughtered and plucked, hung upside down and treated to half a pound of sage and onion up its jacksy.

A turkey was never threatened with being sectioned under the Mental Health Act if it didn't pile on the pounds quickly enough.

I was lucky. I did manage to make the deadline, though not quite as rapidly or as noticeably as the average Christmas bird.

At least Christmas was bearable. While it might be traditional to have things on sticks at Christmas parties, I don't think that it's actually meant to be the guests. And anything with asymmetric shoulders or short sleeves is a definite no-no. 'Would you like to get rid of those half-gnawed chicken drumsticks, dear? Oh, I'm sorry, they are your upper arms.'

For *Ms London* magazine, she wrote about gadgets in the home; coffee, telly, ice cream and chocolate. She even had the temerity to advise men about health matters.

She was also providing topical gags for Bob Monkhouse as well her 'regulars', Rory Bremner and *Spitting Image*. All this on top of her offerings to various web sites.

Her nocturnal routine did not alter. She was still up most of the night dreaming up gags and eating very little. In the five years since coming to London, Debs had shown she was a supreme gag writer and a prolific generator of ideas. But she wanted to expand into serious writing, albeit in her distinctive bright, amusing, and trenchant style. She decided to contact the editor of *Punch*, the oldest English-language satirical magazine, which had just relaunched after four years of closure.

Punch was a weekly publication founded in 1841 by a group of journalists who had the idea while drinking in a pub in Fleet Street. It was meant to be humorous and satirical and so used as its masthead and name the anarchic glove-puppet figure of Mr Punch. It had grown into a British institution, selling at its peak, in the 1940s, 175,000 copies a week. The magazine was responsible for the modern use of the word 'cartoon', to refer to a comic satirical drawing, and it employed some of the world's great satirical writers and cartoonists.

But through the 1980s it went through tough times as circulation plummeted. After a succession of editors, *Punch* was closed by its owners, United Newspapers, in 1992. But the title was bought by the millionaire proprietor of Harrods, Mohamed Al Fayed, who staged a glittering relaunch party at the store and installed the editorial team in offices opposite in Brompton Road. No stranger to controversy himself, Al Fayed, relished an acquisition that poked fun at the Establishment.

The new agenda appealed to Debs, and as she made her way to Knightsbridge for a chat with the editor, she hoped that the initials D. A. Barham would soon join the *Punch* Roll of Honour that included such illustrious names as P. G. Wodehouse, W. M. Thackeray, and P. J. O'Rourke.

The editor at the time was Paul Spike, who asked to see a sample of her writing. But he left shortly after, to be replaced by his deputy, James Steen, who had made his name in the gossip columns and feature pages of Fleet Street. Interviewing her so soon after Debs had 'come out' as an anorexic, the new editor found an honest and open-minded potential recruit.

James Steen says: 'I remember having a drink with her and it was a very open conversation, telling me quite honestly about her background and her illness. We stayed at the bar for several hours. I was impressed by her work and offered her a column. I wanted her to be herself, come out of the protective shell that was D. A. Barham, and write as Debbie Barham with a picture byline at the top of the column.'

One of her jobs was to write the copy for spoof movie posters that used to run across the centre spread. They needed just 250 words of clever political satire aping the critic's verdicts on films. She would send over 4,000 words! The brief for her column was four or five short pieces, plus a few gags for the postscript called 'And Another Thing'. The editor wanted 900 words, but she would file around 7,000, plus 60-odd jokes. He used to sub it himself because it was so enjoyable! He felt that although she obviously enjoyed writing, and was extremely clever, Debs was insecure about her work and so overwrote considerably. But he also contends that she liked to give editors plenty of options on what to use.

When he took over the editor's chair, James adopted the moral message of the magazine's very first edition, back in 1841, 'Punch Hangs the Devil', or as one member of staff put it, 'getting the baddies'. There were a number of much-contested public executions. During his editorship, *Punch* fought forty-five legal battles and won thirty-nine. Lawyers' letters and libel writs were flying about every fortnight. Among its adversaries: a deputy prime minister, the son of a former prime minister, a duke, a viscount, two world-famous singers, an international bank, mercenaries, a detective inspector, two boxing promoters, Stanley Kubrick, the BBC, and the British Government.

Despite her cruel cutting edge, Debs skilfully managed to avoid any legal conflict, but she was extremely supportive of James Steen and the magazine's no-nonsense reputation. *Punch*'s most infamous case was when it and the editor were sued by the Government over an article by former MI5 officer David Shayler, which, the Treasury

Solicitor argued, breached an injunction forbidding him to comment about his work. Debs went to the High Court on many days, watching the proceedings from the public gallery. Between the first hearing and the judgment, her editor asked her to write a colour piece about the hearing in which she likened the judge to the comedian Ronnie Corbett.

James and Debs became great friends – he was later to try to help her conquer her addiction. He recalls: 'Everyone adored her. She was extremely funny and highly intelligent, a very sweet person.'

To mark the birth of his son Billy, Debs sent a gift-wrapped photo album wrapped in the most delicate, meticulous way.

> If you had gone to the best department store in the world it could not have been wrapped better. My wife said with so much attention to detail, the parcel just had to have come from Debbie.
>
> She was like that with her copy. I was always taught to read, re-read and read again. Many people these days do not. Although her copy was obviously bashed out and came across as a stream of consciousness, she obviously polished it, and took great care, although a lot of people didn't think she did.

Food of course is the fountain of life. By refusing it, we deprive our bodies of the essential nutrients needed to survive, effectively embarking on a long, slow suicide course. That's why, for the layman, anorexia is the most baffling of conditions. We all need to eat. Most of us love to eat. But the anorexic is hooked on consuming nothing.

By the time Clive Anderson got to know Debs she was already anorexic, rapidly going from very slim to dangerously thin in a matter of months. As she once joked to him, she was losing weight faster than he was losing hair.

Debs was in a cycle of deep despair. Her urge to produce more and more written work seemed intimately bound up with the state of mind that led to her anorexia. The anger that caused her illness fuelled her writing. She starved herself both as a reward and a punishment. And the more she worked, the less she ate. So for Clive, and the rest of the people who paid Debs for her services, there was a massive moral issue involved. How much are we, by continuing to employ her, putting her life at risk?

The Digital Village had already taken a stand. Now, some of the country's most powerful comedy producers were about to follow suit. Hat Trick Productions was one of the UK's most successful independent production companies. Among their award-winning shows were *Have I Got News For You, Father Ted, Drop the Dead Donkey, Room 101, Whose Line Is It Anyway?* and *The Kumars at No. 42.* They were also the company responsible for Clive Anderson's C4 and BBC shows.

The company was founded by the comedian Jimmy Mulville and producer Denise O'Donoghue, who both understood how the pressures and insecurities of working in the performing arts can trigger dependency. Denise O'Donoghue summoned Debs to a showdown meeting at the company offices near Oxford Street and, with Clive in attendance, told her bluntly that unless she agreed to have in-patient treatment, Hat Trick would no longer employ her. She explained that they were taking the decision for Debs' own good. It was a distressing meeting for everyone involved, with Debs breaking down in tears.

Clive Anderson recalls: 'It was not a decision that I would have taken but that's because I would not have been brave enough, but I went along with it. It was meant with the best of intentions to help Debbie with her condition.' Although Debs never worked for Hat Trick again, Clive did continue to employ her in a private capacity to send through topical gags for the awards and after-dinner circuit. He wrote after her death: 'Were we – was I – right to keep employing her while her condition deteriorated? I was not always sure about that when she was alive and I am even less sure now.' Even if that was the right tactic, he points out that with so many media outlets – television, radio, newspapers, the Internet – it would have been impossible for the industry to unite against Debs.

The Hat Trick ban, coming on top of being sacked by The Digital Village over her health, encouraged Debs to pick up, but only enough to ward off enforced hospital admission, and certainly not enough to make friends optimistic that she was anywhere near conquering her condition.

For the next year her weight hovered around a critical level but it did not stop the relentless flow of one-liners, scripts, articles, and ideas. She continued to take on more work, including writing gags for Graham Norton and for a BBC Bridget Jones night. She entered a script based on the experiences of a girl called Kate for a Channel 4 sitcom festival in London. Her opening line was a classic.

> My name is Kate. I lost my virginity on the number 12 bus when I was 13. Or was it the other way around?

Scriptwriter Dave Cohen, who was among an 'inner-circle' of close friends who attended Deb's twenty-first birthday dinner, reveals that at one point they even talked of kidnapping her to force her into in-patient treatment: 'There were several of us extremely concerned. I even tried her same sick humour on her, hoping that might appeal. I told her that if she died it would be great news in the short term because it would create so many writing opportunities. She laughed at that, but to be honest, we were all completely out of our depth in trying to deal with her problem.'

They played a cat and mouse game for over a year. Every time something serious was said, she would say, 'Yeah, yeah, yeah' and that she was seeing doctors, but Dave suspected she wasn't. 'It was hard to get anything out of her that wasn't a gag,' he says.

The main battle for Debs now was not simply tackling

her anorexia: That was virtually a lost cause and she worked her way around it. Her real fight was to eat just enough to stop her from being sectioned – and of course from starving herself to death.

Her next major emergency surfaced in the summer of 1999. Radio producer Bruce Hyman became more and more concerned about her condition. She was becoming paranoid and delusional. He warned her that her work was suffering and it was not fair on her to employ her if she was not up to it. It was virtually his only weapon to get her to respond to her condition.

With the people around her ganging up again, she became desperate. She decided to flee London and land on me. She contacted Bruce.

```
Bruce
Thanks for the e-mails … sorry to be so panicky.


Sitcom. Maureen. And McKenzie. Yes, yes, yes, I
DESPERATELY want to do this. Please. It could be
just what I need. I'm going away tomorrow, and I'll
start thinking around what you've said so far -
outwardly cosy domesticity with a real hard edge. I
had a futon like that, once. Still do, actually, but
I'm not strong enough to operate the bastard thing
any more.


Discuss further when I get back.
```

And thank you, thank you, thank you for offers of
support etc. At the moment, I'll settle for just
being able to turn over in bed and/or walk down a
street without someone shouting Mong or Devil Woman
at me.

Next day her agent Rachel Swann sent her the following
e-mail:

Bruce (Hyman) has rung me as he is extremely worried
about you. He tells me your weight has dropped to
below 5 stone. I am extremely frightened by this as
at such a low weight you could collapse and die at
any moment. You must be feeling absolutely awful and
I am desperately worried about you. I've tried to
get you to chat or come in but you clearly didn't
want to communicate, probably for fear I'd interfere
again?

I care about you very much (why do you think I am
still trying to be your agent?!) and I want to help
you. You wanted to beat this thing alone and you
cannot.

Please, please will you get in touch. I will do
anything I can to help you get the treatment you so
desperately need.

Don't fight this alone. Many people apart from myself
still care very much about you and want you to get

```
better. Apart from anything else, we all need a
writer as good and funny as you are! But you must
face up to the fact that you need outside help.

This all sounds so melodramatic but Debbie, you are
very, very ill. Please call.
```

Debs did not call, but before boarding the train from London to my home in Aylesbury, she sent Rachel the following:

```
Rachel, I'm going away for a few days. Just checking
my E before I leave for station, but will have modem
with me. Back Monday, at the latest, I think. I will
be much, much more sorted when I get back. And I'll
speak to you then. Please don't worry. Well, do
worry. But not quite so much.
Deb
```

She gave neither Bruce nor Rachel any hint of *where* she was going. And the 'few days' she mentioned in her e-mails became nine months.

Part Three

Back From The Brink

Thirty-one

It is now nearly six months since Debs arrived unannounced on my doorstep in such despair. There was so much that had gone on in her life, and so little that we knew about. Naively, we had hoped slowly to nurse her back to good health by encouraging her to eat. It is an obvious but futile strategy, as many families battling against a loved one's eating disorder will testify.

Today we will face a new crisis.

It is 7 p.m., and I am still at the office. I receive an alarming call from Rachel Swann, Debs' agent.

'Look, I have just spoken to Debbie. She's going on about people climbing around in the loft and of men running around in white coats. She thinks she's being watched and that you are stalking her. She is obviously hallucinating. I have seen her get like this before. We have got to do something. She needs help, now.'

Earlier, Debs had phoned me, mentioning noises in the attic, but I'd dismissed it, merely reassuring her that it must be her imagination, or the wind. But although I barely know Rachel, I know how well she understands Debs and her troubles, and I accept her concern without hesitation. This is not the usual cynical, coherent, funny Debs – she is almost scared. Something is very wrong. I drop what I am doing and race home.

My office is only a few minutes from the house. I return home to find Debs in a strange mood. Not rambling, but almost spaced out. I do not beat about the bush.

'I've had a call from Rachel. She's told me about your hallucinations. I've got to get you to a doctor right now.'

Debs gives in, subject to one condition.

'OK, you can take me. But you must let me finish this piece for the *Daily Express*. Then we'll go to the hospital.'

I am surprised how matter of fact her reply is. Clearly she has realized that her delirium has signalled a new serious depth to her condition. But, typically, her work always comes before her health. Why am I not surprised that she insists on finishing an article before going to the hospital?

What is interesting is that reports of other typical anorexics at 4–4½ stone describe sufferers experiencing serious loss of mental ability and almost trance-like states. Although Debs is imagining people in the attic and is becoming paranoid about strangers watching her, at no time does she lose the ability to write gags, hold an intelligent conversation, or write an article for a national newspaper.

Sue and I sit in total silence waiting for Debs to finish her piece. Normally her thoughts are razor sharp. But only sheer willpower and guts will get her through this.

We watch her labour through her copy in obvious mental distress.

Debbie Barham's Diary of a House Hunter

'Teach Yourself Estate-Agent-Speak in 21 Days – or Your Money Back (minus two per cent commission, stamp duty and surveyor's fee). Study in the privacy of your own home.'

Sadly, no such course exists, but it should. Having spent a week perusing property particulars, I've now concluded that the average 'for sale' ad comes about as close to comprehensible English as the average lonely hearts advertisement . . .

She usually types like a machine gun. This is more like a child learning to type. The process takes nearly two hours. It is a testament to her courage and determination that she manages to get it done at all.

Shortly after midnight I carry Debs to the car for the ten-minute drive to hospital. Her physical state is such that I have to place her onto the passenger seat and lift her legs in. I feel elated, but frightened. This is a huge step. At last we are going to get some real help. Debs is quiet, subdued and resigned to whatever is to happen next.

Stoke Mandeville Hospital is a sprawling complex of low-rise buildings not far from Aylesbury town centre. It is perhaps best known as the National Centre for Spinal Injuries, specializing in treating paraplegic patients from all over the world. Not surprisingly, in the early hours of the morning, there is little sign of life as we drive into the hospital grounds.

Passing the outdated single-storey wooden shacks that

comprise many of the wards at the hospital, we drive into Entrance 4 and follow the red signs round to the more modern section that houses Accident and Emergency and Outpatients. We help Debs from the car and she – quite strongly and purposefully – walks the short distance to A&E reception. The department treats around 50,000 people a year; but as Sue and I help Debs through into casualty, there is hardly a patient in sight. We are seen almost immediately, first by a nurse and then by a young, skinny doctor. You don't need to be a medic to assess the state Debs is in. It is there for everyone to see: emaciated, very weak, very pale, with weary, sunken eyes. She is virtually at death's door.

We explain the day's events and some history of Debs' condition. He comes straight to the point.

'Why have you brought her here at this time of night?'

It seems flippant and inappropriate to mention that we have been waiting for the last couple of hours for her to finish a newspaper article, so I opt for a description of the hallucinations, her bizarre behaviour that day, and our real concern that we have reached crisis point.

'What do you expect me to do?'

His reply shatters my hopes.

'We're not trained to deal with this,' he continues. 'I don't know what you expect me to do.'

I think all three of us are shocked at his response. We are desperate for help. But here is a medic expecting to deal with cuts and bruises and more serious road accidents. Not a person starving themselves to death.

I am angry.

'Look, you are the doctor. What do you expect *me* to do? You can see the state she is in. She is dying. Help us. We don't know what to do to help her.'

The doctor is looking blank and, I would say, pretty helpless.

I have no medical experience. But I did study veterinary medicine at Cambridge and have a pretty good grasp of what makes bodies function. Nevertheless, it seems quite ludicrous that I find myself having to tell a doctor that a good start would be for him to do some blood tests.

I say: 'We need to know if the essential systems are working.'

He seems relieved at my suggestion and, after a rather superficial examination of his patient and a few obvious questions, he organizes a nurse to take some samples.

We watch as she draws blood from Debs' spindly arm. It will be over an hour to get the results. Sue is working tomorrow and orders a taxi to take her home, leaving Debs and myself alone in the cubicle. She is lying on the bed. There is little talk. Our moods are quietly reflective, although underneath I am tired, worried, and dejected.

The doctor arrives with a file. The results are back. A slight raising of hopes, for me at least. Perhaps we'll have some answers, something on which to base a recovery plan.

I'm so disappointed. They show no real problems at all. Everything blood-wise is normal, apart from a slight potassium deficiency which the doctor cannot explain except to say that this may or may not have something to do with Debs' nutritional problem (I think I could have guessed that). He offers referral to a psychiatrist and concludes: 'Take her home and try to get her to eat.'

As statements of the bleeding obvious go, this wins first prize. But it is no joke. This is my daughter's life at stake.

I am desperate for support – and the one hope I have is destroyed. I'd gone to the hospital in a state of optimism, secretly praying that they would keep Debs in and that someone else could take over the burden of rescuing her from her parlous condition. But we are back to square one.

It is only later that I will discover just how vital those blood tests were and how important signals were missed. Low potassium is one of the most serious effects of malnutrition. Potassium deficiency can lead to serious problems with the heart, muscles and nerves, even to heart failure. Hallucinations are a recognized symptom. Supplements can be given in tablet form or, in extreme cases, intravenously. Also, under the Mental Health Act, doctors have the power to force-feed anorexics over the age of 18 provided the sufferer is shown to be incapable of making rational decisions about her condition. Surely, Debs' hallucinations signalled that this was the case?

Without doubt more could have, and maybe should have, been done. But as the doctor said, 'We're not trained for this ...'

It is now 3.45 a.m. I take Debs home in a state of abject despair.

Thirty-two

I prayed that Debs' hallucination crisis and the subsequent hospital visit would shock her into submission to start eating properly, but nothing has changed. In fact, the whole episode has merely strengthened her resolve not to seek treatment.

The hospital had tested the functioning of her organs and they are fine. She feels she has carte blanche to continue as before. So, for the last few weeks, she has returned to the diet of carrot and coriander soup, broccoli and sugar snap peas (although how much she actually consumes is open to debate), plus her endless rounds of strong coffee and white wine. She knows her body better than anyone and has developed a knack for eating *just* the right amount to stave off another hallucination attack.

Her attitude towards us is different too. She knows we are trying to change her and that her control is being eroded. Debs senses our frustration, which in turn makes her more standoffish. The closeness we had has evaporated. The three-way cuddles are out and we are now leading virtually separate lives. The house is split between Sue and me, on the one hand, and Debs on the other. We barely see her and communication is by Post-it notes on the fridge.

Worse, from a personal point of view, my marriage is beginning to suffer.

Sue and I are simply exhausted by the whole experience. We have reached our limit and take it out on each other. She has made it clear that the strain is affecting her feelings towards me. The hospital visit and its futility have deepened the tension between us. She has favoured direct intervention of some sort all along, while I felt strongly that if we did anything heavy handed Debs would run away. It is now so clear that, until Debs herself is prepared to give the problem the importance it deserves, we will achieve nothing.

Debs and I have had several major bust-ups. To meet her demand for perpetual bubbling coffee, she uses a tea light to keep the brew constantly on the boil. The coffee is in a glass supported by a metal holder. The result is that the metal has an almost permanent residue of charcoal on the rim and the base of the glass. This 'soot' peels off, leaving black marks all over the downstairs – on floors, chairs, tables, etc. It is like black dye.

In despair, Sue and I each bought different gadgets to heat the coffee without making any stains, one a hot plate that you warmed in the microwave, another an electric cup warmer. These were given a rather half-hearted trial but failed to meet Debs' exacting and obsessional requirements. Each time she went back to the tea light. Last week, using a new type of tea light gadget made of plastic, the unit melted and burned through the tablecloth and into the polished teak surface of our brand-new dining-room table. I just exploded. Grabbing the whole coffee assembly – glass, metal holder, tea light – I threw it out of the back door, smashing them all to the ground.

I screamed at Debs: 'Why can't you be normal? Why can't you be like other people? Why do you need coffee on the go the whole time? Why do you need ice-cold wine? What is the matter with you …'

As I ranted, part of me was watching myself, disgusted. Me, the mature grown-up, screaming at this weak, defenceless child, her big, sad eyes just staring, bewildered, almost as though they were asking, 'What are you going on about?' I hated what I was doing, but I couldn't stop. I just had to let out weeks and weeks of built-up tension and despair.

The rage must have lasted ten minutes. Debs just sat silent and I stormed out the room. Later, when I had calmed down, I apologized. We cuddled, but this was superficial, not like our long hug on the day she'd arrived at our home.

The late meal sessions, when we tried to lead by example, have failed to work.

The other day I snapped. We had been waiting to go to bed and I could no longer stand watching her just play with her food.

'Why the hell can't you just *eat*? You are killing yourself. Don't you realize this? For God's sake, *eat* …'

23 October 1999

She is now arriving back from London later and later, spending a fortune on taxis. Sue and I frequently have disturbed nights, hearing her come in and listening to the microwave whirring all night. We are on a vicious downward spiral. Losing sleep, losing patience, and losing that bond we'd built up so patiently during the summer.

It has got to the point where the first thing we do on waking up in the morning is to listen to find out if Debs is still alive. Her every movement in the night is an irritation. Her every movement in the morning is relief.

24 October 1999

It is 5.30 a.m. The phone is ringing beside the bed. As I stumble for my senses, Sue has already answered the call. It is Debs. Where could she be? Why the call at this hour? Is she ill? In fact, she is calling on her mobile phone from her bedroom, just the other side of the wall. She says she hasn't got the strength to get out of bed and needs our help. We go into her room and gently lift her up. From now on, she will have to be helped up the stairs.

30 October 1999

Debs has degenerated to 4½ stone, way below the danger-weight guidelines. I believe she is about to die. Sue went to give her a kiss today to thank her for her birthday present and as she leaned forward Debs' head fell back off her shoulders. There is no muscle in her neck to support her. We had the undignified task of putting her head back on her body.

Thirty-three

3 November 1999

An unexpected event triggers a response from Debs which, for the first time in months, gives us hope.

Sue's mother is down from Aberdeen for a memorial service for the man who was due to become her second husband. They met through their shared love of plants and nature, became very close, and got engaged. Shortly before the wedding, he died of a heart attack while on a field trip to Scotland. This seemed unbelievably cruel – they had been so happy and we were both very upset for her.

Not unnaturally, emotions are running high. Sue and her mother prepare to go for a walk just before lunchtime.

Unusually, Debs is still in bed, and Sue wants to speak to her. As they wait, they both become more and more impatient. Eventually Debs appears, in one of her dismissive, 'Problem, what problem?' moods.

Words are said that result in Sue breaking down in tears. 'Can't you understand – I'm scared of you dying – you're just dying in front of my eyes! You've got to start eating.'

Seeing Sue in tears, distraught and scared, somehow breaks through Debs' defences. 'I fancy a croissant,' she says. And with that, Sue breaks open a tin of ready-to-bake

croissants from the fridge. Within minutes Debs is presented with four small, but high-calorie freshly baked croissants, which Sue leaves for her to eat while she and her
mother go for their walk.

12 November 1999

The 'croissant' affair has proved an important breakthrough. Although there is no dramatic change in Debs'
eating habits, at least we have found a crack in her defences
– she is at last beginning to accept the seriousness of her
condition. But the real turning point is about to happen.
Debs starts to complain of feeling strange, and of getting
a 'whooshing' sensation when she stands up. Sue inspects
her legs. Her feet look badly swollen and her ankles are
starting to ulcerate.

'You need to see a doctor,' Sue tells her.

But Debs is still registered with her GP in London. We
ring our GP in Aylesbury, and explain the situation.

'Bring her down to the surgery,' they say 'and we'll take
a look at her.'

They are superb. Debs is seen by my doctor, who is
shocked at her condition, but who also gauges quite quickly the strength and single-mindedness that are a central
part of the disorder. He quizzes her about her condition
and the previous attempts at treatment. Debs is honest, but
somewhat flippant, with a 'been there, done that' attitude.

The doctor diagnoses oedema due to lack of nutrition.

Fluid accumulating in the legs is moving about as she moves, causing the 'whooshing' sensation. The remedy, apart from the obvious need to eat, is to keep the legs elevated, and they are going to need bandaging to limit the fluid build-up and protect the ulcers.

The doctor arranges for a nurse to dress the legs, and because he is so concerned that she should not waste even the smallest amount of energy travelling to the surgery, he insists the District Nurse calls three times a week to replace the dressings.

Travelling to London is now out of the question. A dietician will call once a week to offer advice and monitor her progress. Debs makes her a list of her diet for a typical day:

5 pm	Cappuccino
5.30 pm	2 slices toast and butter
	Cappuccino
	Orange Juice
8 pm	Pretzel
	Cappuccinos
	Carrot juice
12 am	Tuna baguette, salad, sweetcorn
	Fruit Smoothie
	Apple
	Several gallons of coffee through night
5 am	Smoked trout fillet
	Broccoli, carrots
	Purdeys

Unconventional, to say the least, and – sadly – largely fantasy. But at least she is making some genuine attempt to increase her calorie intake. She begins nibbling all day – just Rich Tea biscuits, or shortbreads perhaps, which she dunks in her coffee. Dinner is now salmon steak, plus the inevitable broccoli and carrots.

This is a deeply humiliating period for Debs. She is a prisoner in our house, banned from her daily trips to London. Her legs are uncomfortable: weeping fluid from the ulcers saturates the bandages and has a deeply unpleasant odour. She can only wear slippers, and these soon become sopping wet as well.

She accepts the frequent visits by the District Nurses with good grace, and they soon develop a mutual respect; but she has also to suffer the humiliation of Sue and I changing her dressings when they become too wet. This is an unpleasant and stressful time for us all.

Debs is marooned behind the dining-room table, in an open-plan room attached to the kitchen. She is there constantly, scrutinizing all the activity on the ground floor and aided by one of those 'old person's' sticks with pincers on the end to save her bending down. When Sue is cooking, she feels Debs' gaze behind her, adding a sense of claustrophobia.

The ever-present aroma from the weeping legs becomes a part of our lives. Walking is uncomfortable, and her muscles, more used to trudging around London laden with bags, are gradually wasting away. On several occasions she tries to walk across the room, and simply collapses. She buys a small cycling machine, to use sitting down, but the District Nurse bans it as a waste of vital calories.

1 December 1999

With the imprisonment comes frustration. Debs is growing more demanding as she relies on us for all of her shopping. We get frequent phone calls. 'Hello, it's me. I don't suppose you're going near Tesco are you?' Special trips to the local Italian bakers for biscotti to dunk in her coffee alternate with demands for seemingly huge quantities of peppermint-oil capsules and Nytol.

There is some light relief. Notes would appear for us to find in the morning – they always brought a smile, and showed the sweet side of her personality. These are typical:

I borrowed (OK – took … I can't imagine you'll be wanting it back) a banana. Hope you don't mind.
Debs (little monkey)

And she wasn't ignoring the anorexia either:

Peter (or Sue?)
You wouldn't happen to have 2 envelopes going begging, would you? I'm sure we brought a box of 'em back from the flat. If you have time, could you poss leave a couple on the table (à la letters to Santa, but

whisky, carrot and mince pie optional)
Cheers, Have a good day! Deb

At the top was drawn a cartoon sketch of two envelopes, with a caption 'gummed strip – at least 0.1k calories'.

At first, Debs was grateful for our support. She knew she was in trouble, and we were all she had – her safety net. But gratitude has changed to resentment. The closeness, the hugs, the holding hands, are all gone. Only two or three of her closest colleagues, and her agent, Rachel, have been allowed to know where she is and to be told the extent of her condition. For the rest, Debs produces a range of fantasy explanations for her 'disappearance' from London.

A typical fictional tale transposes actual events from her brief scooter (electric vehicle) episode in the summer and dramatizes it:

```
I'm glad I found the EVUK page when I did, actch ...
'cos I've been racking my brains much of last week
trying to think of a good reason not to sell it. At
the moment it's languishing, poor wee beastie, in
someone else's garage 39 miles away from London. The
first problem, then, is that it only has a battery
range of about 35 miles. The second is that it's not
currently insured and the third is that I've never
actually ridden more than about a mile on it in one
go. I bought it on the assumption that it would be
just like riding a pedal-bike, and that one never
```

forgets how to ride a pedal-bike - forgetting in my
enthusiasm that I never DID know how to ride a pedal
bike, save for one misguided sojourn around the
Shepherds Bush Roundabout on a borrowed boneshaker
belonging to my Aunt. Several sojourns in fact (if
you know the scene in 'National Lampoon's European
Vacation' where Chevy Chase is trying in vain to
negotiate a roundabout in Central London - well,
that was me). I think the experience traumatized
me for good. Anyway, I used to use the Spring for
pottering shakily down to the station and back,
in between fruitless calls to insurance companies
('No, it's not a mobility trolley. Electric bike! You
know! Yes, kind of like a Sinclair C Fi ... hello?
Hello? Bugger!') and trips to the Elastoplast shop.

For a month or so I was Scooterwoman - faster than
a speeding pram. 'Is it a plane, is it a bird … yes,
it's a bird on a bike.' Fearlessly she weaves her
way in and out of traffic, even when there's no
traffic to weave through. Is she pissed? No, she is
the fearless Queen of the Highway - roads hold no
terror, unless they happen to throw up such hazards
as (a) cars or (b) corners, both of which hurl
Scooterwoman into a wild-eyed panic.

Interesting days. I then had a disagreement with a
lamp post, which led to my putting both legs out of
action for 4 months and acquiring a large hole in my
head (other than the usual ones which I use for
eating, drinking, hearing, seeing and vomiting

```
through). Despite this I am still unfeasibly
attached to the wretched machine, but next time I
think we're going to try a different position: Woman
on Top. It's more comfortable that way.
```

She might be using a bit of dramatic licence, but unfortunately the 'large hole in my head' is not fictional. It isn't anything to do with the scooter either, but another ulcer, right in the centre of her scalp. This is a cruel turn of events. Debs has been gaining weight, and her cheeks are starting to fill out, but her skin is so fragile. The District Nurse has to shave away the hair on the crown to keep the wound clean and dress it, and Debs has to suffer the humiliation of hair washing in the bathroom sink. There is no other way, and she accepts it, but her mood changes and she becomes more withdrawn.

She is eating more, and making good progress, but the motivation is now to become well enough to escape her Aylesbury 'prison'.

8 December 1999

I arrive home to find the dining-room covered in packaging, and Debs examining various remote controls, a Garmin III GPS Navigation System, Speech Recognition Software, a Nikon SLR digital Camera, and a C-Pen Scanner. These are all to be the subjects of product reviews for *T3* magazine from a chair-bound critic with an ulcerated head!

She gets frustrated with the installation of the scanner and speech recognition software, and simply makes up most of the review based on previous experience. She persuades my son Sam and me to do a road test on the GPS system and to report back. The reviews are good, witty, and suitably 'techy' – how many readers could ever guess they are written by a 5-stone girl surviving on two hours sleep a day?

Debs is sleeping very little, and continuing to work through the night. She goes to bed at 6–6.30 a.m., just as I am waking up, and asks for Sue to wake her before leaving for work at 8.45. How can anyone exist on that amount of sleep, when so weak already? She can only lie in one position in bed, and we put a duvet under her for softness, pillows propping her up in an almost foetal position, and an electric overblanket.

13 December 1999

Throughout the autumn Debs has been planning her dream of a flat in London's Docklands. Although initial attempts to sell the Chiswick flat have fallen through, she has found a new development in Westferry Road and sets her heart on a flat there. But she immediately finds herself in the dilemma of many self-employed people who strive to make minimum taxable profit, but need proof of maximum consistent income to get a mortgage. Debs hasn't filed a Tax Return since 1994, so this is to be a problem. Her book-keeping is non-existent – surprising, because she had been really good about this in the first few years of her life in London. But the focus on nothing but work soon took over, and anything else was a distraction. So it is now my task to sift through years of unopened bank statements, boxes full of invoices, and the odd receipt, in no particular order, and see what I can make of them.

It becomes clear that, while at first she was reasonably diligent about keeping receipts, the discipline had declined almost completely. She is too impatient, and not sufficiently interested, to wait for me to produce meaningful accounts, so I quickly assess the paperwork and produce gross earnings figures for each year. This is an eye-opener.

For a 23-year-old at the start of her career her earnings are astonishing, and she had gained thousands in equity in the Chiswick flat. She soon has a mortgage offer on the table. But this only fuels her impatience and resentment of her imprisonment in Aylesbury, and she becomes a difficult and very intolerant client for both her solicitor and estate agent.

While Debs is distracted by the process of selling her old flat and buying her new one, the strain for us in our own house is as bad as ever. There seems no immediate prospect of Debs being well enough to live on her own, and it doesn't seem sensible anyway.

So we also start to look around for a larger house, where we can provide her with an 'office' and at least a decent-sized bedroom. She doesn't show any real reaction when we tell her about the plans, although we will learn years later that she was quite upset by it.

For us, it is a question of emotional survival – for her, it is removing a piece of essential stability at a difficult time.

22 December 1999

As Christmas approaches, we try to include Debs in our plans, but I know how much she hates this time of year, mainly because it disrupts her work routine. Everyone else is taking time off, and that annoys her. We usually have a get-together with my brother and his family, and will be going down to Surrey one day after Christmas, but I know this means leaving Debs behind – her choice.

Christmas Day 1999

Debs simply stays in bed until the evening, avoiding any festivities or organized meal. She has sent a small number of cards to very privileged friends, but otherwise ignores the holiday.

New Year's Eve 1999

Tomorrow is the start of a new dawn across the world: the New Millennium. People everywhere are planning to party. We have invited Debs to come to some friends, but she made it clear she prefers to stay in, alone in her captive state and work. She isn't one for communal celebration anyhow, and, in the condition she is in, who can blame her for staying in? Besides, we are not on particularly good terms at the moment. I got upset with her the other day because she was smelling really bad. I had blamed her sodden slippers (from the oozing ulcers) and shouted at her. It turned out it was her head that was smelling, where the ulcer in the centre of her scalp had broken out.

18 January 2000

The 'biscuit' diet seems to be working, of sorts. Debs is slowly gaining more strength, and the ulcers are healing slowly. She is looking less gaunt and her emaciated features are softening as the flesh starts to return to her face.

We arrive home from work to find a Post-it note on the fridge saying simply, 'I've gone to London ... because I can.' The District Nurse had called in, Debs' bandages were removed at last, and she was off like a greyhound from a trap.

We can only be happy for her. The last three months have been agonizing for us all. She seems overjoyed to be mobile again, and strong enough to cope with the exercise. Instantly the old routine returns – into London for the evening – home on the last train, and working all night.

7 February 2000

Relieved at the lifting of the tension, Sue and I find a last-minute flight to Malaga and escape for a long weekend to celebrate our anniversary and take stock of the situation.

We return to find Debs upbeat and determined to achieve her dream of the Docklands flat, on which very little progress has been made. It turns out that the contracts had been sent to the wrong solicitors, and no one had bothered to chase them up.

I would not want to be in their shoes – Debs is livid, and her unique command of colourful language leaves them in no doubt about her state of mind. She delivers her assessment of their performance in person – Debs is back in action!

Although the negotiations on the flat are kick-started instantly, it was not an easy ride. The seller of the Docklands flat is very shrewd, a lawyer herself I believe, and probably senses how desperate Debs is to clinch the deal. The price rises and an absurd figure is requested for the furniture. Debs agrees, although not without some further demonstration of her in-depth knowledge of profanity.

The estate agents are probably frightened and in awe of this intensely determined, very striking, skinny woman. She probably realizes she is being quite entertaining – years later I will find a note to one of them in thanks, and promising to send him a couple of her articles ridiculing the estate agency profession!

5 March 2000

Sue and I have at last found a larger house, and our transactions are equally fraught. At the start of March we had no idea whether we would be moving with Debs or without. We had no completion date, and couldn't make any start on packing because there was no space to put anything.

17 March 2000

I come home from work to an e-mail:

Subject: A moving story

Phew. Despite last minute hassle re release of keys, am finally in new flat. Much of the anticipated furniture isn't, but that's par for the course, & at least I have a lovely sofa. And a cleaner (the human sort) but no cleaner (the Hoover sort), the absence of the latter coming as rather a surprise to the former, who had been assured that it was staying. Still haven't figured out how to work my video entry-phone. Also pissed off by failure of computer to arrive, but compared to the last 9 months these problems are mere chickenshit.

Phone number won't be changed until next week so I'll give it to you when I've got it.

Here beginneth the list of stuff I'd be grateful for car trip to bring …

Microwave
Printer

Hoover

Toastie Sandwich Maker, if we kept this from Church
Path?

Hifi & Speakers

Portable CD player

Time projector clock

Hot water bottle

Juicers(s)

Coffee paraphernalia (percolator and candle thing,
cups and coffee, electric whicker thing)

Bottles of bubbly (four?)

Bathroom stuff (on shelf)

Extension lead and adapters

PSU for Psion (plugged in downstairs)

Peppermint Oil and Lactaid

Palm V (& docking cradle - beside your PC)

HP Palmtop (& docking cradle)

Other mobile phone

Other Psion (on table)

Universal remote

Mini TV

Black clipboard thing on table

2 bottles of shampoo (in bedroom)

Odd bits of jewellery etc

Small orange-coloured 16 Meg Psion disc on table

Debenhams Direct catalogue

La Redoute catalogue

Can I have your Argos catalogue, because it's
probably nearer for you to pick up a new one?
I am nowhere near an Argos unless I go back out

to Hammersmith or Shep Bush Green.
Clothes (in bags, some on bed & jackets etc on
hangers)
Grey furry coat
Scarves (on chair downstairs & in bedroom)
Remote control adapter (it is stuck behind that
white cabinet in the bedroom with the heater plugged
into it) and remote control handset (on bed)
Passport (on top of accounts stuff box)
Cuddly Toy!

Shit, that sounds like loads ... hope you don't mind.
Can I leave my accounts stuff with you until you
move? I guess the other piles of documents/papers
etc could come down & I'll sort through them when I
have time.

Also do you mind collecting a telly from John
Lewis's? It's all paid for, etc, but I don't stand a
cat in hell's chance of being able to carry it
anywhere, put it on stand etc.

And so Debs is gone. This list is the sum total of the possessions she started her new life with – plus the audio cassettes from her teenage years.

She was never to come back to Aylesbury.

Part Four

A Fresh Start

Thirty-four

In the third week of March 2000, Debs finally moved out. She had spent 267 days with us in Aylesbury, during which we had nursed her slowly back from the brink.

It was another new start. And another new home. Her move to Docklands wasn't without hassle, but it made entertaining copy for friends and commissioning editors following the saga on Debs' daily e-mails.

```
Having just increased my offer by 12 (yes, 12)
thousand to stop my vendor pulling out on the deal,
I got the list of Fixtures and Fittings yesterday -
apparently the daft cow wants 20 quid for a TOILET
ROLL HOLDER. She can stick it up her arse for all I
care. Highlight of the whole business so far - apart
from persuading Clive Anderson to witness my mortgage
deed, on account of him being the only other
solicitor I know who I don't want to see ritually
disembowelled - has been walking across town carrying
ten grand in real folding picture-of-the-Queen type
money because my bank wouldn't do an electronic funds
thingy after 2pm. You don't half feel like an extra
from Pulp Fiction. If I'd only had the Uzi and Harvey
Keitel to match I'd have gone round to my solicitor's
office and let her have both barrels through the
```

ribcage. Fuck foxhunting, it's flathunting that's the
really cruel sport - ah well, back to my ES property
supplement to check out other potential abodes for
when this all DOES fall apart ...

Then great news about the Chiswick flat.

Unbelievably, we finally completed on the sale at
5.30pm today (only 8 months! Must be a record). After
buyer no 1 (ran off to Spain), and buyer no 2 (were
buying for student daughter who fucking well dropped
out) did the dirty on me, buyer no 3 (appears to have
financial arrangements similar to Lester Piggott. And
has taken 3 weeks to come up with deposit) finally
hands over the cash. Huzzah. Not sure whether this
is good or bad ... means we CAN now exchange on the
purchase, but since we HAVEN'T, it makes me officially
homeless as of 17th March.

Hmmm. Please address all cheques, commissions etc to
No Fixed Abode, 3rd Jaffa Oranges Box from the left,
Oddbins Doorway, Puddle-of-Urine-on-Thames,
Cardboard City DSS1 P45.

I *think* this is progress. I'm still not paying 20
quid for a bog roll rack tho'.

Sue and I delivered some items in two car loads, and saw
the flat for the first time. It was a very trendy ex-wharf
development, with a central courtyard, underground

parking, and fully equipped fitness centre and pool. We were pleased for her, and she was evidently very happy. It was a Sunday, and we had arranged to meet her at the back of John Lewis in Oxford Street to collect the TV. It would have helped if she had checked that John Lewis was open.

In that first week Debs was in full swing, pitching, writing, researching, doing what she enjoyed most. Her move coincided with our own. We bought a house across town in Aylesbury, right near Stoke Mandeville Hospital. I was packing up amid cardboard boxes when I got a frantic call. She was surrounded by flat-pack furniture, but didn't have a screwdriver – hers had somehow gone missing. In my own turmoil I e-mailed her, trying to give her support and expressing my feelings about the trauma we had lived through in those last nine months:

```
Subject: Ex files and screwdrivers

Hi,
… I suppose you posh Londoners don't use
screwdrivers (except for cracking car door locks
and scratching down the side of expensive BMWs -
especially now). All of yours were nicked, which
was a shame, 'cos I would have nicked them if the
cleaners hadn't. Especially the electric
screwdriver.

This week I've felt, I suppose, how a parent feels
when an offspring leaves home for the first time.
```

```
I haven't had to cope with that before. It's a
strange feeling, and I have really missed you. I may
not have seen much of you the last few weeks, but you
were there, and it was strangely comforting to hear
you come in at night. We've never really had the
opportunity to spend time together - I only wish
there was more.

PLEASE take care of yourself. If nothing else, I
hope that these last few months have shown you that
there are people who really care about you, and are
always here for you when you need us. Don't leave it
so long again before asking for help, or just
phoning for a chat. (Have you got a new number yet?)

Hope you get some sleep this weekend ...
See you soon
Peter xxxx
```

That was it. End of the episode. Time to move on.

I had gained a daughter and, I hoped, a friend. I tried to repress any inner fears about her illness and prayed this was the start of a new, lasting relationship for both of us.

I was only ever to see her once again.

Thirty-five

Moving out gave Debs fresh impetus to sort out her life. She quickly put the conveyancing hassles behind her and was a proud property owner again, enjoying the creative joys of making a home, choosing furniture and organizing her domestic life afresh.

```
Bruce ...
Thank you SO much for the lovely flahs. Yer a gent.
I don't deserve 'em, guv, not an 'umble East End
girl like me.
```

She was determined to kick-start her social life too. Living with dad had its obvious restrictions on freedom, plus of course the sheer impracticality of living so far out of town. But, as always, work was the priority – and she threw herself into it.

She had her regular commitments – columns in the *Sun*, *Punch*, spicing up links for TV shows, fairly regular requests from Clive Anderson for topical material for his after-dinner circuit, plus articles for various magazines; but she wanted more.

She fired off barrages of e-mails: to Radio 4's *Loose Ends*; to Planet 24, an independent production company; to a comedian who was writing a column for a website ('This e-mail guaranteed virus-free – I always wipe my outbox thoroughly on exit, and never leave my files unzipped in public areas'); rattling off more ideas to the *Sun* (amongst the possible subjects: 'It's rich, it's thick, it's full of fat, and it needs a good slap on the bottom to get the most out of it. And it's just had a face lift. No – NOT Vanessa. Heinz Salad Cream. WHY WE STILL LOVE HEINZ SALAD CREAM?' She also suggested a piece for Mother's Day on 'Why Your Mum is Better Than Your Man', which got a positive response: 'Can we do the Mother's Day one please? Sounds like a laugh! Luckily my mother is going away the night before Mothers Day – so I don't have to cook for her! hurrah', to which Debs replied: 'Sure thing. The nearest I'll ever get to cooking for mine is shoving her head in a gas oven …'); pitching to the Royal Society for the Prevention of Accidents; and again to the *Sun* with suggestions on what Tony and Cherie Blair might call their imminent new-born (the suggestions included 'MANCHESTER UNITED: President Clinton's daughter shares her name with a Pre-miership football club, so why shouldn't the Blairs go one better? Young Man U. Blair would surely be a winner in life – and if she's a girl, a lucrative marriage to Brooklyn Beckham would be a dead cert').

To *The News Huddlines* – the show that gave her that first break when she was at school – she was still offering a mountain of topical gags ('The Australian Olympic team have posed nude for publicity photos. Apparently they just misunderstood the concept of the Five Rings'; 'Barbara Cartland passed away at the age of 98. Friends say it was totally unexpected – the day before she went she was absolutely in the pink'; 'Hugh Grant is splitting with his girlfriend. Apparently he just doesn't have enough energy to get up Hurley in the morning' ...).

As well as dreaming up a constant stream of gags and one-liners, Debs was as usual also responding to whatever was on the radio. In fact, she was such a frequent contributor that all the presenters felt they knew her personally, even though few did. In May she put herself in the shoes of an American in London, when submitting links for *The Jerry Springer Show* ('TV here is totally unlike America. Over here the programmes are longer than the adverts'; 'I even went to the ballet. Don't look at me like that ... ballet is no job for wimps. You need INCREDIBLY strong arms to be a professional ballerina. All that sticking-your-finger-down-your-throat – it's not easy, you know...'), an assignment that earned her thousands of pounds. But such was her zeal for work that when the *London Evening Standard* approached her to submit regular technical articles on Information Technology she readily agreed for a fraction of the money she could earn from TV. Her commissioning editor there was Mark Hughes Morgan, who got in touch with her by e-mail after someone on a computer magazine recommended her. He recalls: 'Her copy was very enjoyable – a rarity in people writing about techie things – but it was often a bit hyper, coming out like machine-gun

fire. And it was filed at odd times – sometimes 3 or 4 in the
morning.'

Soon after commissioning her, Mark invited her to lunch
at Kensington Place near the *Standard* offices. Unaware of
her condition, he was completely taken aback.

> A puff of wind would have blown her away. Lunch was
> uncomfortable for her and quite disturbing for me. I was
> worried that if she drank wine she would keel over. In fact
> she had a glass or two. She ordered a salad, but I don't
> know if she ate a single leaf. Quite honestly I wondered if
> drugs were involved, she had an occasional sort of loose-
> eyed look about her. It was obviously an effort to
> focus/walk/etc, but she seemed pretty steely.
>
> After, I tried to contact people who knew her to express
> my concern. I just thought someone should do something
> about this.

Subsequent communication between Mark and Debs was
almost entirely by e-mail. They had a comical exchange
when she sent him a photograph of the contents of her
larder, stacked with weight gain supplements. 'Professionally, she was phenomenal, although a lot of the stuff she
wrote was hyper and took a lot of producing. She had this
shtick, which at its best was great, but no one can produce
at that level when she was doing so much and to so many
deadlines. It was obvious she could not switch off. It was
bizarre, given the level of her writing, that she wanted to

write a £400 feature for the *Standard* but she certainly brought life to a potentially dead subject area.'

Never mind how much work she'd got on, Debs would never say no to doing a quick turnaround. The buzz it gave her was immense. Life in a national newspaper office is a cauldron of pressure as journalists work frantically against the clock to fill the paper. Britain's biggest selling daily, the *Sun*, paid Debs around £600 for a feature in the Women's section. But they also knew that, when the chips were down they could rely on her to provide entertaining copy at the drop of a hat. Ideas are tossed around at the morning meeting – and sometimes order is thrown out of the window when a story breaks and the editor wants a follow-up – all in time for a mid-afternoon deadline.

```
Date: Tue, 18 Jul 2000
Subject: CALL ME URGENTLY!

13:21
Hi Debs, I can't find you anywhere so if you are near
your laptop call me. I need someone to write a piece
on why the male pill can go fuck itself basically!

It's for tomorrow so ARRGGH!


13:37
Okay ... what sort of piece? Quickie points, eg,
'Why The Male Pill Is A Shit Idea' sorta thang?
```

13:48:

The Ed wants to take the line - 'Trust a Man to
take the male pill? You must be bleeding joking!'
and wants a piece written by a woman (you're one
aren't you?) saying that the scientists can produce
these pills but in reality no woman in her right
mind would trust their partner take them.

So you'd need to talk about if a single girl was
on a date and they were getting frisky and the guy
turned round and said: trust me darling I'm on the
pill - what she would think? Also the implications
for other women and also for the men.

It needs to be written in a semi jocular fashion
but also taking in all the social implications etc
etc so semi serious too.

It would be the cover story turning to page five so
would need about 800 words?

Does this all make sense??? What number are you on
by the way???

You are a life saver.

13:56
When's the absolute latest you can take this by?

14:05

Is 4.30pm ok? I can't go later than that. eek!

14:11

4.30pm fine, sure.

15:56

Is it going ok? Do you have everything you need?
Any idea what time you will be filing?? Do I sound
manic????

16:04

Fuck! I already HAVE filed it! Have you not got it?

16:47

Not had your copy! - can I at least call your mobile
to check if you have sent it and you can tell if
I've got it!

16:59

Got it!!! It's brilliant! Took an hour to come
through because it was so chockabloc with great
lines! Thank you thank you thank you!

The piece was actually filed at 15:52:

It's the same old story. A night out, a few drinks, a fumbled grope in the back of a taxi and before you know it your pants are adorning the lampshade and you're flat on your back murmuring those oh-so-important little words. 'It's OK, darling, I'm on the pill.'

Because, hey – you're just a typical guy, right?

Hang on – a typical guy? Correct. Because doctors this week announced '100% successful' trials of the first ever male contraceptive pill. Encouragingly, two in three men said they'd take it. More worryingly, nearly half of all women said they'd trust him if he said he had. I'm warning you now: 'It's OK, darling, I'm on the pill' is set to be the latest addition to the list of Great Lies Men Tell – right up there with 'The cheque's in the post', 'This never normally happens', and 'I had one three feet long, but it got away' (with reference to angling, naturally).

Let's examine the facts. Two-thirds of men say they'd take it. How many of those two-thirds are lying? And how many MORE of them would be lying when they said they HAD taken it, and there was a game of hide the sausage at stake? Obviously, there are guys with a conscience. Guys who will see the male pill as a chance for them to 'do their bit' and take responsibility, without the unwanted having-a-bath-in-a-sou'wester connotations of condom-wearing.

But wise up, girls: if he can't even pop his todger in a little rubber lifejacket before playing sink the submarine, how's he going to feel about shovelling God only knows what kind of chemical cocktail down his throat as a precursor to getting jiggy with it? This is the man who won't go within a 5-mile radius of the doctor's surgery even if his leg's dangling by a single sinew and his head spouting blood like something out of a Quentin Tarantino movie. Do you really think he'll be pitching up at the family planning clinic every month or so, for a repeat prescription at six quid a throw ('Strewth, darlin', you can get three pints for that!' – make it seven pints and you won't need a male contraceptive, since Brewers' Droop will do the job for you).

Research so far is based on a sample group of just sixty men – which is, what, less than Tara Palmer-Tomkinson gets through in a year? – and like any new drug, the male pill is new enough to be potentially risky. Sure, they say it's completely safe. But they said that about thalidomide. And beef. And the Millennium Bridge. And no man I know is going to gamble on something that could muck up his hormones and affect his 'masculinity'.

Being on the male pill would mean having – and admitting to – a sperm count totalling a big fat zero, which in male-bragging terms is like announcing the fact that you drive a Skoda and drink small white wine spritzers instead of pints of Heavy. So if he is taking the pill, girls, watch him like a hawk. He'll probably end up trying to spit instead of swallow.

There are doubtless ways to make the idea of a pill seem more appealing to the average lad-about-town:

market it in 'Vindaloo Flavour', maybe, or have them dispensed not by draconian matrons but by pushers in clubs for a tenner a throw with the promise that 'It'll help you pull, mate'. There's even been talk of administering it via implants, although when it comes to having something fired into their arm down a hypodermic elephant-gun, I suspect that's one form of penetration most guys won't be so enthusiastic about. Or by injections: I can see it now. 'Not to worry, sir, you'll just feel a little prick ...'

But whilst it's all hunky-dory for those shining examples of New Manhood who read Nick Hornby books and knit their own papooses, your average Old Lad is just going to see 'I'm on the male contraceptive' as another easy chat-up line to get gullible birds into the sack – when in reality, he's not on the pill but on the PULL. And what if, despite his best intentions, he simply forgets to take it? Unless it's coupled with an anti-amnesia medication, there's a minefield of uncertainty here.

Then there's the side effects – if it's anything like the female pill, guys all around the country will suddenly start getting bloated, gaining weight and experiencing all kinds of unpleasant mood swings. Although come to think of it ... they do anyway after a couple of jars in the Ferret and Firkin.

And the damn thing takes three months before kicking in, for goodness' sake. How is any man going to remember to start taking his pills three months before having sex? Most of them can't even remember that you're supposed to start the foreplay a bit more than five minutes in advance. OK, three minutes if you forget the pizza.

At the end of the day, it all boils down to the same reason why we've always ended up taking responsibility for contraception. The simple fact that if Mr Sperm and Ms Egg do manage to arrange a romantic head-to-head, who's the one who suffers the consequences? I'll give you two guesses. Clue: it's not him. Until men start getting pregnant, they won't give – literally – a toss about contraception if it could jeopardize their chances of rumpy pumpy. At least if it's me who has to take it, I know I've taken it. And if I'm too drunk to remember, there's always the Morning After Pill – and potentially now, the 'Morning Before Pill' as well.

But even if you trust the guy, do you trust the pill itself? Personally, I'd put no more faith in any new wonderdrug than I would in Gary Glitter to babysit. Particularly not a new wonderdrug that actually claims to be '100% successful'. A typical male boast, and guaranteed to turn out to be a load of old balls. And what about the other risks? The male pill is not, however successful a contraceptive, any defence against AIDS and STDs.

I'm sure there are better methods to stop men from fathering unwanted children. If he's that serious about never skinny-dipping in the gene pool, there's always the good old vasectomy (a snip, compared to all those £6 prescription charges). Failing that, just taking away his other pills would be a start – you know, the little blue ones that 'refresh the parts others fail to reach'? Yeah, Viagra. If this were a bad Hollywood movie, I'd suggest that the male pill was simply a profit-making scam by the manufacturers of anti-impotence drugs to cash in even more – but maybe I've just been watching too much *Mission Impossible 2* with that whole virus/anti-virus blackmail thing.

It's a nice try, and as a supporter of female equality I ought to give it a big thumbs up. But frankly, the male pill is no more likely to be successful than the female condom – and unlike the Femidom, you can't even use it as a spare sleeping bag, rubbish sack or insulation jacket for your hot water tank. No, if the market really is crying out for a guaranteed way to stop men getting women up the duff, I've got a much better – and cheaper – solution. It's called a David Mellor mask, and it's clinically proven, 100% certain to stop any woman going to bed with you.

Thirty-six

Soon after starting her new life in Docklands, Debs received an unexpected blow. Her agent and confidante Rachel Swann unexpectedly wrote to tell her that she was giving up the business to concentrate on her family. Her new agent was Chris Cope, who had been Rachel's assistant at Casarotto Ramsey and Associates for several years but who was now taking over many of her clients. He wrote to Debs explaining the new arrangement, adding that he had managed to negotiate an improved rate for a TV series with ITV – up from £4k to £6k. She replied that she was happy, 'anything for a quiet life', as she put it.

Quiet life! Hardly. The work – and the money were rolling in – as this family e-mail reveals.

```
I was sorting through a pile of stuff this evening
and found just over £17,200 worth of cheques. Yes, I
am a complete fuckwit. Trouble is, one of them is 7
months old. Is this still legal tender? What will
the bank do with it? I normally post cheques to
Sheffield but haven't all the Sheffield banks turned
into one big (black) whole, and will my non-valid
cheque end up being swallowed into it, never to be
seen again? I know cheques do have an Eat Before
date, but I'm never sure what it is.
```

```
Fucking News International owe me over ten grand
too, and I bet they won't pay AT ALL because the
relevant editor has left/been fired, the supplement
barely exists any more and I was way late with my
invoice.

Buggery hell. I *try* to be organized, and look
what happens. Why can't I get a spam filter for my
snail mail like I can for the online stuff? Mind
you, then those shysters at Con-screwya (or what
ever the Royal Mail/Pissed-Office are called now)
would want to charge me 14 quid a week on account of
my not receiving more than 20 items of mail per day.

Aaaargh.
```

It had certainly been a hectic – and lucrative – few months.
Worrying that I had not had any contact with Debs since
we had dropped off her remaining possessions at the flat,
and still coming to terms with her sudden absence from
our lives, I wrote the following:

```
Hi Debs,
I miss you ... really ...

Sorry I haven't got round to ringing again ... this
week has been MAD. These three short weeks have
piled the work up to such an extent that we have
been really struggling. Long nights ... early
mornings ... you know them well!
```

How are you? How's the flat now you've been there a
while? How's the cleaner? I'll call over the next
couple of days to catch up on the gossip.

What do you want me to do with the data on your old
computer and mine? I can dump it all on CD if you
like. Or mail it with a message saying I Love You.

Hope work is OK and that you, in particular, are
feeling good. Is your head OK now (outside - can't
do anything about what's inside - you were born that
way!)?

Look after yourself. Eat well, sleep well and
everything else will take care of itself.

Lots of love
Peter

I don't recall getting a reply. Nothing got in the way of the
whirlwind of work. Shopping trips were rare: Debs purchased virtually everything online – food, goods, even
medication. She constantly complained to Tesco about defi-
ciencies in their online service until, after three months in
her new flat, her frustration boiled over. I can only imagine the reaction of the poor customer services employee
receiving this:

Dear Sir/Madam

I wish to complain, in words which I shall refrain from using here to avoid undue wear and tear on my 'F' key, about the appalling quality of your so-called 'service'.

This has been going on for a number of weeks now. I order approximately 30 pounds worth of groceries from you at least three times a week, and have had problems with approximately one in every two deliveries.

Normally you manage to omit at least one of the items for which I have paid, e.g. not those listed on the receipt as 'unavailable'. In individual cases I am prepared to overlook this, although on one occasion you failed to deliver an entire bag full of items and were not even able to locate them on the van. This meant that not only had I wasted the morning waiting for the delivery, I then had to waste the entire afternoon travelling to the supermarket from which this delivery had come, in order to purchase the missing items. This is not my idea of 'labour saving'.

You have also maintained a consistent 100% success rate at utterly disregarding any comment I append to my order (via the small green pencil icon). I have come to the conclusion that this icon is for decorative purposes only. Perhaps your web designers would like to replace it with something more suitable, such as a small artistic representation of two raised fingers?

The badly chosen, irrelevant, or just plain f***ing stupid substitutions are presumably down to the whim of the picker and as such beyond my control. You will no doubt gain satisfaction from the thought that I now have a small European Food Mountain of unwanted groceries which will at some point be donated to a more deserving cause. I suspect the local junior school Harvest Festival is in for quite a windfall.

Today you managed to surpass yourself. Not only did my order arrive 40 minutes late, I was subsequently informed that my chilled goods had been 'placed in the freezer compartment by mistake'. Since no replacement could be dispatched until the following day, I elected to take the frozen items anyway on the assurance that they were 'not ruined, just frozen' and that I could de-frost them this afternoon.

Naturally, your staff are as incapable of reading the phrase 'Do not freeze!' as they are of reading my appended comments to certain orders. I am now the proud owner of, amongst other things, four large pots of rancid/curdled cream, which is of course completely ruined. As is the occasion for which it was purchased.

I have contemplated consuming this repugnant concoction, which looks and smells (for your information) not dissimilar to certain more obscene bodily excretions, in order to give myself food poisoning and thus sue Tesco for every miserable penny they've got. However, under the circumstances it's not worth the effort. Particularly since I would be unable to order over-the-counter medication for said complaint without it being 'substituted' with something 'reasonable', such as a piece of halibut or tin of pickled gherkins.

I read recently about one dissatisfied Barclays Bank customer who sprayed his local branch with raw sewage in protest at their shoddy service. Had your incompetence not left me so far behind schedule, I would have made an extra trip to Tesco with my inedible dairy produce and deposited it on your premises in a similar manner.

It was recently brought to my attention that Tesco Online has just created another 10,000 jobs. I take it 9,999 of these are in the complaints department, whilst the other will be appointed to the coveted post of Head of Just Generally Pissing People Off For the Sheer Hell Of It?

Meanwhile, next time I encounter someone whose breathtaking stupidity, unhelpfulness and smug self-satisfied arrogance reaches levels I had never before believed humanly possible, I shall naturally be recommending them for a job at Tesco.

Apologies for the lack of goodwill in this letter. Goodwill is currently unavailable, so I have substituted 'extreme annoyance'. In case the above has been a little too subtle for someone of your intellectual level to understand, I shall reiterate: you are a bunch of clueless, cackhanded f***wits who have succeeded in making my life substantially more unpleasant and difficult. Congratulations.

I wish you all the best in your new career, which I hope you will be starting very soon after your speedy dismissal from Tesco.

Kind regards,

Ms D. Barham

There is no record of any reply.

Debs had been in Docklands for nearly four months. She seemed to be on a 'high', with plenty of work and jolly e-mail exchanges with her acquaintances and business contacts. But loneliness was gradually creeping in. She rarely went out socially, but – despite her frail state – she continued her nocturnal beat of cafés in the West End. She had few, if any, 'bosom' friends that she could just call in on and share a bottle of wine with; but she decided to make contact with Scott Colvey, a former boyfriend, whom she'd met online when she was 17 and who was now acting editor of *Computeractive* magazine.

They eventually met at Debs' club, Blacks, where they stayed until 2 a.m. Then, both in a drunken state, they somehow ended up on the roof of Broadcasting House, having successfully avoided all forms of security! Debs managed to blag a BBC car home, emerging from the building saying she'd been working all night and giving some spurious programme code number, while Scott was left to his own devices to get home to West London. His e-mail the afternoon after, tells it all.

```
This morning and I find myself asleep, quite
literally on my doorstep. I stumble around a bit and
then an elderly neighbour appears from nowhere to
help me in and up the stairs. An old codger helping
a fit youth up the stairs - life is not supposed to
```

be this way. This is all your fault. I have to go
and be sick now.

… And just what the fuck did I do to my knee, such
that it hurts to even look at it? And why does my v.
expensive suede jacket now sport two expansive piss-
like stains on the pockets? And how come I took £100
from a hole in the wall at 8:55pm and wake up
shivering the next day with just £3.57 in change? My
evening with you resulted in personal injury and a
quite spectacular loss of earnings. I will sue.

S.

As does Debs' response:

Six o'clock ...
This morning and I decide it's probably time to go
to bed, having spent 90 minutes staring at computer
screen and produced a total of three words. None
of them are in the dictionary (not the English one,
anyway) and neither do they contain any vowels.
There is also what appears to be dribble on my
keyboard (goddamn that Internet porn – those fake
celebrity nudes of Brad Pitt are always my
downfall).

Eight o'clock ... This morning and I wake up,
stagger to the kitchen, drink the equivalent of Lake
Windermere in cold water and try to locate the

source of a pervasive wine-like aroma. Eight fifteen
... And I conclude that the source of the pervasive
wine-like aroma is me. Eight thirty ... And I go
back to bed. Eight forty-five And my dynamic
downstairs DIY-obsessed neighbour starts drilling
holes in his wall. Again. Headache ahoy. Eight
forty-seven And I fall asleep aided by several
Nurofen and another three pints (of water). Eleven
o'clock And I consider getting up because There Is
Work To Be Done. Oddly, I feel not-too-trashed,
provided I don't even think about thinking about
food. Twelve fifteen And the doorbell rings. I flip
on my fancy video-entryphone to reveal a nice beardy
man from Tesco.com come to deliver me thirty quid's
worth of groceries, which I had totally forgotten
about. Suddenly I feel like shite. Twelve twenty
And I give the nice man a large tip in the hope
that this will deflect his attention from the fact
that I'm still wearing a dressing gown, look like
Bela Lugosi in Invasion of the Bodysnatchers and
smell strongly of wine. Twelve twenty-five And I put
the groceries in the fridge. Now I really feel like
shit. What I could do with is some strong black
coffee. What did I forget to order from Tesco.com?
Yup, you're ahead of me here. I go back to bed.
There is Work To Be Done, but fuckit. Six o'clock
In the evening. And I consider getting up. There
is Work To Be ... etc. On the other hand, there is
something inside my head saying 'Tonight, Matthew,
I'm going to be the drummer from AC/DC', the Nurofen
don't appear to be working, I still smell of wine

and my mouth feels like something died in there.
Seven o'clock And I stumble blearily out of bed, find
some clothes (mine, good - cleanish, good), draw the
curtains, check my e-mail and wonder how you managed
to actually be conscious enough to send anything
coherent at 1pm. Seven thirty And I leave the flat,
not smelling so much of wine. However, my bag, I
discover, smells very much of wine, and has a small
European Wine Lake residing at the bottom of it.
There is also a pair of (surprisingly clean) male
underpants on the steps outside my flat. This I hope
is nothing whatsoever to do with last night, but I
think worthy of note since it's not something you
see every day. Well, not since Sam Fox moved out.
Eight pm And I make it as far as Baker Street for
what is the most sublimely, wonderfully, deliciously
welcome cup of coffee I've drunk in weeks. Despite
being produced by Starbucks. I trawl the papers
looking for a subject for next week's column,
wishing I was one of those slackarsed columnists who
just wrote about their own pitiful little boring
life, since I could then write about what I know:
namely, getting slaughtered and smelling of wine. I
notice my bag is given a wide berth by other coffee-
drinkers, although a strange gypsy type lady with no
teeth and a shopping trolley does sidle up and try
to engage me in conversation about My Fortune. She
also smells of wine. A kindred spirit indeed. I
suspect she may have been me in a past life. Ten
thirty pm And I finally feel almost human again.
However, my bag still smells of wine and so (I

realize) does my very wonderful, very expensive
(despite being second-hand) very comfortable Harrods
sofa, on which I dumped my bag last night.
Fortunately the cleaner comes tomorrow, and she
KNOWS I'm a pisshead.

This is ALL your fault. I shall be consulting
Autonomy with regard to whether it's worth suing you
or not. Deb.

Last word from Scott:

Yeah. Still, it was a laff.

Thirty-seven

The parties at *Punch* were always wild boozy affairs, paid for by the magazine's proprietor, Mohammed Al Fayed. As a *Punch* columnist, Debs decided she would now make a rare public appearance to wine, if not dine, at her boss's expense and enjoy the company of her colleagues.

Among the fellow partygoers was John McVicar, a former armed robber turned journalist who, according to his website, 'brings the same attitude to journalism that he had in crime'. No prisoners, presumably. Despite sharing the columns of the esteemed journal, he had never met Debs – until, that is, he spotted her across the room with a drink in her hand. 'I saw this stick insect, so I merely rushed over to make some brutal joke. I said: "If you are going to kill yourself, why don't you use drugs, it's far more pleasurable."' Her response was typical Debs – quick, deflective and funny. 'It's a lot cheaper.'

The exchange was the start of an intense friendship in which John tried desperately to help Debs overcome her illness. Delving through her e-mail correspondence from the autumn of 2000 and the winter of 2001, it is clear he gave his heart and soul to try to halt her decline, and for that I will always be extremely grateful.

After the *Punch* party, he called her and left a message.

She replied by e-mail.

```
Hey there - thanks for the call.
Yes, I'm fine and managed to make it home without
losing a) consciousness, b) my credit cards, c) my
way, d) all remaining dignity or e) the contents of
my stomach in the back of any taxis. The only item I
did manage to lose was a small but vital piece of
computer cable, which subsequently turned up down
the back of the Punch sofa (Christ only knows what
else is down there … a couple of ex-editors, I
suspect, and a few million rejected cartoons dating
back to the 1840s) …
```

Over the weeks they met occasionally for drinks and games of Scrabble, competitive affairs between two excellent word-smiths. Their friendship grew alongside concerns about her health. John was aware that she had tried therapy, which had failed miserably, and that she also found relationships difficult. A fitness instructor with a degree in sociology, he felt that her womanhood had been suppressed by her psychological complexities. He wanted her to love her body, not reject it; to cherish intimacy, rather than allow her insecurities to squash it. And the first step was exercise.

Twenty minutes a day would, he told her, regenerate what her degenerate habits had run down, build her character, and kick-start her metabolism and appetite. He suggested she join his gym at Battersea Arena, invest in a rowing machine for use at home, and begin a course of protein and vitamin supplements along with body-building milkshakes – easier to digest, and probably better for her than her usual intake of carrot and tomato juice. He would oversee her exercise programme.

It must have been a strange sight for the gym regulars – a strapping six-foot man of steel barking orders at a five-stone 'walking skeleton' in a skimpy tracksuit and trainers. His determination that she should enjoy exercise was matched by her determination not to.

Having once been sentenced to twenty-six years in prison, John was used to single-minded personal challenges and was a patient, well-meaning, but formidable trainer. As he told the congregation at her funeral service: 'I think everyone has got a bit of a prison warder in them, a screw, and I certainly have. There is nothing I like more than training people. I got her on the Concept rowing machine and I really did push her. I had a heart rate monitor on her one day and I didn't tell her this, but her heart bombed up to 180. At one stage I was pushing her along as she was rowing and she suddenly stopped in the middle of the gym and said: "Fuck Off."'

Away from the gym, Debs was sweating over her workload, which was as demanding and compulsive as ever. She spent Christmas 2000 at home, working day and night to meet deadlines, which even included a magazine article about fellatio. Some of her pleas to editors *for more time* were bordering on frantic. John McVicar was appalled at her punishing work regime and spelled out to her that she was gravely ill and slowly killing herself. The gym sessions were gradually drying up; and he told her that witnessing her walk up the stairs of his apartment was like watching someone climb Mount Everest without oxygen. She called the ascent 'Death Flight 103'.

The next time he saw her was a few weeks later at the launch of a book by David Price, one of the lawyers in the infamous David Shayler case when *Punch* was taken to court by the Government. Debs had sat through some of the hearing and had got to know the defence lawyers quite well. John McVicar noticed she'd lost weight between Christmas and the New Year. The day after the party, he phoned the *Punch* editor, James Steen, a good friend of both John and Debs, to express his concern. James had also been shocked at her emaciated state.

Neither James nor John had first-hand experience of dealing with anorexia. However, they were both aware of people who had died from the disorder. As a 17-year-old working in a Bernie Inn, James had worked alongside a waitress who was anorexic. What had touched him then was how, despite struggling physically, she was determined to work. There was a kind of parallel with Debs.

John too had witnessed the heartbreak the disorder brings. He told Debs about a woman patient he saw when visiting a friend in hospital. He used to watch her eating with her father, who never noticed that all she consumed was mushroom soup. The father assumed that, as she was in hospital, his daughter was being cared for. In fact when she was weighed she always drank five cups of water to trick the scales; and after visits she would walk around the ward perimeter in a frenzy to burn off calories. She died in her mid twenties of a heart attack. Her case made him frightened for Debs.

James and John could not stand by and watch Debs kill herself. Soon after the book launch, the three met in a bar in the basement of a hotel in Marylebone Road. James, of course, already knew about her illness. But it was the first time he became aware of Debs' frenetic lifestyle and work pattern. Over white wine and her trademark black coffee, the men hammered home their concern and made it clear they would do anything to help her. Debs was openly touched by the gesture. She cried a little, cracked a few jokes about her pathetic condition, but was adamant that she wasn't going to seek help.

John and James then hatched a plan to try to 'trick' Debbie into eating. They arranged a series of regular informal dinner parties for just the three of them, with the men sharing the cooking. They would chat, gossip, drink, and eat. John and James hoped that the friendly atmosphere might somehow result in Debs actually getting something inside her. It was amateur psychology, naive, but dreamed up with absolutely the best intentions.

They were a fearsome partnership – James, a Fleet Street journalist and magazine editor, who had taken on the might of the British establishment, and John, once Public Enemy Number One, and the subject of a 'Wanted: Dead or Alive' notice. But they were taking on a highly intelligent, stubborn, and manipulative opponent who'd already seen off several therapists armed with every professional trick in the book.

Their first supper-club date was at James's place just off Clapham Common. They discussed the menu in advance. Believe it or not, Debs said she wasn't fussy, and that she liked most things. John, a nutrition expert, advised James on what to prepare and they settled on seafood risotto. John turned up with a bag of mussels and James laced the risotto with hundreds of hidden calories – half a pack of butter and huge dollops of cream.

She arrived late. Physically, she looked more like a 90-year-old than a woman in her early twenties and had to be carried from the table to go to the loo upstairs.

The pair adopted a sort of 'Good Cop, Bad Cop' routine. James's layman assessment was that they were dealing with a case of arrested development. He detected a girl trapped in the body of a woman, a wounded child stuck at an emotional age of 13 or 14. While James tried to win her confidence with a concerned, softly-softly approach, John delivered brutal but honest home truths.

James recalls: 'It was a nice atmosphere and the conversation flowed. I was concerned to find the root of her illness. I saw it more as baby steps but John was more cajoling. He wanted her to commit to something.'

As she pushed a mussel around her plate for half an hour, John interrogated her like a detective questioning a suspect: 'Do you want to die, do you? Look at me Debs, I'm asking you. Do you *want* to die?'

John asked her if she had made a will. She replied with a joke.

'Seriously. No? You have got to do one. You are killing yourself so you have got to do it.'

The supper ended in tears but she said she really appreciated their help and agreed to more dates. They met for these dinners twice a week, with Debs always arriving late and playing cat and mouse with the patience and tolerance of her friends. The driving force of anorexia is control – and she was in the driving seat. James says: 'One time at John's place she turned up at 10.30 for a nine o'clock start. It was her way of controlling us, sending a text message saying she was on her way, would be there in half an hour and turning up one and a half hours later.'

James would praise her for munching a few morsels; John was more sceptical about achieving any success. James remembers: 'Stupidly I remained optimistic. In February 2001, the morning after one of our dinners, Debbie e-mailed me to say she was feeling frail, but positive.' She wrote:

```
Progress report. Still alive, despite John's
predictions. I'm not going before the Queen Mother
and General Pinochet, I swear. I think I had a
little bit of a breakthrough today. I got home
feeling rotten (that's not the good bit. The good
```

```
bit is coming), so I thought I'll have something to
eat. So I had a rice pudding. And for the first time
in - ooh, ages - I actually enjoyed the sensation. I
didn't feel guilty about what I was doing. I ate
MORE … I had some fruit smoothie as well - I was
really craving sweet stuff.
```

How much of the above is true, or merely telling James what he wanted to hear, is hard to gauge. James says: 'Her ambition in life was to eat something on impulse rather than under supervision and she seemed pleased with the way things were going.'

'It was as though a little window had opened up,' she confided to James. 'I was suddenly able to eat normally and fast (eat fast, I mean, not fast as in eat nothing). I don't know whether the window will stay open or, like so many windows these days, end up being sealed shut again by some psychological equivalent of an Everest double-glazing salesman. But God, I hope it won't.'

She certainly appeared to be in the mood for at least going to restaurants. In one week she dined at the Groucho Club with her friend and radio producer Bruce Hyman and sent out a celebratory invitation to dinner to her scriptwriting mate John Langdon.

Dear Mr/Mrs/Ms/Rev/Sir/Anything but Doctor
LANGDON

You are cordially invited to an

'At Death's Door'

to celebrate the sad passing of
some actual food into D. A. Barham
(May She Ingest In Peace)

Bring Your Own Bodily Hangups
Complimentary little things on sticks (i.e. Debbie)
will be circulated After-thinner speeches will be given by
friends of the decreased-in-weight

Cocktails: told until novelty of old Huddlines joke wears off.

Disease of the Day: Hungry 'n' Ghoulish

Time: 30 minutes after arranged. Obviously.

Dress code: Sindy's castoffs or Posh Spice's out-shrunks. Or
trad. Langdonian.

Venue: Probably Not Big-Uns Ribs

Starters at 9 pm, Main Corpse at 5 stone. Dancing Until Legs
Ulcerate and Ooze Fetid Oedematic Fluid
No Fucking Taxis at 11 pm.

If wet, you are probably Hugh Grant or John Selwyn
Gummer.

Toasts: To John Diamond, who like all the best diamonds is
now buried underground.

As for the supper club, it could not last. The whole point had been to get her to open up about the cause of her illness. She never did. And she was cheating her friends (and ultimately herself) when they weren't around. While she maintained that the dinners were helping her, the truth was that she was getting worse. John told her after one dinner that her face was like a death mask, that her body was devouring itself, and that she looked like she was going to die any day. He accepted he was no longer on a therapeutic mission, more a friend of a victim of a grotesque illness driven by emotional forces beyond her control and who would now have to be responsible for her own actions.

She replied: 'Oh, John, I can't respond to this now am just going to bed. But I HAVEN'T lost the will to eat. I had more to eat tonight. I didn't feel about the oil in the risotto the way I would normally be averse to it. I thought the meal was delicious. It made me think I really CAN change my attitude to food, conquer the irrationalities etc., try to stop getting depressed about work, though I'm the last person who can justifiably say that.'

As if to prove her point, she arranged an appointment with yet another eating disorder specialist, this time in Highgate – the subject of a round-robin e-mail to her inner circle of concerned friends.

Have now been to see posh and fearsomely Jewish
Highgate doctor. Jolly convenient for the Cemetery,
I suppose. Am now very glad I did, despite obvious

reticence. He is brilliant - no bollocks, straight
up. Really like his manner. Very different from most
of the other medical personnel who've seen me. He
did the customary weights (5 and a half in clothes -
actually a little better than I anticipated) blood
tests etc, and reckons I can definitely be treated on
an outpatient basis by being referred to a
nutritionist… Anyway the Doc is hoping to find a
suitable nutri person. I await his call. And
presumably the results of the bloods as well. They
always take such a LOT. Surely in my case I need as
much of the stuff as possible? Perhaps they'll give
it me back in a Thermos when they've finished with
it. Or at least bung me some free Children's Organs
(congratulations, it's a perfect fit) as compensation …

John felt that by agreeing to see a nutritionist, Debs was deluding herself. He compared it to someone on judicial review going to the Citizens Advice Bureau for legal advice. She was failing to address the central emotional issues. James says: 'John slowly lost confidence. He spoke to experts and as a result felt we were wasting our time. I felt we were getting somewhere. But then she started lying to us, saying she had eaten things when we knew she hadn't. Also her illness was getting to me. My first thought every day was Debbie's eating problem. A friend who is in Alcoholics Anonymous told me Debbie's condition was making ME ill. I was mentally drained and became exhausted by the whole experience.'

Gradually, personal contact with James and John, and with the Highgate doctor, dried up. Debs was consuming just enough to survive, but was inflicting hidden and fatal long-term damage on her organs. In a eulogy to Debs at her funeral, John McVicar said: 'She was in the thrall of this and she couldn't do much about it. We tried and we failed. She did get on with her life and for that I will always remember and love her.'

Thirty-eight

In early May 2001 I became determined to see Debs, partly to check on how she was, and partly because I had missed her. I e-mailed to say I would be in London, and asked if we could meet, either at the flat or elsewhere. She was evasive to start with, then accepting.

The Thursday that I had suggested was a Tube strike day, so that was no use, but the Friday seemed possible. She wouldn't commit to a time or place, and on the Friday morning I felt like a villain waiting for instructions on where to make a drop with a brown envelope. Just as I was about to leave to catch the train, the rendezvous details arrived by e-mail. We were to meet at the Tate Modern at lunchtime. As I travelled in to London on the train, I was not at all certain that she would turn up.

I was early reaching the gallery, on the south bank of the Thames adjacent to the new Millennium Footbridge. We were to meet outside, and then go to the café on the top floor, from where you have a stunning view across the river towards St Paul's Cathedral. I waited in the sunshine outside – it was a lovely warm day, and although it wasn't busy there were plenty of tourists milling about. I watched out for Debs, but I didn't know what I was looking for. Many taxis came and went, and I must have waited for over half an hour before I spotted her – or at least I thought I did. The familiar all-black, long skirts of the past had been replaced by a gold mini-skirt, maroon strappy top, and noticeably thick tights. She spotted me and strode purposefully across from the taxi, looking slightly self-conscious, but with a smile. I kissed her on the cheek, but didn't risk a hug – she seemed a bit tense, but we chatted freely as we took the lift up to the top floor, squeezed together amongst the Japanese tourists listening intently to their audio commentaries.

For the whole afternoon we sat and chatted over several cappuccinos and chocolate cake for me, just cranberry juice for Debs. I have never felt so relaxed and at ease with her, and she seemed the same. She was bubbly, open, not at all evasive. There was constant eye contact and she looked well and happy. We chatted about everything, from work to politics, her cats, her cleaner, and current events, and she asked with genuine interest about everyone in the family. She didn't talk much about her own work, but then she never had done. It was clear enough that she was busy, and happily so.

Debs did not want to eat anything there, and after five hours we got the message that if we weren't going to buy anything else we should move on. At no time had Debs given the impression that she was in a hurry, or wanted to leave, which was unusual.

We continued chatting as we took the lift back to the ground floor and walked up the ramp into the sunshine. I was mentally tossing up in my mind how to say goodbye, but with a couple of throw-away words she was off – striding towards the nearest taxi. Before I knew it, she was gone. She never looked back.

I never saw her alive again.

Thirty-nine

Debs once said that her illness was the only thing she would ever allow herself to fail at. For most of the time anorexia was an obstacle to negotiate around, not a barrier to crash into. A perfectionist in every way, she had become an expert on control – knowing exactly how much, and when, to eat simply to stay alive. But what she couldn't control was a return of ulcers on her legs. She endured several transfusions, in an attempt to increase nutrients in the blood, joking to friends from hospital that she was in for an oil change.

In terms of income, this had been the best period of her life, and she seemed to all the world to be on a high. Portraits taken for the *Sun* and used in many of the obituaries and tributes show a beautiful, elegant woman. She spent over £12,500 on cosmetic dentistry to repair her decaying teeth – probably the result of her parsimonious diet and damage to the tooth enamel from frequently being sick over the years.

But the lack of mobility caused by her ulcerated legs damaged her morale.

Clive Coleman, an admirer of her work during their time on *Huddlines*, contacted her to add some depth to the main character of a BBC television sitcom of his centred on the world of barristers called *Chambers*. They met up at Television Centre to discuss the project. She ordered a black coffee with literally a spec of milk. He never used a line of her work. Worse, he received distressing e-mails from her saying she'd lost the use of her legs. He was so concerned that he contacted her local Social Services department, asking them to visit her. They did, but she refused to let them into her flat, fobbing them off with some excuse.

Obsessively immersed in her work, she went to ground, ignoring e-mails and phone calls, striving to achieve impossible deadlines. Her demons were unpredictable. Spells of small weight gain were followed by weeks of weight loss.

By the beginning of 2003, Debs had descended into another and, as it proved, final health crisis. Her weight had slumped to four and a half stone again, a critically dangerous level at which many human beings cease to function. On a rare visit out, she visited a doctor about various ailments brought on by her anorexia. Sleep was a major problem, along with constipation, stomach pains, and premenstrual tension, even though her periods had long ceased. With so little muscle protection, her skin was frequently sore at the various contact points. When registering at the surgery, Debs gave her Aunt Melanie as next of kin, even though of course both Ann and myself were still alive. Why she did this is hard to guess.

Debs had always been close to her aunt, in whom she confided and whom she felt was on her level. As a troubled teenager she had sought her advice before telling her mother that she wanted to leave school. Melanie had also put her up when she first came to London and the pair had met sporadically over the years when Debs' extensive work regime allowed.

Shortly after moving to Docklands, Debs entertained her aunt at home; they talked into the evening, drinking wine and eating chocolates, and Debs entertained Melanie with her latest gadget – a voice-activated robotic dog. Later, Debs would arrive at Kew by taxi at Christmas or New Year with a bottle of champagne as a gift for her favourite aunt, looking painfully thin but, with unflagging energy, sitting up late with Melanie's husband Owen discussing electronics and computers.

Perhaps by giving Melanie's name she secretly hoped that the doctor would contact her and raise the alarm about her condition. This in fact is precisely what the doctor did. The medic took the unethical step of contacting Melanie on an 'off the record', basis, without Debs' permission, and expressed extreme concern at her malnutrition.

Melanie needed to see Debs in person without raising suspicion that the doctor had broken a confidence. So she wrote to Debs saying she needed urgent one-to-one advice about a problem with her daughter Faye's schooling. Although this was true, it provided a perfect cover for Melanie to see for herself the state Debs was in.

On seeing her niece, Melanie was shocked and concerned in equal measure. Afterwards, she sent a long, plaintive e-mail saying she had never written anything in her life upon which so much hung. She said she'd been doing some research and had discovered that beneath four to four and a half stone, the body virtually packs up.

Melanie warned Debs that she was now critically ill, and possibly days away from the point of no return. 'I don't want to lose you and I know you don't want to lose you either,' she wrote.

Melanie begged Debs to seek help and offered to accompany her to a private clinic to ensure that nobody manoeuvred her into anything that was against her will. This was the first time that Melanie had actively intervened beyond offering advice in a low-key way. Debs would cut people off if they interfered, and although there was considerable trust between her and her aunt, Melanie had never been sure how far she could push it.

Debs' reply was typically defiant and illustrates the impossible position that faced everyone who tried to help her.

```
Date:     Tues 04 March 2003
From:     D.A. Barham
Subject:  Re: Support etc


Dear Melanie,
Thank you for being so supportive. I really DO
appreciate it, and the first thing I'll say is that
I'd love us to meet up on a more regular basis.
Weekly if necessary - so that you can 'keep tabs' on
me.


But as for clinics, therapists, medical personnel
etc ... No. I can't stress this enough. I am NOT
```

prepared to visit any more clinics, either with or without a chaperone. I've been feeling so much better during the past couple of days, my appetite is coming back.

I've finally got a bit of a breathing space work-wise and I'm feeling far more motivated. And hungry, which is the more important thing.

This is something only 'I' can fix. And I can fix it. External interference just antagonizes me. If anything, it'll drive me in the opposite direction, because I'm stubborn like that. I have fortnightly appointments with the doctor anyway, so at least I'm not completely off the radar, medically speaking.

And believe me (this isn't necessarily an excuse, merely an observation) I've been in an infinitely worse state than this in the past. Last month was a definite 'down' curve, and you happened to encounter me at the nadir of it – I am now on an 'up', and convinced that it will continue in the same direction.

And I've still got a big supply of protein powder, Complan and 'Olympian Crash Weight Gain Formula' which I had from a couple of years ago and resort to if I feel really unable to eat anything else.

This is obviously a psychological thing – and the key with anything psychological is positivity. Going

to any kind of clinic, support group, what-have-you
- however well intentioned - will kill that
positivity STONE DEAD.

Don't make me do it. If you have my best interests
at heart, which I'm 110% certain you do, otherwise
you'd not have made such an effort and written me
such a lengthy e-mail - then you'll understand and
not try to push me down this path.

You can't push me anyway, because I'm fucking stubborn
when I want to be. And I'll only end up exerting more
energy fighting YOU as well as my own ... demons,
insecurities, whatever you want to call them.

Stay in touch. Please. Keep caring. Be supportive. I
need that. But this is MY PROBLEM. I've seen enough
therapists etc in the past 5 years to convince me
that they are, universally, the wrong option, and
will merely exacerbate the situation.

Let me take things easy for a while. Let me eat, let
me sleep, let me have some breathing space and give
myself a bit of TLC.

If you don't want to lose me, THAT'S the way to go
about it. Oh, and TRUST me.

And I'm not normally as low as 4/4.5st - that's
what comes of a week on an involuntary soup fast.
And obviously when I'm this low, it's relatively

quick to reverse the process and stabilize at a
higher (not that MUCH higher, I'll admit - but
higher nevertheless, and thus safer) weight.

I'm not saying 'stop worrying' - you're right to
worry, but please, try to feel that some of your
worry is reassured by the fact that I'm answering
this straight away (so hey, I'm still in the land of
the living).

Sorry if I've tended to go a bit quiet on you in the
past. Consider me 'missing, presumed fed' if I do it
again, but I'll try my utmost not to.

But no doctors and no clinics and no anything else
that might come under the same umbrella. I can't say
that strenuously enough. NO. NO. NO. NO. NO. I am
screaming this from every last pore and particle in
my body, and if you continue trying to persuade me,
I WILL go silent on you and disappear. I know you
don't want that, and neither do I. Don't make me
waste energy arguing over this.

The last thing I want you to think is that I'm
spurning your help, but at the end of the day I DO
know what works and what doesn't. You have to trust
me. I DO care about my health, more so than you
might think.

If I say anything else, I'm just going to be
repeating myself. And wasting energy in the process.

I hope this reassures rather than antagonizes you,
which is the last thing I want to do.

Please stay in touch, and I promise to do likewise.

Cheers
Deb

Melanie discussed Debs' e-mail with Ann. They concluded that forcing her into hospital might save her body but
would destroy her self-respect to such an extent that her
spirit would be broken – her independence and freedom
seemed more vital to her than health and long life. I would
have agreed, though I was not consulted or informed of
this downturn in her condition.

But there was a crumb of a concession. Her refusal was
no longer a dismissive, humorous brush-off. Instead her
reply was a cry from the heart, acknowledging the risk of
death and begging Melanie to accept fears and feelings she
could not hope to understand: 'Let me take things easy for
a while. Let me eat, let me sleep, let me have some breathing space and give myself a bit of TLC,' Debs had written;
yet her work schedule was as hectic as ever. *Celebrity Driving School*, Olivier Awards, books, regular columns for
newspapers and the www.bluesq.com website, radio work
… it was unrelenting. Yet she constantly pushed for more.

There was not much Melanie could do except take up
Debs' offer of 'keeping tabs'. Melanie hoped that, in time,
she might gain her niece's confidence enough to persuade

her to accept medical intervention. Melanie insisted that Debs 'check in' every day and meet up every couple of weeks. If she did not call, text, or e-mail, Debs agreed that Melanie could raise the alarm.

So began the strangest, most intense two months. Each day a text or e-mail arrived, including one day: 'In the immortal words of John Major, I'm still here.' The correspondence gradually turned into a flood of longer e-mails, complete with digital photos of bread, cakes, cats, scones, and domestic equipment.

Aunt and niece became extremely close. It was as if Debs was resigned to her fate and yearned to turn the clock back, trying to rekindle some of the magic innocence of her childhood – discussing the wonders of the natural world, hoping to reclaim the part of adolescence that had been cut short by her running away to London and lying about her age.

Melanie says: 'She entirely suppressed and "lost" the second part of her adolescence, the time when you are neither adult nor child, and feel like setting the world to rights and do not mind whether people think you foolish. Yet for about four years she had to maintain with almost everyone she knew in London the careful front of an older person. It is one thing not to be age-labelled, quite another not to allow any clue to your age to slip out.'

Melanie speculates that this disrupted adolescence might have been a factor in her developing anorexia. During the early years of the illness she noticed that some parts of

Debs' emotional make-up seemed not to have developed and even almost to have reversed. Melanie avoided discussing work because, whenever she did so, Debs would slip into a 'pseudo-older' persona, which was more tense and harsh, almost angry.

'Watching other adolescents grow up, if I had to name just one emotion typical of the "up and down" adolescent years it would probably be "anger". It is striking to reflect that this very anger, artificially prolonged, was part of what continued to fuel her writing.'

Now, with Debs gravely ill, Melanie was 'talking her way through' this missed-out stage of development. They met on Saturdays in cafés and had long, rambling conversations about 'life, the universe and everything' – a phrase they borrowed from Debs' childhood hero Douglas Adams.

In e-mails, they tried to relate to each other the sounds and senses of their respected worlds, the aroma of coffee, freshly baked bread, the splash of the fountain down in the square, or a voice on the radio in the small hours.

It was like a love affair – each culinary success or disaster savoured afresh in the telling; each nocturnal feline prank doubly enjoyed; the exhausting task (for her weakened body) of defrosting a completely iced-up freezer lightened by the fun of sending 'before and after' pictures down the e-mail. In a way it was indeed a love affair – a love affair with life, her rediscovery of the long-forgotten pleasure and refreshment of having someone always 'there' with her (thanks to modern computer technology) to share the simple everyday details of her life, the gradual unfolding of something stifled for years, packed into a mere fifty days.

But was everything what it seemed? The digital images were genuine, but while they appeared to be of, for instance a pudding baked by Debs, she was simultaneously buying online from the Bakewell Pudding Shop. In e-mails Debs talked of her freezer overflowing with bread and rolls, but no evidence was found of that after her death. We will never know.

'A kind of long-distance empathy developed between us, as can happen with people in close contact,' says Melanie. '"Oops, psychic vibes again," Debs would say, as yet again we would find ourselves having e-mailed at exactly the same time.'

One day an unexpected parcel came. Opening it, Melanie found Claire Rayner's autobiography and a lovely little message from Debs saying she had just invented 'Aunts' Day', so that she could send her a present. This is the touching sort of gesture I came to appreciate so much when Debs lived with me – examples of her softest, most genuine side.

'We had mentioned in passing listening to part of this book on Radio 4,' recalls Melanie, 'but she did not know that just the day before she ordered it I had been holding it in my hands in a bookshop, almost on the point of buying it?'

I'm convinced Debs knew how dangerously ill she was and that her passing was imminent. I believe she was trying to evoke the inner peace and solitude of when she was happiest – her childhood. She had rediscovered the joys of keeping pets – Ellie, her cat, and two hamsters – and had even purchased episodes of Kipling's *Just So* stories, which her grandfather read to her at bedtime when she was a little girl.

And were those baking sessions that she discussed with Melanie a throwback to junior cookery lessons? There is no evidence she was actually eating any of her culinary creations of home-baked bread, scones, flapjacks, bread and butter pudding, rice pudding and Belgian biscuit cake, if they were indeed happening. Some may have gone straight into the freezer. What little went into her mouth was probably vomited up soon after anyhow.

Forty

The end came during the Easter Bank Holiday weekend. Melanie and Debs had discussed trying to meet up but had been thwarted by Debs' work commitments and Melanie's diary. After rejecting Good Friday, Saturday and Sunday, they settled on Bank Holiday Monday. I had also tried to make contact the previous weekend, but my messages had gone unanswered.

On Good Friday morning at 7 a.m. (Debs had obviously been up all night) she sent Melanie an e-mail confirming their Monday meeting, announcing an overwhelming desire to bake her own Bagels, and saying she was feeling 'crap' and was eagerly anticipating a nice, long sleepful rest over the holiday. Just before 8 a.m. that day she sent Tesco Online an e-mail, adding mascarpone cheese, vegetable soup and a prawn and avocado sandwich to her Saturday order of a few groceries.

Debs spent most of that Saturday in bed, surrounded by an assembly of gadgets and her cat. In a footnote to one of her last e-mails she said: 'Have been enjoying bed too much, ably assisted by combined hot water bottle/furry foot warmer/therapeutic vibro-massage unit/portable alarm clock/earwax remover (a.k.a. lovely Ellie). And listening to footy/cricket on radio all afternoon ... bliss. Then got sent unexpected flowers and Get Well balloon, which brightened flat up (until investigated by probing paw and converted into new form of natural floral carpeting).'

Around ten o'clock that evening, she sent Melanie a collection of poems about sleep, 'my new favourite hobby'. These were researched on the Internet, downloaded, and edited by Debs into a flowing chapter of verse.

```
From:       D. A. Barham
Subject:    My new favourite hobby
Date:       Sat, 19 Apr 2003


O sleep! it is a gentle thing,
Beloved from pole to pole!
To Mary Queen the praise be given!
She sent the gentle sleep from Heaven
That slid into my soul.
- Samuel Taylor Coleridge


O magic sleep! O comfortable bird,
That broodest o'er the troubled sea of the mind
Till it is hush'd and smooth! O unconfined
Restraint! imprisoned liberty! great key
To golden palaces.
- John Keats


Golden slumbers kiss your eyes,
Smiles awake you when you rise.
- Thomas Dekker
```

The innocent sleep,
Sleep that knits up the ravelled sleave of care,
The death of each day's life, sore labor's bath,
Balm of hurt minds, great nature's second course,
Chief nourisher in life's feast.
- William Shakespeare, Macbeth

O, Sleep! the certain knot of peace,
The baiting place of wit, the balm of woe,
The poor man's wealth, the prisoner's release,
Th' indifferent judge between the high and low.
- Sir Philip Sidney

Take thou of me, sweet pillowes, sweetest bed;
A chamber deafe of noise, and blind of light,
A rosie garland and a weary hed.
- Sir Philip Sidney

Sleep, rest of nature, O sleep, most gentle of the
divinities, peace of the soul, thou at whose
presence care disappears, who soothest hearts
wearied with daily employments, and makest them
strong again for labour!
- Ovid (Publius Ovidius Naso), Metamorphoses

Fast asleep? It is no matter.
Enjoy the honey-heavy dew of slumber.
Thou hast no figures nor no fantasies
Which busy care draws in the brains of men;
Therefore thou sleep'st so sound.
- William Shakespeare, Julius Caesar

Come to me now! O, come! benignest sleep!
And fold me up, as evening doth a flower,
From my vain self, and vain things which have power
Upon my soul to make me smile or weep.
And when thou comest, oh, like Death be deep.
- Patrick Proctor Alexander

Sleep away the years, sleep away the pain, wake
tomorrow - a girl again.
- Hal Summers

The footnote reads:

Boy did I need THAT. I think I could sleep for a
week ... (am e-mailing from computer in bed w/one
finger, so 'scuse typos ...!).
... Will e you properly tomorrow re meeting
arrangements etc.
Happy Easter, btw!
Cheers Deb

Having got to know Debs' psyche during her long stay at
my home, I am convinced that these poems were a massive
warning sign about her state of mind. To my knowledge
she had never sent poetry before – and certainly not about
sleep. The very last extract was particularly significant.

Sleep away the years, sleep away the pain, wake
tomorrow - a girl again.

Something was desperately wrong. If I had received this, I would have been there in a flash. I doubt if there would have been anything I could have done. But I would have *been* with her, holding her hand in those final moments of her life.

I was not even aware that Debs had sunk into this new crisis. Both Melanie and Ann had failed to tell me, fearing that Debs might get wind that we were discussing her behind her back. So I spent that Easter in blissful ignorance that Debs was at death's door.

Melanie did not read such sinister overtones into the poems. She received a text message from Debs on Saturday night that said: 'Have just sent you e-mail. Check your inbox.' Melanie read the poems before retiring to bed, regarding them as a beautiful collection of verse, reflecting Debs' strong appreciation of a long and restorative rest and certainly nothing to worry about. The subject had preoccupied Debs for ages and they had discussed poetry in the past, with Melanie often reading poetry to her niece in those last few months. She was delighted that Debs had at last got some sleep, something that had eluded her of late.

On Sunday morning, at 09.17 a.m., Debs completed her last professional act. In bed, she transferred some gags for the *Daily Mirror* from her laptop over to her main computer ready to refine and send off later.

To: Debs
From: D. A. Barham
Subject: Gag Stuff

It's been revealed that multi-millionaire J. Paul
Getty gave several million pounds to the Tory Party
just before his death. That would at least explain
what he died of. Shame and embarrassment.

It's been revealed that multi-millionaire J. Paul
Getty gave several million pounds to the Tory Party
just before his death. That would at least explain
what he died of. Irrevocable senility.

It's been revealed that multi-millionaire J. Paul
Getty gave several million pounds to the Tory Party
just before he died. Makes a change - most people
don't become donors for tragically sick cases until
just AFTER their own death ...

West Ham's Joe Cole is being investigated by police
after reports that he deliberately hit an opponent in
the face. That's hardly likely. When was the last
time a West Ham player actually got a shot ON TARGET?

The MoD is claiming that future wars will be more
high-tech and feature new innovations such as
'inconspicuous miniature drones' on the battlefield.

Something that hasn't been seen since - well, since
Iain Duncan Smith left active military service ...
The MoD is claiming that future wars will be more
high-tech and feature new innovations such as
'miniature drones' on the battlefield. We can't see
that happening. Robin Cook wouldn't go anywhere NEAR
a battlefield ...

The MoD is claiming that future wars will be more
high-tech and largely fought by people safely
located thousands of miles away from the actual
battle zone. Or as they're currently known - 'the
French'.

Crippled boxer Michael Watson has successfully
completed the entire London Marathon - despite
taking six whole days to complete the journey from
Blackheath to the Mall. On the positive side, he
still made the trip quicker than every train
currently running on the Central Line.

David Beckham has suggested that England's next Euro
qualifying match should be played behind closed
doors. Scotland's next qualifier, meanwhile, will as
usual be played behind closed eyes.

armed forces slashed
schumacher coma
dictionary
tracy
rebuild iraq

```
Tory leader web
Coltrane marriage breakup (crush, heavy)
Getty millionaire cough
Tara £250k biog
Nazi hunter
```

The first cleaning operation in over a century on Michelangelo's 'David' has been suspended due to a row between the two women doing the job. The statue has now been officially renamed: Michelangelo's 'Bob Geldof'.

Education secretary Charles Clarke snubbed the TUC by refusing to attend their annual conference. To be fair, he DID send a note ... a fiver, we understand, to cover their entire salary increase for the coming year.

A row is already brewing in Iraq over whose face should replace Saddam on the proposed new currency. Best suggestion is George Bush – at least that'd stop people wanting to nick the stuff from all the country's banks ...

A survey has discovered that women are twice as likely as men to have a vehicle collision in a car park. There's a reason for that. Men won't go within a mile of a supermarket car park ...

All day Sunday, Melanie tried to raise Debs as part of the 'keeping tabs' agreement. Her e-mails went unanswered, but this was not unusual since Debs often slept during the day. She did not ring in case she woke Debs up.

By the time Monday arrived, there was still no word from her. Melanie became more and more worried. By the afternoon, Melanie and her husband Owen decided to drive to Docklands. They travelled praying for the best, but fearing the worst.

The discovery of Debs' body was not without farce – something that she herself would no doubt have made a joke out of. On the way to East London, their car was stopped by the police for speeding. After explaining the situation, the officers let Owen off with a warning.

When the couple arrived at her block they rang Debs' doorbell for ages, but there was no reply. They went to the estates office, where staff produced a spare key. But Debs had double mortise-locked the door from the inside, and left the key in the lock, making access impossible. They all had no option but to phone the police to make a forced entry.

Three officers turned up – two male PCs and a woman. Almost like a comedy sketch, they shoulder-charged the door several times before giving up, bruised and exhausted. They radioed back to base to summon a battering ram – an enforcer – which police usually use to break down the doors of drug dens. But, incredibly, they had lost them all.

Melanie suggested calling the Fire Brigade. So, Melanie and Owen, the three police officers, and the man from the estate office all sat waiting on the stairs for the brigade to arrive. Melanie and her husband had been there for nearly an hour. With so much commotion going on, if Debs had been alive she would surely have come to the door.

The fire fighters were much more adept and gained entry relatively easily by removing part of the door frame. The emergency services went inside, telling Melanie and Owen to wait at the door. They found Debs slumped on the bed. There was no pulse. Death had been sudden and painless. Her heart had been damaged by her anorexia and had simply packed up.

The officers broke the news to Melanie and Owen and asked if they wanted to see the body. Entering her bedroom, they both felt it was as if Debs was not there. They had to look twice to see where she lay. They both felt that her spirit had left her. Her body was almost invisible.

Melanie made the heartbreaking call to her sister Ann. Then she looked around the flat. There were the flowers and the helium-filled balloons with the 'Get Well Soon' message that Debs had sent to herself a few days before. Then, amongst the debris in the kitchen, Melanie found a blue Post-it note with a list of memory jogging subjects.

Debs had been planning a long letter to Melanie that she was hoping to write over Easter. A deeply religious person, Melanie is convinced that Debs' spirit led her to finding that note, which she keeps to this day. Melanie's explanations are on the right.

The list read:

Dream	(probably about Melanie and her cousin Faye's recent dreams)
Kittens/Ellie	(the behaviour of Debs's cat?)
Territorialism	
Religious Beliefs	
Talking Tired	
Send You Smells	
G'pa Cakes	(a recipe?)
Jaoi baby	(?)
A present	(for Melanie)
Positivity	(a word that crept up in Debs' defiant e-mail refusing treatment)
Ask God For	(a reference to sleep?)
Mental dialogue	(?)
Adapting/PMT	(Debs' additional health problems)

Melanie feels that, in her final days, Debs was operating on two levels – a conscious and a sub-conscious. On one level she knew she was going to die; on the other, she carried on the best she could. One part of her was sending herself flowers and 'get well' balloons; the other was receiving them as a welcome gift.

It was only after Debs died that Melanie saw the sleep poems in a different light. She now feels that these were composed by the subconscious side of Debs – the side that knew the end was near. Verses were put intentionally in a particular order – especially the last three verses – to give a lasting impression of looking towards some sort of renewal or restoration.

In an essay for this book, 'Memories of My Niece', Melanie writes:

> Deb's stock-in-trade was a ready wit, with a delight in the bold and vulgar. Yet all that is suddenly laid aside, and the only medium adequate to express her thoughts and feelings seems to be this, which is at first glance just a hymn of praise to sleep and the promises which sleep brings, woven out of verses taken from other people's poems, but arranged in such an order that the whole seems full of new meaning, the style and content both quite unlike anything else she had ever written to me.
>
> Over and over again I have read these words, wondering if I am really reading into these small verses something which is not there, subconsciously trying to make a tragedy seem less tragic. Yet the reaction of most of those with whom I have shared her borrowed words has been rather like mine and I bear in mind that subtlety was part of her stock-in-trade and she did not tend to do things haphazardly.
>
> There is something rather similar in Maureen Dunbar's moving book *Catherine*, about her daughter's seven-year battle with anorexia, where Catherine's last day is full of sleep and rest and somehow suffused with an atmosphere of peace and a half-knowledge that she will soon depart.
>
> What adds to my sense that I am in the presence of

something beyond the ordinary is the matter of the balloons. To believe that she felt so sorry for herself that she had to send herself best wishes and pretend about it afterwards does not fit with even the most intimate glimpses I had of how she felt, the sort of glimpses you get when you hug someone goodbye.

But there is another explanation available, one recorded by Dr Bernie Siegel in his books about his 'exceptional' cancer patients. As part of his therapy he would get people to draw pictures to give insights into the nature of the person's condition and even the prognosis. He records at least two people having drawn kites or balloons and that this had indicated a nearness to death.

His explanation for this phenomenon was that the subconscious was expressing symbolically something of which the person themselves was not necessarily consciously aware.

We are all so prosaic and ready to pooh-pooh such observations. But Deb was the first to acknowledge that there are mysterious aspects to our existence – which was why we often had such interesting discussions on 'life, the universe and everything'.

Who dares categorically to deny the possibility that she might have been operating partly on a different, deeper level, from that of our normal existence? Even if I did not believe in a spiritual aspect to our lives, with these other observations in mind and knowing her the way I did, that would still be my conclusion.

Part Five

Aftermath

Forty-one

5 May 2003

I receive a call from the funeral directors. Do I have a recent photo of Debs – and could I send them one of her wigs? It dawns on me – and this comes as quite a shock – that they need these to see what she looked like, to do the best possible job for the Chapel of Rest.

They had asked if Ann and I wished to see Debs in the Chapel of Rest before the funeral. I had known that this would be traumatic, but I needed to do it as part of my own emotional closure. Ann was less sure, but we both made the request. We will say goodbye to Debs separately.

10 May 2003

Sue and I drive across London to the funeral directors. I have only ever seen one dead person before – my father an hour after his death from cancer in 1996. When I kissed him goodbye, I understood how people can know immediately when a person has died. The life is gone and the whole essence of that person goes with it, leaving an eerie coldness. It will be the same with Debs, I'm sure.

Hand in hand, we open the door and step into the Chapel of Rest and edge our way over to the open coffin. There, looking very peaceful, and surprisingly small, lies Debs' body. But to me she isn't here. I had left her, and said good-bye at the very spot where she had died in her flat. She looks thin, but we had seen her far worse three years before. I stand for quite a while holding Sue tight and just thinking, looking, remembering, then I slowly kiss her cold forehead, silently whispering 'I'm so sorry – sleep well' and leave her for the last time.

13 May 2003

It is now the day of the funeral. I am standing in London's Covent Garden in the shadow of St Paul's Church. I, along with four hundred friends, family members, and colleagues from the press, television, and radio are about to remember the life of Deborah Ann Barham.

The arrangements have been a source of much tension. Ann wanted a quiet family affair in Debs' birthplace, Sheffield; but I felt strongly that this would be a mistake and would exclude the vast majority of her friends and colleagues. Besides, Debs had too many poor memories of that city and never went back there, even for a day, after leaving for London as a teenager. Her chosen home was the capital. And her 'family' was her world of work. I argued strongly that we should have an open funeral in London at which we could bring everybody together. I knew already that many people felt a need to say goodbye properly, and in the end I persuaded Ann to go with my plan.

The next problem had been a venue. Where do you stage a funeral when you discover that your daughter is a celebrity? Debs was not in any way a religious or spiritual person, and had no connection with any church or community. We all racked our brains, and the answer came from the actor Bob Kingdom, Ann's brother-in-law – St Paul's, Covent Garden, otherwise known as the 'Actors Church'.

The Rector has been extremely helpful and understanding. We decided on a memorial service followed by a smaller crematorium service, to which we have invited everyone. Again, I felt strongly that Debs' closer friends should be here with the family, and even at the crematorium if they wished, and was able to persuade Ann.

The biggest dilemma was the choice of speakers and music. I wanted people who spanned Debs' life and who meant something to her. We decided on John Langdon, a senior scriptwriter who became a close confidant; radio producer Bruce Hyman, for whom she did much work and who was a close friend; Clive Anderson, for whom she 'gagged up' speeches; radio compare Ned Sherrin, who delivered so much of her best material, John McVicar, fellow *Punch* columnist, who desperately tried to persuade her to eat in the depths of her illness; and fellow writer Hugh Rycroft, a soul mate when they'd both started out at the BBC. Her Aunt Melanie would close the service with Debs' own final writings.

Music is hugely important to me. I wanted time for emotion and time for laughter, using music to complement the readings, but I had no idea what anyone was actually going to say. I think I shed more tears while choosing the music than at any other time. We were going to start the service with traditional organ music and a hymn, but what else? I listened to album after album, searching for tracks with that special 'something' that makes your skin tingle.

We had a recording of Debs herself, aged 17, on *The Ad Break* (BBC) to use early on. The first music track I had quickly decided on – the mellow, breathy voice of Diana Krall. The simplicity of her solo piano introduction on her version of Billy Joel's 'Just the Way You Are' was meant to echo the feelings of so many – that we all loved Debs as herself. We may have all wished she would eat, but we didn't want to change her. It brought tears flooding to my eyes, and still does.

I carry that album in the car permanently, and play that track after stressful, difficult days. It takes me back to Debs, and puts the world back in the right perspective. If only I had realized what was truly important when she was young – I should have been there.

Her favourite band was the Doors. 'Break on Through (to the other side)' was from Debs' own collection, as was the final exit music, John Mayall's 'Why Worry'.

I wanted everyone to leave smiling, not sad, and this track did it for me. John Mayall is a personal favourite of mine, and a love of blues and jazz was something that I shared with Debs.

The other essential choice was the deep, hauntingly beautiful voice of Karen Carpenter. This may have seemed like some sort of sick joke to some of the congregation, but to me it was doubly poignant. Karen died from heart failure due to anorexia nervosa, just as Debs had done, and the morning of her death in February 1983 when I woke to the sound of her voice on Radio 4 has remained crystal clear in my mind. Her singing sent shivers down my spine, and for the rest of that day I felt very emotional, and had premonitions that something terrible was going to happen.

I can't explain those feelings, but shortly afterwards my electronics business failed and I hit the first big crisis in my life. I've never forgotten that day, or Karen Carpenter's voice, and I knew that it had to be a part of Debs' day too. 'Look to Your Dreams' seemed to strike just the right note, and reminded us that Debs could have a rest at last.

St Paul's dominates the west side of Covent Garden piazza, London's first square. It's an appropriate setting, in the heart of theatreland and near many of the bars and cafés where Debs spent so much of her time. I stand and take in this historic structure.

Many famous names have been connected with the building – John Wesley preached here, W. S. Gilbert was baptized here, and the very first victim of the Great Plague – one Margaret Ponteous, a doctor's daughter – was buried in the churchyard in 1665. The church has hosted memorial services for stars as diverse as Charlie Chaplin, Hattie Jacques and Adam Faith.

For most of the journey to the church on the Docklands Light Railway I give an interview to the *Daily Telegraph*. They have decided, very unusually, to cover the funeral in their Court and Social section.

As I walk into the church, I notice several memorial plaques to famous stage names, including Vivien Leigh and Dame Edith Evans, whose ashes repose here. A sign above the door says: 'We are unafraid to reason, laugh and explore.'

Now it is to remember the Invisible Girl, whom few of the public knew, but who put a smile on so many faces. Today, as we lay her to rest, Debs herself is about to turn the holy air blue as the congregation revels in her professional work and personal letters.

In my pew, I take in the scene as I wait for the proceedings to begin. There are few in the congregation whom I have met before, but there are familiar faces: TV performers Clive Anderson, Roy Hudd, Ned Sherrin, and Ian Hislop, editor of *Private Eye* and a panellist on one of Debs' favourite shows, *Have I Got News For You*. The church is adorned with two tall black banners carrying two hauntingly elegant portraits of Debs. I had made those banners myself, after realizing that many people attending the service would never have met her. I worried for days about whether it would seem tasteless, but they look perfect, standing each side of the coffin.

We had chosen a simple wicker coffin – I didn't discover until two years later her entry on www.mydeath.net in which she requested a coffin 'made of MDF, draped in purple velour and hand-stencilled with gold-effect spray paint. I know my "Changing Rooms"'. On the same site she had also expressed a wish that her funeral should 'look like a cross between Kew Gardens and Danny La Rue's dressing room. It's not that I like flowers. It's just that a lot of my relatives have hay fever.' Well, the flowers look wonderful, nestled around her portraits. As the organ plays its haunting refrain, I stare into her eyes, bringing her back to life again, and allowing me to have a private chat with her and say in my head some of the things I wished I'd said to her.

The service is opened by the Rector of St Paul's, the Reverend Mark Oakley, himself a regular contributor to radio on church affairs. I listen to his opening address with a mixture of sadness and pride.

> You are all very, very welcome to St Paul's Church today as we come together to do something beautifully but painfully simple – to celebrate Debbie and to give thanks for her being the quite remarkable person she was. And I know I don't need to tell you, those who feel her absence most, about her huge talent professionally as a comedy writer; about her backstage work, as it were, for this country's leading comedians and comedy shows; about what has been called her Mozartian fluency and delivery – as Victor Lewis Smith has said, 'Debbie only had to whistle and an entire herd of gags would thunder towards us, every one a winner.'

As well as celebrating these professional talents and acknowledging how poorer British comedy will be without her, we are here also to say thank you for the person she was; for her modesty and her creativity, her ability to befriend; for the fact that although she poked fun, she did not slip into maliciousness, her drive of cynicism not leading her off the road into negative attitudes towards life. She had high standards of course, and did not suffer fools gladly – although she wasn't the world's best businesswoman, always losing vital bits of paper, or actually losing herself, as she had a hopeless sense of geography. And not always brilliant at managing domestic issues, such as how to defrost the freezer, which always bore a close resemblance, I'm told, to Antarctica. Needless to say that once the task was completed she wrote one of her famous e-mails comparing the whole process to colonic irrigation.

We meet here as the church celebrates Eastertide. Indeed, Debbie died on Easter morning. Another flame burns here, that of the Easter candle, reminding us of the hope – the hope – that love is stronger than death. Debbie died far too young. None of us here knows why. All we can do is come here, where we do not need to be ashamed of our tears or laughter, where we can direct our words and feelings of thanks and hurt and anger. And we give up all our admiration, affection and our pride in her alongside Ann and Peter and their families and we will commend her to the embrace of her creator. And we will

pray that she rests in peace now. For in the words of the
Koran, the one who makes his companions laugh is the
one who deserves paradise.

In his eulogy, radio producer Bruce Hyman tells the congregation: 'Essentially, our memories and impressions of
her are the same because she had no side to her; you will
hear from everyone who knew her that she was prodigious-
ly talented; that she was sweet and kind about the people
she knew, but ruthlessly and savagely funny about anyone
in the public eye. Even when I was thinking about what I
wanted to say this afternoon, the one person I really wanted to ask for help from was Deb.'

For the next hour or more we will be treated to rounds
of wicked gags and outrageous personal correspondence
from various friends and colleagues. Bruce quotes some
sample gags, Debs' alternatives to *Big Brother*, a series she
apparently loathed, but always kept an eye on for potential material.

Gibb Brother – three members of the Bee Gees share a studio
with host Clive Anderson. Each Friday one of them walks
out in a strop while the remaining group members celebrate
their survival with a rousing burst of 'Staying Alive'. [This
was written before the death of Maurice Gibb.]

Big Buddha – like *Big Brother* but with less sex, more
Karma than Kama sutra; Ten monks live together in a cave

hoping to be the first to meet their Nirvana, rather than simply meet Davina; each week a holy brother is evicted to the sound of one hand clapping. Host, Jade off the last *Big Brother* if it meant she would agree to be sworn to a vow of silence; and Bagel Brother, kosher version, ten nice Jewish boys and girls share a house. Every Friday their mothers phone in to ask why they haven't rung them all week. From the producers of previous Orthodox game shows such as Challenge Hanukkah, They Think It's All Passover and Have I Got Jews for You.

Hugh Rycroft, a colleague from her early days at the BBC, says that although he did not see Debbie at all frequently over the past few years, as a Radio 5 listener he was reminded of her brilliance on an almost daily basis: 'At any hour of the day or night, the jokes that she had texted in would be read out to general hilarity in the studio. Of course, she wasn't being paid for doing this. And in a way, that sums her up. Because first and foremost Debbie wrote not for the money, not for the kudos, but for the sheer joy of it.'

Clive Anderson explains to the assembly how in one e-mail she was bemoaning the trials of moving into her flat in Docklands:

I've now sprained my other knee carrying a microwave down the corridor, but other than that everything has gone surprisingly smoothly, except for John Lewis' steadfast reluctance to deliver my new telly. I tried to pick it up in a cab today, only to discover that they are the only store in Oxford Street that don't open on a Sunday. Thus I now have a video recorder in East 14 and a TV in a warehouse in Acton somewhere. Does anyone with a really, really long extension lead exist?

John Langdon, a close friend, who met Debs when he was script editor of Rory Bremner's show, remembers an e-mail sent to him after he had written simply to say that he had heard her monologue – read by Ned Sherrin – on *Loose Ends*.

Hello you. I didn't hear it. It was too painful. Those poor, innocent gags being mercilessly mown down by Twinkie's machine-gun delivery. But on the assumption that he only name-checks the writer when his material goes down like a cup of cold sick, presumably that's not favourable news.

I'm having a day of feeling sorry for myself. Clive Anderson is pissed off with me because I got roped into doing an extra Loose Ends at short notice. Neil Shand is sick. Yea, sick, presumably with having his gags murdered by (see above); I ended up having to re-cycle some stuff I had already sent to Clive for a thing he was doing in the West End the day after Loose Ends when the jokes would already have been on the radio. Now I know why they say the secret of good comedy is timing.

Victor Lewis Smith is pissed off with me because I
have not been answering his e-mail. I don't answer
anyone's e-mail. If I did, I would have to admit
that I did not approve of the way he edited the
programme we did last year which would then
exacerbate his degree of pissedoffness (or should
that be offpissedness?) - they never teach you
useful grammatical rules like that at school
languages.

The tax office is pissed off with me because they
don't think I live in Sheffield. I don't know why
they think I should live in Sheffield. Last time I
paid any tax I did not send it to a tax office in
Sheffield, yet the tax office in Sheffield keeps on
ringing me up asking why I am not known at that
address. If they have my fucking phone number,
surely that's a clue!

Oh no! He didn't just swear did he? I glance nervously
across at Mark, the Rector, and a discreet grin spreads
across his face. As the panic in my own face changes to
relief and a smile, I realize that most of those present are
also laughing. John carries on unabashed ...

My dentist is pissed off with me because I cancelled
my appointment. Suffice to say that my dental bill
was even larger than my tax bill last year. But he's
a very good dentist and I did enjoy those four hours
of total sedation. Tonight I am having to make do

with local election coverage - similar effect but
substantially cheaper.

My friend is almost certain to be pissed off with me
because I agreed to look after her hamster for a
week and the fucking thing escaped last night. It
has now gone completely Bin Laden. I wasted several
hours at the garden centre trying to obtain a humane
rat trap which has been rather optimistically baited
in the bathroom with some McVities digestives. I
wait in hope. Perhaps I'll catch the hamster,
perhaps I'll attract a rather large rat population
to the area, thus giving the rest of my neighbours
reason to be pissed off with me. The hamster is
pissed off with me for obvious reasons.

Some woman from a publishing company is equally
hacked off with me because I am steadfastly refusing
to do a 'spot' at a book launch for a book I
inadvertently contributed to. Just what manner of
spot does she expect me to do? Hamstertaining? Fire-
eating? At least it's low in calories. I mean,
honestly, there's going to be an audience for
Christ's sake who have paid for tickets. Get a
bloody performer to do it. Get Ned or Clive. Same
gags, just different delivery.

My local election candidate is probably pissed off
with me for not voting. It's not my fault, my life
is under no overall control. And I don't care if
some biddy did throw herself under a horse in

pursuit of female emancipation - or was it female
emaciation (I tried that one as well).

I am pissed off for being stupid enough to sign up
for ITV Digital. I don't know why. I watch on
average less than an hour of telly a week. At least
I now get to keep a large free and extremely ugly
digital clock on top of the TV. I suppose it might
deter burglars. They'll feel sorry for me and decide
not to steal my telly. Hurray, I can switch this
telly off now because the monkey has won Hartlepool,
thus the only joke-worthy result is done and dusted.
Apart from that, though, life is a bed of roses.
Sorry, New Roses.
Cheers Deb

Oh, wow, 2.41 a.m. and I have just had my first laugh
in 24 hours, courtesy of the Duke of Edinburgh.
Apparently he went up to a blind woman and quipped:
'Do you know, they now have eating dogs for
anorexics?' I take back everything I ever said about
that man. He is a comedy genius and ought to be
given a job presenting Loose Ends immediately.

John McVicar tells the congregation that, despite her illness, she got on with her life. 'She worked all the time, she
paid her own way and she carried her own water. She did
not whinge and whine. She worked at making people laugh
and she did make people laugh and she's still making people laugh – the best laughs today have come from her

e-mails. There is something admirable, exemplary and I suppose honourable in how she lived … she did not let the counsellors come in and feel sorry for herself and breast beat.' He ends on a quotation from Hilaire Belloc.

From quiet homes and first beginning,
Out to the undiscovered ends,
There is nothing worth the wear of winning,
But laughter and the love of friends.

Next, it is the turn of veteran broadcaster Ned Sherrin. He recalls that he only met Debbie twice, at end-of-season parties on *Loose Ends*, but that she had written hundreds of one-liners for the programme, all showing how quickly she had learned the tricks of her trade and, above all, her 'cavalier attitude to taste'. He too quotes some of her gags ('Doctors warn that teenage girls who drink to excess run the very real risk of not just becoming alcoholics, but also of ending up as Chris Evans' girlfriend' . . . 'Big Brother Three features a flight of stairs for the very first time. It will be nice for the contestants to have an intellectual challenge to grapple with'…).

Finally, it is the turn of Debbie's Aunt Melanie, who shared so many intimate secrets with her, particularly during the final weeks of Debs' life. She focuses on the central question in Debs' truncated life, addressing her niece direct.

Years ago, your pursuit of freedom, your asking to be taken seriously when you were 15, left us one legacy you never realized. In setting you free to do things your own way, far from the usual career routes, we, your family, broke the mould of our thinking and never quite returned to the old patterns.

These last years, too, you were asking to be taken seriously to try to return to health your own way despite the huge risks. In the end, no one overrode you or robbed you of your dignity or self respect.

Did we do right? Was freedom and trust worth more than length of days? Who could ever presume to know the correct answer to that question. But I already know your answer because you made it very clear. And you were, at the end, exactly where you chose to be – busy living and looking forward.

Melanie ends by reading Debs' collection of poetry about sleep, sent to her aunt a few hours before she died.

The service over, we make our way back out into the courtyard gardens for some fresh air and to take in the tears and laughter of the last two hours.

The rector will say later he has never heard so much laughter in church. We will even receive press coverage as the holders of some sort of record for the number of profanities in a church service. Debs has written her own send off in her own inimitable style.

Then we travel in convoy to the cemetery, and the light-hearted banter in the car changes to a much more sombre atmosphere as we reach the crematorium.

The service is brief but very subdued and moving. Even though I feel I have already said goodbye, I cannot look as the curtains finally close, and I am too numb to shed more tears.

Forty-two

It is now two months since the funeral. The grief is still here, but is being diluted by the practicalities of dealing with Debs' affairs. She left behind what I can only describe as financial chaos: no will, no tax returns, plus of course an empty flat that has been cleaned, cleared, and is ready to sell.

Debs' last tax return was in 1994, leaving me with nine years to complete. The accountants will deal with the tax calculations and advice, but providing the data for them to work on is down to me. The next ten months of my life will be dominated by a slow unravelling and documenting of her affairs, and the successful submission of tax returns by the next January deadline. Her tax bill will be horrendous, but the money is there to cover it.

Today I am making my last visit to Debs' Docklands flat to say my last goodbye.

This morning I listened to a tribute to Debs on Radio 4, introduced by Clive Anderson. I taped the programme and played it several times. It was a hurried, but moving tribute to her, and now, standing alone in this dark, empty flat, I am feeling very emotional.

I have felt awkward coming in the flat. It is pleasant

enough, and tidy. Burrells Wharf is a superb development. But this is where my daughter died, alone. Visits have been practical, lasting only as long as necessary. It was the place that Debs had dreamed of, and created herself, and I feel like an intruder, uninvited.

For Ann it appears to have been different. She has been staying here with John on trips to London, and sleeping in Debs' bed. I felt she was using the place as a hotel, and that Debs would have been horrified. This really got to me and in the end I had to say something.

I was still aware of the particular smell in the flat, and through this hot summer have left windows, and even the balcony door, wide open to try to get fresh air through the rooms. A potential buyer has emerged who already has connections with the Burrells Wharf estate. We have left him just the basic furniture, which we hope to include in the sale.

The atmosphere is eerie. As I look out of her bedroom window across to the ever glowing lights of Canary Wharf, I imagine Debs enjoying that view through the long nights of work. Like her, I feel so lonely. This place was her dream and, as far as I know, she was very happy there; but to me it is full of sadness and isolation.

The long corridors and heavy doors remind me of so many hotels, with the same impersonal, unfriendly feeling. I spend an hour, maybe more, just sitting on her bedroom floor, alone with my memories. It seems a stupid thing to say, but in this hour I feel closer to her than ever.

As I finally lock the door and go down to the car, I feel

so sad and useless. I just sit and cry and cry, releasing weeks of pent-up emotion.

One week later

I get a call from the agents to say that the buyers are concerned about the smell, and that they had heard 'rumours' around the estate about what had happened in the flat. They will consider going ahead, but want all of the carpets replaced, all wallpaper stripped, and the flat professionally cleaned.

I am horrified – this is just 'Chinese whispers'. A girl has died, men in white coats had been seen going to the flat, there was a smell – and the gossip has done the rest.

I act fast. I ring the agents and agree to do most of what has been demanded next weekend.

That weekend

We return to the flat – Sue, myself, Ann, Melanie, and John. In a very long day we totally disinfect and clean every surface and crevice, washing, scraping, brushing, and vacuuming. We paint large areas and I replace all the carpeting. By the time we get home it is nearly midnight. We have left the place sparkling and completely clear.

On Monday I ring the agents – only to be told the buyers have pulled out. However, a new purchaser will be found quickly.

Forty-three

Two years before she died, Debs was contacted by a book editor called Jessica Berens who was looking for female writers with 'deviant perspectives and adverse ideas' to contribute to a provocative collection of essays on subjects such as guns, bestiality, and satanism.

The book was entitled *Inappropriate Behaviour*, and was designed to be uncompromising, witty, and subversive – 'resisting the mainstream pap that is served up under the guise of "women's interests"'. The front cover depicted a devil woman, scantily dressed and seductively licking an ice cream cornet. Debs agreed to join 'this bunch of trouble-making provocateurs ready to make mincemeat of mediocrity and propel feminism into the 21st century'.

The idea certainly had Debs licking her lips as she savagely dissected the cult of *Bridget Jones's Diary* and the proliferation of BJ spin-offs, calling it the rise of Fuckwit Fiction. Debs was at her best when she was angry and to me it was one of her best pieces of writing, a wonderful example of how she could absorb a style, and mimic it.

You're Never Alone With a Clone

Single? Thirtysomething? So desperate for a ring on your finger that you'd even marry a member of the Royal

Family? Calm down – there are plenty of agencies positively gagging to sign you up. Not DATING agencies, obviously. Literary agencies.

Thanks to the sacred cult of Bridget Jones (Peace and Cellulite Be Upon Her), millions of women are now convinced that they're exactly like you. And they're spilling their guts onto sheets of foolscap quicker than an inaugural meeting of Bulimics Anonymous. These days, every female author – and a fair few male ones, to boot – wants to be Keeping Up With Bridget Jones.

There's no denying that Bridget was a big advance for the Modern Woman. The modern woman in question was Ms H. Fielding, and the big advance was somewhere in the region of half a million quid. Not bad, for someone whose heroine made a career out of chronic self-pity and abject failure to achieve 'personal goals'. Then again, it's a good thing Bridget wasn't an exact reflection of her creator's lifestyle. I can't see many Miss Averages relating to 'Helen Fielding's Diary'.

Monday (Pounds gained today: £500,000 – not v poor. Positively rolling in it, in fact. Units of alcohol: 24. Units of 'Bridget Jones' sold by Waterstones: 30,000. Calories: 1250. Salary: £12.5M. Editor's opinion of new book – v v good. Public's opinion of new book – aaargh!)

9am Wake up. Argorblurryhell! Still pissed from yesterday's lunch with film producer. Bugger. Shit. Fuck. Bollocks.

Looked in Thesaurus for more expletives to pad next book out. Discovered I'd used them all, except 'arse'. Arse.

9.30am Try to locate clean apparel which doesn't render self reminiscent of back of bus, or hideous Anne Widdecombe-type person. GAH! Cannot get rid of ghastly unsightly bulge in top of new boot-cut Joseph trousers. Bulge finally identified as wallet. Uuurgh! Can see huge great rolls of excess poundage spilling out of zip. Am clearly horrible, overpaid, greedy cow. Hence reason everyone hates me.

9.45am Self-loathing thoughts today: 12. V V good. Should fill at least 3 minutes of film script.
10am Look in mirror – disgusted to see no eight-page serialization of new Bridget Jones book. Ring agent in panic. Agent reminds me I have exclusive deal with *Telegraph*, not *Daily Mirror*. Phew!

10.15am Drop into Coins Coffee Shop in Notting Hill for triple-skinny half-caff no-whip Viennese Mocha Java latte macchiato with soya milk, drink-thru lid, wings, two-way dry-weave top-sheet, five Chocolate Croissants (Aaargh! Oooops!) and a quick product-placement for Coins Coffee Shop ...

10.25am Stroll casually past bookshop. Pleased to note presence of 20 Bridget Jones copies in window.

Disappointed to note that none of them are written by me. Make mental note to send poison pen fan letters to A. Weir, A. Jenkins, J. Green, I. Knight, J. Lloyd etc etc ...

Yes, they're everywhere – first came Dolly the Sheep (and equally bleating); now we're witnessing the invasion of the Bridget Jones Clones. Legions of DNA-identical, self-loathing Singletons who can't get a shag – but somehow manage to breed like herpes, infecting every bookshop from Land's End to John o' Groats.

The same scene is being played out in editors' offices nationwide. Prospective authoress tippy-toes in, clutching example of previous work (e.g. a 'What I Did In My Holiday' composition that her Infants Teacher was really proud of, or something she painted in the Rehab Centre as part of the therapeutic process). 'So!' leers the moneygrubbing agent, 'You're twentysomething?' Check. 'You work as a temp in a Soho PR company?' Check. 'You've got big boobs, a little black dress, all your own teeth and preferably an adolescent tragedy to reveal in post-publication interviews?' Check. 'Can you write? No, bugger that. Here's a cheque.' Check.

And so it went on for 4,000 words of caustic parody. The piece made such an impact that both the *Spectator* and the *Daily Mail* ran abridged versions. I had bought *Inappropriate Behaviour* when it was published, not because Debs had told me about it, but as a result of my regular web searches to find out what she was doing. So during my searches for important financial paperwork in the days after her death I was not surprised to find an envelope from the publishers with a final proof.

What did surprise me was to find a proof of a second essay in the same envelope, written apparently by someone called Helen Hastings. I went back to the book and, sure enough, the main essay was by a woman of that name, advocating matricide. As a child, Debs lived in Hastings Road in Sheffield, so I didn't need Hercule Poirot to deduce that this was written by Debs under a *nom de plume*. Besides, the style was unmistakable.

I started to read, and as I did so my heart was pounding. To any innocent reader, this was a savage fictional essay; but as I read it, I encountered familiar phrases that I had heard before from my own mother, and from Debs herself. This essay was to have a profound effect on my understanding of Debs' life and feelings. As a piece of writing it could have been forgotten quickly, but much of the resentment and anger that came off the page was echoed by my conversations with Debs' friends, colleagues, family and doctors.

The essay had been written in 2001, just when her ulcers returned and, I believe, when she probably felt she had reached the point of no return in her battle with anorexia. The theme is based on her expensive sessions with a psychotherapist in 1997, after she became seriously ill. It was entitled 'Matricidal Mayhem.' 'Helen' is, of course, Debs herself.

Just what is my problem?

'Look at you. You're continually wracked with guilt and inadequacy. You're an emotional cripple who's mentally incapable of forming normal healthy relationships with either men or other women. You're hopelessly obsessed with your own failure, verging on obsessive-compulsive and you have the most severe self-destructive streak I've seen outside the Japanese Kamikaze pilots' training campus. In many respects, Helen, you have the psychological maturity of an eleven-year-old.'

Thank you. That's the sort of personal critique only a trusted friend and confidante can really deliver. Unfortunately it's not being delivered by a trusted friend and confidante, but by a poker-faced individual with a Hitler moustache who sits bolt upright beside the couch in a large, uncomfortable-looking leather chair. Her name is Doctor Goldmann, and she is currently charging me a hundred and fifty quid for the privilege of being deeply insulted in a slightly foreign accent. No wonder it didn't take her more than three minutes to spot my talent for self-sabotage.

'So ...'

For that price, she'd better give me someone to blame for my fucked-up life – other than myself. What I get is a classic straight out of '101 Chat-Up Lines For Psychoanalysts'.

'... Let's go back to your childhood.'

I was eight. Old enough to be intrigued when I found a

vibrator in my mother's bedside cabinet; young enough to
wonder why she needed to whisk eggs in the middle of the
night (illicit midnight feasts, presumably: when you're
eight, that's the kind of perk which makes adulthood seem
so enviable). The house was empty but I, being an eight-
year-old dragged reluctantly through Montessori school,
force-fed Usborne Junior Encyclopaedias and given a
Speak 'N' Spell when what I really wanted was a Sindy
pony, was not up to no good. I wasn't raiding the fridge
or my mother's make-up drawer. I was attempting to
expand my Inquiring Young Mind by raiding the
bookcase. I'd often raided the bookcase before, but
tonight I was really going for it – above the Conan Doyle,
above the Agatha Christie and the Edgar Allan Poe, loftier
even than the Jerome K. Jerome and the P. G. Wodehouse.
I found myself mountaineering up the shelves to the very
top, to the highest literary pinnacle where, I was sure,
some forbidden delight lay. And that was where I had my
innocence cruelly shattered.

The shelf was full of soft porn. High quality soft porn,
to be fair – not your typical thirty-something Single
Mother fare of Jilly Cooper and Black Swan. This little
library included *Lady Chatterley's Lover*, *Fanny Hill* and
Tropic of Cancer by Henry Miller, along with a smattering
of sex manuals in the 'Joy of . . .' mould. But those didn't
interest me. I was far too horrified by their sordid tales of
throbbing love muscles and red-hot nubs of womanly
passion. The cover of this book bore a picture not of some

dashing rogue in riding breeches ripping the bodice from his swooning Mistress, but of a small boy and a large, well-developed organ. It was a human brain – and above it, the title: *Give Your Child a Superior Mind*.

That's when I knew I was going to have a lousy childhood. I wasn't my mother's beloved daughter at all. I was just a chance for her to redeem all the academic failure that had landed her – once a promising student – on the single parent scrapheap at the age of thirty. Now it all made sense: why the reports I trotted back from school with concerned her so much more than the grazed knees I hobbled home tearfully nursing. Now I understood: why it was so imperative that, every Christmas, shitting myself even more than the average infant, I stood up and recited stumbling tracts of pre-rehearsed Kipling to paralytic pervy uncles.

This appears to be a common theme in anorexics – the feeling of being unloved, or at least not showing the child that they are loved. The essay continued:

Lizzie Borden took an axe
And gave her Mother forty whacks
And when she saw what she had done
She gave her Father forty one.

Oddly, that was one nursery rhyme I never remember my Mother using to lull me to sleep. Which isn't that odd, actually. I never remember her using ANY nursery rhymes to lull me to sleep. I never remember her kissing me, cuddling me, reading me a bedtime story or, indeed, showing any outward sign of affection towards me. And I never once called her 'Mum'. Nor 'Mummy', 'Main', 'Ma', 'Mama', 'Momma', 'Mother' or even the princessly 'Mater'. No, it was always 'Janet'.

Well, not 'Janet' of course; but certainly 'Mum' left Debs' vocabulary very early, probably in an attempt to be practical and avoid confusion when Ann moved in with John, but it was also why I also became 'Peter' instead of 'Dad'.

My therapist told me I'm probably in denial. From, she said, a repressed urge to return to the womb. And she could well be right: I'd love to return to the womb. Not because this might encourage the rekindling of emotional bonds, but because I'm now three inches taller than my mother and BOY would it hurt her when I forced entry.

I can only assume I must have hurt her like hell on the way out; that would presumably explain her desire to get revenge by fucking up my life for the subsequent two decades. Or maybe she doesn't need a reason. Maybe she IS just a bitch.

I wish I'd been a stillbirth. Nine months of misery, all the pain of labour and all she'd get out of it would be an extra-large helping of placenta pâté. The Ancient Egyptians had the right idea: they dumped their Mummies in formaldehyde, bound them head-to-toe in those Tennis Elbow bandages and locked them in a tomb for a few thousand years. I wish I'd thought of that when I was twelve: it might almost have muffled the sound of her carping and castigating. Almost.

Oh, how eagerly I anticipated my eighteenth birthday when (in my pitiful young fantasy) she would finally take me aside and break the news to me that I was adopted and she WASN'T my real mother. Tell me I had been found in a wheelie-bin on some piss-soaked council estate, callously dumped by my teenage smack-fiend prozzie parent after accidental impregnation by the maths master. Of course, she didn't. Though since I'd left home three years before my eighteenth birthday, she might have had a job tracking me down to pass on the glad tidings.

Debs had no reason to question at all that she had genuine parents, but she had, in her own way, cast aside the family in which she had grown up when she walked out of the door at the age of 15. She never once returned to Sheffield.

Nowadays she has another source of disappointment: my persistent refusal to produce any visible grandchildren. The fact that she disapproves of every boyfriend I ever had (too old, too young, too fat, too unemployed, too mad, too married ...) doesn't come into it. I swear she wouldn't mind if I hung around in a Budgens car park and swiped the first unattended pram that came along,

if it meant she could call herself 'Granny' and inflict
unwearable hand-knitted garments on some wretched
infant. I suspect, having abandoned all hopes of seeing
ME achieve anything worthwhile, she's hoping to transfer
the burden of her unfulfilled ambition onto a second
generation of innocents.

I've only seen her a few times since I left the family
home. Most memorably at a funeral: she, in mourning
dress, was looking even more witch-like than usual; I
was the one desperately resisting the urge to throw her
the wreath and beam 'Ooh, you'll be next!'

Debs is referring here to my father's funeral in 1996. From
what I can remember on what was a terribly upsetting day
for me, she spoke very little to her mother, and stayed with
me that night. I had stayed with her for a fortnight the year
before.

'You don't LIKE your mother??!' colleagues boggle,
seemingly unable to grasp the concept that someone with
whom I never chose to associate, have nothing in common
with, am over two decades younger than and who has
been single-handedly responsible for my life being a bed
of neuroses is NOT top of my Friends and Family list.

I have barely seen the evil woman since I left home.
Now our sole communication is a one-way process: the
annual arrival of the Family Christmas Newsletter,
diligently word-processed and touchingly personalized

with the help of Microsoft Word's mail-merge feature which she clearly hasn't quite mastered.

Dear [HELEN]. Phew! Another eventful year for the Hastings family draws to an exhausting close. It has certainly been an Annus Nonstoppus (!!!!). As you probably remember from last year's Newsletter, Helen is still off in the 'Big Smoke' doing her own thing – but the others are still regularly popping back to check upon us oldies and make sure we're not overdoing it!! Rebecca got the promotion as expected, and ...

I don't remember at exactly what point I became a matricidal maniac. I suspect it was some time between that unhappy convergence beneath the maternal duvet of Mr Testicle-Tadpole and Ms Soft-Boiled Ovum and the point at which I emerged bawling into the NHS ward having spent the most satisfying nine months of my existence doing nothing but kicking my mum and ruining her figure.

Perhaps someone should set up a Support Group for it by now. Matricidals Anonymous, or 'Ma' for short. It would be like Alkies Anon, I guess, but they wouldn't make such a point of getting your relatives 'involved'.

I would not want people to think my mother's murder was an impulsive act of madness. I may be a dangerous psychopath, but I can bide my time. As the years go by I will gradually start to mimic that same, patronizingly

chivvying tone she so kindly acquainted me with during
my tortured teens. 'Come on, mum. Are you just going to
mope round the house all day doing nothing? Haven't you
got FRIENDS you can call? What do you mean they all
say you SMELL and wear funny clothes? You're ninety-
three, you know! And I suppose you failed your kidney-
function test JUST TO SHOW ME UP, didn't you?
Hmmmmmm? Yes. Charlotte's mother didn't fail HERS,
did she? If you don't pull your bloody socks up – I mean,
your surgical socks up, old lady – it'll be straight up to
your room in the Twilight Towers Nursing Home with
NO supper for you.'

Having never murdered anyone before (despite the
temptation presented by several ex-bosses, ex-boyfriends
and ex-Tory Ministers) I haven't decided yet on my actual
weapon of choice. Poison? Cyanide pills could easily
replace her Mothers' Little Helpers in that old brown
glass jar, and it would be great payback for the years of
clammy Tesco Economy Chicken-Roll baps I was forced
to take for school lunch – despite every other kid within
our Local Education Authority's jurisdiction being
permitted pizza from the tuck shop. I could beat her to
death with a rolled-up copy of *Give Your Child a Superior
Mind*: 'Thwack! Take THAT! That's for the haircut and
the second-hand school uniform.' 'THWACK! That's for
making me watch Interesting Documentaries About
Indonesia instead of *EastEnders* and *Grange Hill*, thereby
denying me my rightful education in early eighties pop

culture.' 'BASH! BASH! BASH! And THAT'S for the string of revolting men you dated once you'd packed me off to some hard-faced childminder for the evening, despite my being unable to sleep properly anywhere except my own bed and thus developing a prolonged bed-wetting dysfunction.'

Hanging's too good for her. A hitman could probably be arranged (but I wouldn't waste my money on one). A traffic accident, maybe. It's so easy for old ladies to get disorientated in the middle of the road and mown down by a passing Juggernaut: the only trouble is, I don't have an HGV driver's licence.

I think I'll plump for starvation. It's a satisfyingly long drawn-out process: cheap, too, and everyone knows how careless those disorientated Old Folk are about eating properly. More to the point, it'll be deliciously ironic: revenge for the continual, heavy-handed hints she dropped about my weight which subsequently drove me into a four-year battle with anorexia, threatened sectionalization under the Mental Health Act and eventual hospitalization when I tipped the scales at four stone. I suppose she was just disappointed that I never managed to shake off that final puppy-fat and return to the weight I was when she first 'met' me: a svelte 7 lb 8 oz, according to my birth certificate.

If I really couldn't wait for the starvation to run its course, I could always finish the slag off with a sawn-off. Would I miss her? Not a chance. But just in case I did, I'd keep another bullet in the chamber for a second shot. Then, the dread deed done, I'd hack her lifeless bony corpse limb from limb – not methodically, not carving the joints in a careful 'Shall I Be Mother?' family-round-the-table-for-a-Sunday-roast sort of way – but stabbing and swiping at random, amply demonstrating the clumsy, haphazard way of doing things which she's never missed an opportunity to castigate me for. Then I'd feed her to the cat. She never liked the cat. I think she was jealous of it because I used to prefer its company to hers, even when it vomited in the bed.

I could grind her bones up – 'Fee, fi, fo ... fuck you, you poisonous old hag' – to make some glue. Then distil it into an aerosol can, sniff her, and get high as a kite on my own matricidal bliss.

It will be the perfect crime. No evidence (unless that cat vomits her up in the bed). No witnesses, no concerned colleagues reporting her sudden disappearance to the police. But if it did come to a trial, I'd just plead guilty, as I have spent twenty-four years feeling guilty, thanks to her.

I reckon I would get off. It's not as though I have any OBVIOUS motive for bumping off the old bitch. The last thing I want is to inherit any of her revolting accoutrements. I suppose I could burn them as a cathartic funeral pyre, but I could happily do that when she was still alive.

To give the shrew her due, she was never negligent. Far from it. Ignorance is bliss, and being left alone would have suited the teenage me to a T … I do hope my dear mama doesn't take this the wrong way when she reads it. It would be very easy to confuse a serious statement of matricidal intent with a light-hearted, flippant essay – nothing more than a gentle bit of fun-poking. But this ISN'T 'just a bit of fun'. This is deadly serious – and I just hope she realizes so she can make the most of her remaining time in the land of the living. Enjoy herself: dig out those old family photos and remember how I wasn't in any of them because I resolutely refused not to wear 'a face like an inside-out laundry bag'.

Maybe what I'm suffering is the female equivalent of the Oedipus Complex. A similarly frustrated desire to perpetrate that most basic of primal urges upon one's begetter? Not sex, but death. And OK, maybe I DO come across as some sort of soulless, psychopathic bitch from hell. What can I say? I blame the parent.

I was simply stunned by this piece. My daughter, blaming her mother for her illness, and wanting to *kill* her. So much anger, so much vitriol, an expression at last of all the hurt she had carried inside her for most of her life. But was it fact or fiction? Was she simply writing to her brief – 'trouble-making provocateurs' – performing a role, rather like an actor on stage? Or was this the genuine out-pouring of a tormented soul?

I read it again – and again. The essay is littered with fac-tual reminders, events that I knew had happened, phrases

I knew had been said. But what was Debs' motive? Did she *really* want Ann to read it and discover her rage? If so, then why not write to her direct, or publish it under her own byline. But if she wanted to remain anonymous, then why leave clues – Helen Hastings, the road where she lived – plus so many detailed recollections that her mother would surely recognize the author?

Maybe, the whole exercise was therapeutic, intended to get years of pent-up anger off her chest. Sometimes, as a step during counselling, it is suggested that sufferers write down how they really feel in a letter to someone with whom they have issues, but never actually send it. Was Debs in effect doing this?

Is this rancid resentment simply the illness taking hold? Was she latching on someone to blame? We'll never know; but I never understood her absolute refusal to talk to her mother during her time with me. She expressly forbade me to talk to her too (although I felt that Ann had a right to know how ill she was, and we spoke weekly, if not more often, for most of that nine months. I think there might have been one occasion when Debs could not avoid a conversation, and this was curt and monosyllabic to the point of rudeness).

Was this the result of too much love, a natural desire to want your child to be successful, or too little love? This is the fine line that we all, as parents, have to draw; but I suspect that neither I, nor Ann, will ever know the answers.

Forty-four

Did my daughter have to die?

When I set out to write this book, there were many parts of Debs' life that were a mystery. I was reminded at so many stages of our research how she led a life of such contradictions. She dedicated her working years to making others laugh while rarely laughing herself. She was very often intolerant of the standards of other people while being useless at running her own affairs. She was a consummate professional, always delivering on time, but could never be bothered to remember birthdays. She loved food, but died because she wouldn't eat.

Neither I, nor any of her friends and colleagues, ever really understood why she became anorexic, and I do not believe she ever knew herself. What I do know is that Debs' 'problem' was the making of her professionally, although she paid the ultimate price for it.

'They say that comedy is about conflict and pain,' wrote Ben Elton in his novel *Inconceivable*. Through the decades there have been so many comedy performers and writers who have had to deal with a tormented private life. As with so many troubled geniuses before her, there was nothing that anyone could have done to help Debs, because she was not prepared to help herself. This is the one point of agreement about anorexia – only the sufferer can overcome this destructive illness. Therapy, love, support, and firmness can help, but the individual has to want, above all else, to get better.

From the day that she walked back into my life in June 1999, I knew that I had a choice. I could hospitalize her and completely destroy her spirit and her life, although keeping her from actual death; or I could help in as many practical and emotional ways that I could and allow her to be the intelligent, funny, successful girl that she had worked so hard to be, and let her continue to enrich all of our lives.

For me, that wasn't a difficult call. Perhaps I found it easier to understand Debs because I have spent my own working life surrounded by creative minds, under very considerable stress, but for whom the 'buzz' of success is worth any amount of pain.

I was reminded how difficult it was to judge the balance between help and intrusion when I found a very long letter that I had sent to Debs on her birthday in 2002, just six months before her death. Towards the end I had written:

> After you left Aylesbury, I was aware how unwelcome you would probably find anything that could be misinterpreted as 'checking up' on you, so I kept my distance. I know that you found those months awful, and were probably thrilled to get away, but although we had some very difficult times, I really treasured that time with you.

So, I kept my distance, partly because I didn't want to intrude and partly because I'm frightened of being pushed away I suppose. But I do wish that you would keep in contact – because I miss you. I'll make an effort if you will …

I have, through the writing of this book, gained a much better understanding of the emotional turmoil that Debs had to cope with. I have also been able to put my last meeting with her in context, and understand just how much we were able to achieve in those tortuous nine months together in 1999. I only realize now what a major step it had been for Debs to open up her very private life to me. Perhaps because I had confided in her through my most difficult years, and felt that she would understand, she knew that she could trust me.

I am completely satisfied in my own mind that Debs knew towards the end that she was going to die. I have no doubt about that at all. I also have no doubt that she was content with that, and that she was not afraid of death. Innocently, for the memorial service, I had chosen Karen Carpenter singing 'Look to Your Dreams', which contains the phrase 'And tomorrow may be better for you and me'.

How ironic it was that Debs had sent herself flowers three days before she died with the message 'Chin up babe – it gets easier from now on'. And the poems that she sent to Melanie on the night before she died were a way of sharing how she felt at the end. If only she had sent them to me I would have realized what they were saying. But it wouldn't have made any difference. I am just very, very sad that I was not told how ill she was becoming. I understood enough of what drove her creative mind, and enough about the damage already caused to her body to have respected her choices and not interfered. But I could have been with her so that she didn't have to die alone.

This book has given me plenty of opportunity to reflect on how Debs' life could have been different. That can't change anything, and I am not a person who looks back or has regrets. I have always made conscious decisions that I believed to be sensible at the time, but that doesn't always mean that those decisions were right. What I have tried to discover from the many hours of conversation with family, friends, and colleagues is why an otherwise happy young girl became an anorexic, and how that understanding can help other parents.

She claimed that she used eating as a reward mechanism, but I do not believe that was a major factor. I think that, for Debs, the anorexia was the ultimate demonstration of her control of her own life. Was she doing it deliberately to deny her mother grandchildren, as she wrote herself? We will never know.

Whatever the underlying causes, the anorexia, for Debs, became an irrelevance. She lived to write, and nothing, or nobody, was going to get in her way. There was never any possibility of hospitalization, or any form of professional intervention or help that compromised her working routine. With very minor exceptions, she never let the anorexia interfere with her career. She created a career *around* the anorexia, and became 'The Invisible Girl'.

I do not want her to be remembered as an anorexic. She was a fabulously talented writer who just happened to be dealing with a health problem. Although her untimely death stopped her developing her writing talent, her illness never affected her work, only the people working with her. So we should only celebrate the laughter that she brought to the world, and thank her for it.

And because she wouldn't put that computer down, not even for a moment, not even for a blood transfusion, we should let Debs have the last word …

Hey, like does anyone mind if I unplug this life-support machine to plug my laptop in? No? OK …

'Preparing to Die'*

Religion

Jehovah's Witness. I would like two slightly suspicious bespectacled people with no dress sense to wheel my cadaver round the local neighbourhood, knocking on doors and asking the occupants if they would like to let a decomposing stiffy into their life.

Humanists

No no, humorists. I would like either Alan Coren or Simon Hoggart to pen a pithy vignette satirizing my demise. With a few irreverent quips about Peter Mandelson into the bargain.

Other

Auction me off on eBay. Some idiot is bound to bid.

Disposal

I would like to be scattered on the pitch at Elland Road. If the board of Leeds United object, my solicitor may consent to have me cremated first.

* Submission by D. A. Barham to www.mydeath.net (3 June 2000).

Additionally

My liver, kidneys and other vital organs are to be left to medical science, on the grounds that they are donated to Jim Davidson. Whether he wants them or not. The idea of this vile Nazi shit undergoing horrendously painful and possibly fatal transplant surgery will make my soul rest easier in its celestial berth. The tips of my fingers should be cut off prior to cremation, and inserted into the curtain-poles of all my least popular relatives. I will therefore remain in their thoughts as a lingering, inexplicable rotting flesh smell until they are forced to move house. This will also ease my tortured soul.

Undertaker

Light the blue touch paper and retire.

Coffin

It's got to be something made of MDF, draped in purple velour and hand-stencilled with gold-effect spray paint. I know my 'Changing Rooms'.

Venue

Anywhere but Center Parcs. I wouldn't be seen dead in Center Parcs.

Flowers

The biggest, most stunningly elaborate bouquet that Interflora can come up with. None of that 'donations to a local hospice instead' nonsense. I want my funeral to look like a cross between Kew Gardens and Danny La Rue's dressing room. It's not that I like flowers. It's just that a lot of my relatives have hay fever.

Music

Celine Dion's 'That Godawful Titanic Song'. DO I want to hear that again? Yeah, over my dead body.

Readings

Reading's a moderate sized town just outside London, isn't it? I guess I might as well die there as anywhere else. Death is probably one of the more interesting activities one can partake of in Reading.

Mourners

Barred: Jimmy Savile. I've heard the rumours.
Invited: all my nearest and dearest. You can book the telephone-kiosk now.

Dress Code

Vicars and tarts.

Wake

Hmmm … a rave from the grave? A little wine and corpse evening? A louch 'at Tomb'? I think I'd like to hire McDonalds for the evening. Each mourner would get a themed 'Unhappy Meal' (containing Rigor McMortis, Regular Flies – and maggots – and Coffin McNuggets). When they left, the surly pustule-ridden staff would invite them to 'Have a nice die now'. I reckon death is a small price to pay for such an elaborately staged crap pun.

Epitaph

Sorry, I thought the deadline for epitaphs was 'next' week.

Famous Last Words

Hey, like does anyone mind if I unplug this life-support machine to plug my laptop in? No? OK …

Suicide Note

Jim Davidson did it.

D.A. Barham CV

Television

Sitcom pilot *Eureka!*; Rory Bremner Christmas Specials and *Who Else* (series 2, 3, 4, 5); *So Graham Norton* (series 1, 2, 3); *Clive Anderson Talks Back*; *Clive Anderson All Talk*; *The 11 o' Clock Show*; *Spitting Image*; *20th Century Stuff*; *McBeal Appeal*; *Bob Monkhouse on the Spot*; *The Drop Dead Show*; *To Diet For*; *I've Got the Music in Me*; *Lily Live*; *Bridget Jones Night* (*In Search of Mr Perfect*); *Bridget Jones Night* (*Truly, Madly, Singly*); *Top Ten Love Songs*; *Top Ten Heartbreakers*; *Top Ten Losers*; *The Jerry Springer Show*; *Dotcomedy*; *Gayle's World*; *Jonathan Ross in Search of Hamlet*; *In the Dark*; *Haywire*; *Fred MacAulay Show*; *Planet Mirth*; BAFTA Scotland Awards; *Evening Standard* Drama Awards, 1996 and 1997; *The National Lottery Live*; *The National Lottery on Tour*; *The Girlie Show*; *Is That It?*; *The Russ Abbott Show*; *The Big Stage*; *Brian Conley's All the Best for Christmas*; *No Limit*; *Jim Davidson's Generation Game*; *A Royal Gala: 20 Years of the Prince's Trust*; *Prince's Trust Comedy Hour*; *21 Years of the Prince's Trust*; *The Double Deckers* (30-minute pilot script); *Saturday Live* (pilot); *Bobby Davro* (pilot); *Le Show* (pilot); *The Treatment* (pilot); *Do or Die* (pilot); *Seaside Special* (pilot); *Chapter One TV*; *Cliff Richard Christmas Special*

1998; *Chambers* – script consultancy/editing work for BBC1 sitcom; 30-minute sitcom script commissioned for Channel 4 Sitcom Festival 1999; *It's a Girl Thing*; *Modern Histories*; *Real Comic Icons*; *Jo Brand's Hot Potatoes*.

Radio

Sitcom *The Elephant Man* (first series of 8 shows); *Loose Ends* (R4); *The Sunday Format* (R4); *I Can Do That* (series of 30-minute spoof documentaries, R4): *A Guide to 20 Years Hitch Hiking* (R4); *The News Quiz* (R4); *Week Ending* (R4); *The News Huddlines* (R2); *I'm Sorry I Haven't a Clue* (R4); *Dead Ringers* (R4); *The Radio 4 Christmas Pantomime* (co-writer for 1998/1999 shows); *Graham Norton's News Lasso* (R4); *Paris, London* (R4); *I'm Glad You Asked Me That* (two series, R4); *Four Individual Tarts* (half-hour sketch show pilot, R4); *The Treatment* (R5); *The Christmas Box* (half-hour one-off sketch show, R5); *Cross Questioned* (R4 panel game); *Bits from Last Week's Radio* (R4); *Patrick Barlow's Compleat Life of Shakespeare* (R4); *Alan Davies' Big One FM* (R1); *The Miles and Millner Show* (R4); *NewsNet* (R4 pilot); In 1994/95 one of the BBC Radio Light Entertainment Contract Writers.

Newspapers

The *Sun* – regular column 'Debbie Barham on the Loose' (plus other features); *Evening Standard* – regular weekly features for IT section, plus general features; *Independent* –

regular columnist: approx. 1 year as 'Mystic Deb' and 'Corporate Strategies'; *Daily/Sunday Express* – features. Regular column in *Express Magazine* 'Diary of a Househunter'; the *Guardian*.

Magazines

Punch – regular columnist for two years; *Private Eye*; *Cosmopolitan*; Condé Nast: *Hot*; *Computeractive*; *Palmtop and Palm User*; *Focus*; *Broadcast*; Weekly column in *Ms London*; *Stuff* magazine; *T3*; *Wired*; *.net magazine*; *More!*; *Deadpan*.

Books

Girls Behaving Badly; *The Net Head Handbook* (contributor).

Other Miscellaneous Writing

After-dinner speech/presentation material for Clive Anderson, Bob Monkhouse, Ned Sherrin, Ronnie Corbett; Material for Bob Monkhouse for BAFTA TV Awards; Multimedia writing work with Douglas Adams (on project 'Starship Titanic'); iVillage – topical 600-word features/columns for new Internet Portal; 'World Cup Diaries' (short packages for Radio 5 during 1998 World Cup); *Newsrevue* (stage show, London/Edinburgh fringe); Creative Consultant to Comic Relief '97; Corporate video work; Material for humorous greetings cards.

Index